THE SCULPTURE OF DONALD DE LUE

GODS, PROPHETS, AND HEROES

The Sculpture of
DONALD DELUE

Gods, Prophets, and Heroes

By D. ROGER HOWLETT

With contributions by

JOSEPH VEACH NOBLE, JONATHAN L. FAIRBANKS,
JOHN P. AXELROD, and M. DARSIE ALEXANDER

DAVID R. GODINE, *Publisher*

BOSTON 1990

First published in 1990 by

DAVID R. GODINE, PUBLISHER, INC.
Horticultural Hall
300 Massachusetts Avenue
Boston, Massachusetts 02115

in association with John P. Axelrod

Library of Congress Catalog Card Number: 89-45925

ISBN: 0-87923-820-8

First Edition
Printed in Hong Kong by the South China Printing Company

Aldus Manutius, the premier printer of the incunabula period, created
a new typeface for the publication of *De Aetna* by the humanist
scholar Cardinal Pietro Bembo in 1495. Although there have been
thousands of faces devised since then, few can rival Bembo for
readability or graceful letterforms. This book's designer, Richard C.
Bartlett, selected it as a font complementary to Donald De Lue's
handsome sculpture. The composition is by
Crane Typesetting Service, Inc.

For my mother and father,
who expected much but demanded little.

CONTENTS

OPPOSITE:
Bearer of Good Times, 1985, bronze, 19 inches.

VIII

ACKNOWLEDGMENTS

Thanks to the following for their assistance in the publication of *Gods, Prophets and Heroes*:

M. Darsie Alexander, editorial assistant
American Artist
American Battle Monuments Commission
Asbury Park Press
Art News
John P. Axelrod, instigator
Barbara SoRelle Bacot
Carol Banks, Hall of Fame for Great Americans
Richard Bartlett, designer
Msgr. Henry Bezou
Boston University Archives
Domenic Carbone, Philadelphia Art Alliance
Chet Chatman
Janice Chadborne, Boston Public Library,
    and all the fine arts reference staff
Michael Craven
Lisa Cunningham, photography and numismatics
Deborah Sarafin Davies
Lauretta Demmick, Museum of Fine Arts
Eastern Acorn Press
Lawrence B. Eustis, Delta Development Corporation
Jonathan Fairbanks, Katherine Lane Weems curator
    of American Sculpture, MFA
Father Divine's Peace Mission Movement
Katherine Fehrer
Lucy Ferriss, copy editor
Ann Fisk, Rockport Art Association
Dan Friend, West Virginia University
Preston Frazer, Blacksburg, Va.
Marion Giannesi, U.D.C.
David Godine
Angela Gregory
John Griffith
George Gurney, curator of sculpture,
    National Museum of American Art
Walker Hancock
Kenneth Hari
Paul Harbeson

Fran Hegeler, H2L2 Architectural Firm
Mr. Hilton, Sawyer Free Public Library
Robert Hoge, American Numismatics Association
Arlene Holden, John Simon Guggenheim Foundation
Kathy Howlett
Erik Jarnryd, Harvard University
Miss Alice Jones, U.D.C.
D. Wayne Johnson, Collector's Auction, Ltd.
Journal of the American Institute of Architects
Mr. Kenin, Grand Lodge of Pennsylvania Archives
William Kilpatrick, assistant to Donald De Lue
Gloria Kittleson, Minnesota Museum of Art
Réné Lavaggi
Life
James Mann
John Manship
Margaret Manship
Robert Menard
Elizabeth McKeown, Childs Gallery
Morgantown Post
Steven Moore, JFK Special Warfare Center, Ft. Bragg, N.C.
Theodora Morgan, *National Sculpture Review*
Mother Divine, Gladwyne, Penn.
Museum of Fine Arts, Boston
National Archives, Washington
New York Public Library
New York Times
J. Nikolouzos
Joseph Veach Noble
Carl Palusci
Richard Pollich, and the staff of Tallix foundry
Beatrice Gilman Proske
Gwen Putzig, National Sculpture Society
Colonel William E. Ryan, Jr.
Evelyn Scarnegi, secretary to Donald De Lue
Jacques Schnier
Robert Sennett, Fogg Art Museum Library
Arlie Slabaugh, the Franklin Mint
Robert Spring, Modern Art Foundry
Alan Stahl, American Numismatics Society
Elizabeth Stahl

Jim Strandberg, Firestone Public Relations Office
Gurdon Tarbox and the staff of Brookgreen Gardens
Sister Mary Trimble
University of California Press
Viking Press
Glenys Waldman, Masonic Temple, Philadelphia, Penn.
Albert Wein

Thanks also to:

Peter Gill, British Astronomical Association
  and Peter Hingley, Royal Astronomical Society, London
Microfilm and microtext staff of the Boston Public Library
Research staff of Sawyer Free Public Library, Gloucester
British Library, London
Frick Art Reference Library
Library of the Royal Academy, London
Fine Arts Department, New York Public Library
National Sculpture Society
National Academy of Design

*Note: Every effort has been made to secure permission to use
copyright material. We regret any omissions and will make
appropriate corrections in any subsequent printings and editions.*

There are certain people who so helped to shape this book
that it would not be the same, or perhaps would not have
existed at all, without their help and encouragement. First, I
must mention Donald De Lue himself, who gave countless
patient hours to correct misunderstandings and to lead me to
new sources of information; and then his secretary, Evelyn
Scarnegi, who from the first burrowed in his studio to find
scrapbooks, photographs, negatives and drawings that would
shed new light on his career, and Carl Palusci, who worked
with each of them in the preparation of the first research at
the studio in Leonardo to get me started.

This book would not have been written without John P.
Axelrod, my business partner and friend. John did not really
encourage me in the traditional sense; he ordered me to write
the book. When I asked him if he would read a chapter, he
said that if I would just hurry up and get it printed he would
read the whole book.

David Godine of David R. Godine, Inc., and his staff have
been of inestimable help. They assembled for me a team of
editors and designers that could not be better. First, Robert
Sennett helped to shape the contents and form of the book
and Lucy Ferriss red-penciled a mass of manuscript into final
form. Richard Bartlett has given the whole an elegant and
classic design and typography that would please De Lue.

My fellow workers at Childs Gallery have been more than
patient. They have shouldered the burdens of work that
I ought to have done, while I wrote onward. Lisa
Cunningham, followed by E. Ellison McKeown, have done
the vast majority of the photography. The majority of the
gallery staff have read the manuscript at many stages and
made helpful comments.

There have been outside readers, friends, and relatives who
have given careful study, thought, and not a little red pencil
to one or more drafts of the book and I give them my
undying gratitude for this (until this moment) thankless task:
Joseph Veach Noble, Jonathan Fairbanks, George Gurney,
Barbara SoRelle Bacot, Theodora Morgan, Carl Palusci, Louis
Newman, Robert Menard, John Griffith, Ramon Osuna,
Angela Noel, James Kay and Kathy Howlett. Noble and
Fairbanks have generously given of their time and talents to
contribute essays to the book.

Finally, however, I must thank M. Darsie Alexander, who
marched the last miles with me listening to the frustrations
and nit-picking of the revisions, proofs, and designs. She fact-
checked and got permissions, ferried the manuscript to editors
and designers, assembled photographs, and constantly read
and re-read each word, paragraph, and chapter. I thank her
and all of the others who have helped me to bring this
material on Donald De Lue together.

—D. Roger Howlett

AUTHOR'S NOTE

THIS BOOK BEGAN IN 1986 AS A CATALOGUE TO ACCOMPANY THE MUSEUM exhibition of the same name. In beginning to write it, I quickly discovered that the subject was much larger than I had first thought, that there was much more material, scattered widely, than I had originally believed, and that De Lue himself was an enormous resource who remembered conversations, events, and names from seven decades with uncanny accuracy, though he often could not remember in which decade the conversation or event had occurred. I had the enormous advantage of nearly one hundred hours of conversation with De Lue. When new material appeared, or I began to have a sense of a different period in his work, I was able to discuss my ideas with him. This is the first monograph on De Lue since the publication of a book in the University of Georgia American Sculptors Series in 1955. I believe that the following essay will not be the last about De Lue, and I am under no illusion that this is the "final" word on the subject. This book is certainly not a *catalogue raisonné*.

There has been a dirth of books on sculptors of De Lue's generation. While exhibition catalogues have appeared on Manship, Friedlander, Jennewein, Hancock and a few others, there have been few extended studies of this later generation of beaux arts sculptors, and the only book in print is Harry Rand's new work, *Paul Manship*. I hope that this book will lend, through the example of Donald De Lue, some perspective to the goals and difficulties of his generation. There is, I think, much new material in this book and perhaps a new way of looking at very familiar monuments.

The greatest difficulty for me has been dating De Lue's sculpture. While he did not consciously misdate or predate works, I believe that he assigned later dates to some "works in progress" to keep them current. Perhaps all sculptors of De Lue's period have works of uncertain or ambiguous date because of the nature of the working method of their generation and the protean quality of plastiline that they used. For students of the beaux arts tradition in sculpture, the creative process is ongoing, one might say never-ending. Rarely does an artist consider a work "perfect," and should one do so, his or her own vision will change with time so that the same work ten days or ten years later will bear improvement against the artist's new standards. I have tried to assign the date at which I believe that the sculpture was first realized in a concept close to its final form. In some cases, such as *Alexander Astride Bucephalus*, the evolution is well docu-

82

mented. In *Pegasus* it is elusive. In many other works, it is still unclear. 23
Adjusting the dating of many of these works may occupy the time of
scholars in the future.

Donald De Lue was deeply involved in the ongoing creative process,
and the confusion that can result from that process may be illustrated
with two pieces of his smaller sculpture. First we might examine the
dating problems with *Icarus*, which is arguably his best known smaller 19
work. Most public information comes from the catalogue of the Brookgreen Gardens Collection and is correct, as far as it goes. The catalogue
states: "It was this work, exhibited at the Allied Artists of America in
1946, that won for the artist a medal of honor." "Signed on the base at
back: De Lue 1945 Placed in Brookgreen Gardens in 1948." When we
carefully examine this information we discover that the plaster model
was exhibited at the Allied Artists of America in 1946; that the bronze
cast at Brookgreen Gardens was paid for and cast after the exhibition by
Archer Huntington and therefore not placed at Brookgreen Gardens until
1948; and that the date 1945 is arbitrary, referring neither to the date of
the inception of the design nor to the date of the cast. *Icarus* was modeled
while De Lue was still employed by Bryant Baker and before he established his own studio at the Lincoln Arcade building in 1938. According
to best records and De Lue's own recollection, the design was essentially
realized in 1934. Nevertheless, because of the tradition of ongoing refinements, it is possible that the work was being clarified and sharpened
as late as 1945.

The issue of ongoing refinement is well illustrated in the work *Alex-* 82
ander Astride Bucephalus. This work was set up in plastiline while De Lue
was finishing the Edward Hull Crump Memorial (1956) in Memphis. It
was conceived as a public commission of an equestrian statue of Hernando
De Soto to be to be set on the banks of the Mississippi at Memphis. It
soon became apparent that this commission would not be realized, and
by the late 1950s De Lue had converted the figure astride the horse to
Alexander. The horse was reworked to appear Greek rather than Spanish.
Since the sculpture was still in workable clay, De Lue returned to refine
it at regular intervals through 1986, when it was cast into plaster. In
November and December 1986 he refined detail in the plaster before it
went to the foundry for casting into bronze. Our protocol in dating the
works has been to establish, on best authority, the date when the design
first reached its essential form. If major changes took place during ongoing refinements, dates will indicate a bracketing of years. With very
few exceptions, major commissions and noncommissioned works developed over a period of more than one year. Only the smaller commissions and portraits tended to be completed in a short span of time.

The drawings present dating problems of their own. Donald De Lue
was an enormously prolific draughtsman. Until 1985, he rarely dated his
drawings at the time that they were created. Some can be dated by way
of the known dates of the beginning and end of the project for which
they were executed. It comes as a surprise, therefore, to find drawings
for a monument to the Battle of Corregador dated three years before the
battle occurred. The explanation is that in 1985 De Lue attempted, in a
marathon session, to date the bulk of his drawings. Sometimes he was

correct; more often, however, he missed the date by years or even decades. I have attempted to correct those dates in the captions and text, even if the correction varies from the date written later on the drawing by De Lue. After 1985, De Lue began to date most of his drawings at the time that he made them, and the dating is fairly reliable.

A great deal of research has been done to document the dates of inception and completion of projects. Donald De Lue was very helpful in ordering the dates and helping to determine the years. Nevertheless, precise dating is not the primary goal of a sculptor working in the tradition that De Lue chose. His primary goal was perfection in his art, and that is not necessarily compatible with closure in a calendar year.

This book was written for no one more than for De Lue himself. I share Joseph Noble's sorrow that he could not have lived to see the final copy. Nevertheless, no review could please me more than De Lue's comments on reading the manuscript in progress. He said that he had never before thought about the paternal relationships that had been established with Recchia, Pratt, and the Bakers, and he felt that my analysis was quite correct. Saying that the events recounted brought back many memories, he concluded, "Really, you know more now about my history than I do!" Although our working relationship lasted less than four years, knowing him was a privilege and an honor, and the research and writing of this book was a labor of love.

D. Roger Howlett
Childs Gallery, Boston
May 1989

New Bedford Fisherman, circa 1978, plaster.

This study model, now at the Museum of Fine Arts, Boston, was intended as a companion monument to Bela Pratt's *Whaleman Memorial* for the city of New Bedford, Massachusetts.

PUBLICATION NOTE

As a collector my abiding interest is art objects made between
the world wars. This period, which has as many forms as names, has
been largely ignored by the American art community. The issue first
arose when America declined the premiere foreign exhibition space at
the 1925 Paris Exposition Internationale des Arts Decoratifs et Industriels
Modernes (which gave the name "art deco") on the basis that this country
had nothing notable in the way of decorative arts to exhibit. Similiar
attitudes existed toward the fine arts, the underlying feeling being that
only European art was worthy of collecting. To a degree, the notion that
American art died with Winslow Homer (1910) and remained dormant
until the abstract expressionists sprung like Aphrodite out of the artistic
sea became commonly held by writers and readers of art criticism of the
1950s and 1960s. To many collectors and curators who lived during this
period, an earlier figurative tradition was only a distant memory, and all
that they focused on was a Depression with world wars as bookends.

In fact, there were many fine American artists and sculptors who worked
and developed their distinctive styles between the wars. A handful, such
as Paul Manship, Elie Nadelman, Gaston Lachaise, and John Storrs, are
now known (a familiarity accompanied by very high prices) to American
collectors and museums. There are many others whose works are as good
(or better) whose reputations are just starting to emerge in the American
consciousness. This book introduces one of the truly great American
sculptors of the twentieth century: Donald De Lue.

My path to Donald De Lue was long and circuitous. My collecting
started in the late 1960s with ceramic refrigerator-ware (Hall Co.) and
other aerodynamic objects. I soon had accumulated a large collection of
objects and furniture (primarily European). One day, while attending a
New York City auction, I noticed some Martin Lewis prints on display
for an upcoming sale. The desire to have something from that period for
the wall was my segue into "fine arts."

As my collection grew, and space at home became cramped, I made
the tough decision to limit my collecting to American art and objects.
This led to my meeting two very impressive and, to me, important people
at the Museum of Fine Arts, Boston: Anne Poulet (curator of European
Decorative Arts) and Jonathan Fairbanks (curator of American Decorative
Arts). Although it may be fairly stated that neither of these curators had
much art deco in their collections, both were very generous with both

New Bedford Fisherman, circa 1978, pencil on
paper, 19 × 22 inches.

A preparatory drawing for the plaster
model in the Museum of Fine Arts,
Boston.

their time and their energy. Anne helped by relieving me of the better quality part of my European collection, which has become the base of what I hope evolves into a great collection of European decorative arts at the museum. Jonathan has worked with me in grooming what is now my fast growing collection of American decorative art and sculpture.

A problem facing any collector of this period is that there has been, until recently, very little reference work available; therefore information has to be gleaned from periodicals and papers of the time. A lot of time was spent with Jonathan (whose father, Avard Fairbanks, was another great sculptor of the period) and his staff to find and document pieces. Jonathan also has established at the MFA an American decorative arts gallery that rates as the best in the world. One day—and here we tie it all together—while in Jonathan's office, I saw four fantastic plasters and inquired as to the sculptor. It was Donald De Lue. Jonathan arranged for me to visit De Lue at his studio in New Jersey.

I visited Donald and was taken aback by his studio, filled with over a hundred plasters—most of which were better than any American sculpture of this period I had ever seen. A relationship grew, and Donald asked if I would work with him to produce his work. I declined. (At this point, I envisaged lost wax method as being molten metal being somehow dropped into a wax figure—a notion that has since been corrected by hours in a foundry.) A great synergy combining my excitement and interest as a collector, Roger Howlett's expertise, time, and energy as a gallery owner, and—most important—De Lue's unlimited talent (and, at times, patience) resulted in bringing his plasters to life as bronzes and his career to life as this book.

John P. Axelrod
Associate Publisher
Boston, 1989

OPPOSITE:

Faun and Goat, circa 1937, pencil on paper, 16¾ × 13¾ inches.

This is almost certainly part of a series of drawing studies that culminated in the bronze *Faun* of 1937.

XVII

Hᴏᴡ ᴡᴏᴜʟᴅ ᴀ ᴄᴏɴᴛᴇᴍᴘᴏʀᴀʀʏ ᴏꜰ ᴍɪᴄʜᴇʟᴀɴɢᴇʟᴏ ʜᴀᴠᴇ ᴅᴇꜱᴄʀɪʙᴇᴅ ᴛʜᴀᴛ universal genius? The answer is "with great difficulty." I am faced with the same problem in describing Donald De Lue and his lifetime of work in sculpture. Coincidently, Michelangelo lived for eighty-nine years and De Lue even past that milestone. Is it chance or fate that this modern-day Renaissance man lived in a town with the name of Leonardo? It is on the northern coast of New Jersey with a beautiful view of New York City right across the bay.

To start with, here is a man who created more monumental sculpture than any other recent American artist. Simultaneously, at the other end of the spectrum of size, he created some of the most powerful and dynamic medals of our time. This man of genius had the vision to sculpt a bronze figure forty-five feet in height, and he compressed the same figure within the confines of a three-inch medallion. Naturally, the medal fairly explodes with imprisoned power.

He was born in Boston at the end of the last century. As a teenager he entered the studio of the Boston sculptor, Richard Recchia, as an apprentice. Next, he worked with an English sculptor, Robert Baker, who had been commissioned to do several large statues in Boston. Wanderlust took him to that Mecca of sculptors, Paris, at the close of World War I. After a few years he returned to America and in 1938 opened his own studio in New York City. The time was right and his future was assured.

An avalanche of sculpture poured out of his studio: Among them were *St. John the Baptist*, five and a half feet, New York City; *Law* and *Justice*, each nine feet, Philadelphia; *Thomas Jefferson*, nine feet, New Orleans; *The Boy Scout Memorial*, twelve feet, Washington; *Mountaineer*, thirteen feet, West Virginia; *Soldiers and Sailors of the Confederacy*, fourteen feet, Gettysburg; *George Washington at Prayer*, fourteen feet, Valley Forge; *Quest Eternal*, twenty-seven feet, Boston; and *The Rocket Thrower*, forty-five feet, New York World's Fair. He created medals for the Hall of Fame of Great Americans, the National Science Foundation, the National Academy of Design, and two for the Society of Medalists, the first sculptor to have done so. Can you picture that second medal three inches in diameter with the figures in such high relief that it is one inch thick and weighs a pound and a quarter?

Zeus showered gold coins on Danae, and the art world showered gold medals on Donald De Lue. They were received from the Allied Artists of America, American Artists Professional League, American Numismatic Association, American Numismatic Society, Architectural League of New York, National Academy of Design, and three from the National Sculpture Society, which he served as president. He was also awarded a Guggenheim Fellowship.

I had the pleasure of knowing Donald for a good number of years in my capacity as executive director of the Society of Medalists, and as president of Brookgreen Gardens of South Carolina, which has the largest collection of American sculpture in the world. He is represented there by two excellent pieces: *Icarus*, an amusing study of the untimely descent of that young impetuous flier, and the *Spirit of American Youth*, a heroic

102
192

36, 38,
39
147
134, 141
136
155   127
102
207, 208,
209
207, 209
206, 211

19
71

DONALD

DE LUE:

THE MAN AND

HIS WORK

Joseph Veach Noble

Director Emeritus Museum of the City of New York
Executive Director of Society of Medalists
President Brookgreen Gardens of American Sculpture

OPPOSITE:

Genesis-The Evening and the Morning of the Second Day, 1968, bronze, 35 inches.

Genesis won the Hexter Prize at the 40th Annual Exhibition of the National Sculpture Society, 1973. A reduction was made by De Lue in 1986.

figure which also stands on Omaha Beach in Normandy in honor of the American soldiers who were lost in that epic battle.

Each year Brookgreen issues a fine arts medal, and in 1978 I decided to ask Donald De Lue to create one based on the theme of the sculptor at work. I was not sure that he would accept a commission with such an exacting subject. However, with characteristic graciousness, he assured me that he would be honored to create such an important medal for such a distinguished organization. I said that I hoped he could show me some sketches in a few months, and he replied that they would be ready in a few weeks. Naturally, I expected a sketch for the obverse and another for the reverse of the medal. True to his word, in three weeks he phoned me and said that the sketches were ready. I was apprehensive that such an eminent sculptor would present me with a pair of sketches as his finite and unchangeable interpretation of the subject. Upon his arrival in my office you can imagine my astonishment when he produced from his bulging portfolio no less than thirty-three drawings. These were no hasty thumbnail idea sketches, but rather all were fully rendered as thirty-three different approaches to the subject. Each one showed a sculptor and a

Joseph Veach Noble reviewing 33 drawings proposed as alternatives for the Brookgreen Gardens medal, 1978.

statue. In some the sculptor was modeling in clay and in others he was carving in stone. Typically, De Lue had chosen classical themes with Apollo, the sun god, as the male figure that was being carved, and Diana, the goddess of the night, as the female figure that was being modeled. All were excellent, and I simply chose the two that most complemented each other.

200   A few more weeks and he had finished the clay models. Again he wanted my approval and when I made several picky suggestions, he adjusted the models almost before I had finished speaking. So much for my worries about artistic temperament. Certainly the greater the artist the easier the relationship is. It is the ones with little talent who are the most difficult to work with.

210   The medal was a triumph, one of the finest ever struck in America. In fact, it was one of the small group chosen to represent America in the exhibit of medals of the world in Lisbon in 1979 under the auspices of the Federation International de la Medaille.

    Early in his career Donald De Lue achieved his distinctive heroic style. It can be traced back through the work of Michelangelo, who in turn was influenced by classical Greek and Roman sculpture. Indeed, it was Michelangelo who said "I am the pupil of the torso," a fragmentary late Hellenistic powerful marble torso by Apolonius of Athens that had been excavated in Rome, and today is in the Vatican Museum. I see the influence of this torso in all of De Lue's work.

    As time passed, the fickle art styles of the twentieth century kept changing, but Donald De Lue did not. He stayed true to his vision of what sculpture should be. Some critics thought him to be old-fashioned and outdated. He fooled them all, and had the last laugh, by living long enough to see abstract, minimal, found objects and conceptional styles run their course. Here was Donald De Lue still sculpting in his heroic mode, the art world came full circle, and Donald's style is "in" again.

Job, 1986, bronze, 9 inches.

Job, as much as any work of De Lue, shows the male torso in repose. De Lue cannot make him emaciated or covered with sores; instead, he focuses his attention on a single star or spiritual point of light for Job to think on God.

Study for Justice, circa 1939, pencil on paper, 16¾ × 13¾ inches.

THE SCULPTURE OF DONALD DE LUE

GODS, PROPHETS, AND HEROES

. . . For this is he who is able to make not only vessels of every kind, but plants and animals, himself and all other things — the earth and heaven, and the things which are in heaven or under the earth; he makes the gods also.

PLATO   *THE REPUBLIC X*[1]

My mother was rather artistically inclined. When I was twelve she took me to the new Museum of Fine Arts on Huntington Avenue in Boston. We went up the stairs together into the great sculpture court. There were casts of the Medici tombs by Michelangelo, the high reliefs of the pediment from the temple at Pergamum, and the two great equestrian statues — Verrochio's Colleoni *and Donatello's* Gattamelata. *The power and arrogance of those Renaissance knights and the magnificence of the horses' rumps in shimmering white plaster — as white and clean and pure as you can possibly imagine — transfixed me. When I saw those, there wasn't anything else in the world I wanted to do. I knew then, I wanted to be a sculptor.*

DONALD H. DE LUE, 1987

LEARNING THE CRAFT

NEARLY EIGHTY YEARS AFTER THAT MUSEUM VISIT, STILL ACTIVELY PURsuing his first love, sculpture, De Lue reflected on a career of success after success, which created hundreds of works. His enthusiasm for fine sculpture had not dulled one bit, but he would have agreed that with all the honor and fame, sculpture is still a hard mistress.

Early Training

Donald Harcourt De Lue was born October 5, 1897, in the Dorchester section of Boston, to Harry T. and Ida M. De Lue.[2] When he was nine they moved to Roslindale,[3] another area of Boston. As a schoolboy De Lue created his own Sistine Chapel of sculpture and drawings, a feat that impressed his teachers.[4] De Lue's mother, also impressed by his interest in sculpture and believing in his talent, tried to enroll him in the School of the Museum of Fine Arts in Boston. At age twelve his drawings were reviewed by Bela Pratt (1867–1917), the head of modeling at the school. Pratt was impressed by young De Lue's work, but judged that he was too young to enter the life classes at the school. He therefore recommended that De Lue enter the studio of his own pupil and assistant, Richard Recchia.

Before being accepted as an apprentice by Recchia, De Lue had tried to get a job with the British-born Boston stonecarver John Evans. Evans said he had a job, but it was for a man — not a boy. This rejection was probably a great stroke of luck for De Lue. Evans was a successful architectural carver with a great deal of work, but he was an indifferent sculptor and not a carver of fine sculpture. Had De Lue found a successful berth with Evans, he might never have been offered the better opportunities that followed.[5]

OPPOSITE:

Seated Woman, 1934, bronze, 14¾ inches.

This work is one of several De Lue maquettes which reflect the modernizing trends in American figurative sculpture of the 1930s; it is simple, compact and round.

(Courtesy of Childs Gallery, New York)

The Cast Room at the Museum of Fine Arts, Boston, after 1909.

The photograph shows the equestrian statue of the *Gattamelata, upper left*. It was here that the twelve-year-old De Lue had his first experience with the great sculpture of the Western world.

Richard Recchia

Richard Recchia (1888–1983) was less than a decade older than De Lue and at the age of twenty-one had impressive credentials. He had been born into a family of Italian stone-carvers and sculptors. His father, Francesco Recchia, who had moved the family to Quincy, Massachusetts,

Donald De Lue posing for Richard Recchia's *Whistling Boy*, 1909–11.

As an apprentice, the young acolyte swept the studio, posed nude and began to learn to manipulate clay, build armatures, cast in plaster, and master the other basic skills of the sculptor.

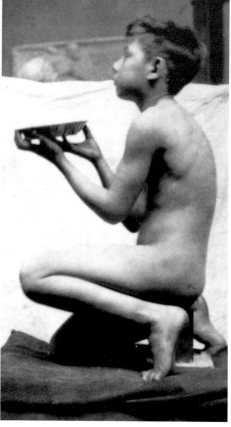

from Italy, was often called upon by Boston sculptors to carve their designs into stone. De Lue later remembered him as a magnificent marble carver who carved beautiful nude figures for Bela Pratt. The elder Recchia was also critical of his son and held him to a high standard. He insisted that if his son were not going to be the best that he could be as a sculptor he should become "a floor walker at Jordan Marsh in Boston."[6] Richard Recchia, who had grown up in this rigorous atmosphere, then entered the School of the Museum of Fine Arts in 1904. He continued there until 1907, assisting Pratt both in his studio and as teacher of modeling. After graduation he continued as Pratt's assistant until 1912. In 1909, when De Lue joined him, Recchia shared Pratt's St. Botolph Annex studio; by 1911 he had his own studio adjoining Pratt's in the same building.[7] De Lue later wrote to Recchia of

> . . . many happy memories of the days I spent with you in your St. Botolph Studio where I certainly learned the fundamentals of what I would be doing for the rest of my life. I was most fortunate of having the privilege of being with you in your studio, seeing how beautiful work was done and being guided in the right direction for me — opening my eyes to the Wonderful World of the Arts.[8]

Donald De Lue's first job, aside from sweeping up, was to pose for Recchia's *Pan*. In that same year, Recchia modeled *The Golden Age*, which received a bronze medal at the Panama-Pacific Exposition in San Francisco in 1915. De Lue posed for Recchia's *Faun* as well. He did casting for Recchia and began to do modeling on his own. He also did some restoration work for the Museum of Fine Arts; most notably, he restored the left arm of the famous gold and ivory Cretan *Snake Goddess*.

Perhaps Recchia and Pratt served as more than teachers and mentors. Donald De Lue had never been close to his father, who imported Sheffield steel and was seldom home.[9] Family life was not good; his parents fought, and there was very little harmony in their household. At the age of fourteen, telling his family that he was going into Boston to English High School, he began to slip away to Recchia's studio instead. Within a year he had left home and school and moved to a furnished room on St. Botolph Street near Recchia's studio. In June, 1914, when De Lue was sixteen, his father died; he was on his own.[10]

Bela Pratt

De Lue remembered, "I saw Pratt's *Art* and *Science* being worked on in the studio. I was at the Boston Public Library the morning that one was set [in spring 1912].[11] Bela Pratt was there. He said, 'I'm surprised that you're this interested.' I said, 'Well, being a sculptor, I have to know all of these things.' He liked me very much and he had a five dollar gold piece that he had done. He took it out of his pocket and handed it to me."[12] Pratt said that it would not be so very long before De Lue would be setting the same kind of monument in Boston.

Recchia was in Europe[13] during the first six months of 1912, and Pratt had taken over Recchia's studio[14] to model his *Whaleman Memorial* (New

Pan by Richard Recchia, modeled between 1909 and 1912 as a half life-size statue.

De Lue posed for this as he did for other Recchia sculpture. This cast is part of the American sculpture collection at the Museum of Fine Arts Boston.

5

Bedford Free Public Library, Massachusetts).[15] De Lue assisted Pratt on this project as he often assisted Pratt when Recchia was traveling. De Lue, Pratt, and Recchia were all on St. Botolph Street in Boston: De Lue was still in his furnished room and Pratt and Recchia had adjoining studios. Recchia was boarding with Pratt in Pratt's house at 30 Lakeville Place in Jamaica Plain. In 1914 Pratt and Recchia both moved around the corner to studios (in the same building) at 4 Harcourt Street.[16]

After De Lue's father died Pratt continued to be an influence in his life. De Lue wrote to Pratt on July 27, 1915, "I thank you most sincerely for the check and the letter that you sent me. I shall always keep the letter and shall make your check go as far as possible. I appreciate all you have done for me and hope some day to be able to return it and be worthy of your generosity towards me."[17] Pratt had arranged for De Lue to enter the School of the Museum of Fine Arts under a special scholarship starting in October of 1914.[18] De Lue quickly found out that the instructors there were teaching him what he had already learned as Recchia's assistant. More importantly for De Lue, Pratt himself was the major teacher of sculpture at the school. He tried to get De Lue to follow his own style of fine, smooth finish. De Lue said later, "I didn't like the school at all. It was too 'sweet.' I was inspired by Michelangelo and Rodin; they were my idols. Anything less was nothing." Nevertheless, Pratt continued to advise and encourage De Lue and to support him with money; and De Lue dutifully attended classes in modeling taught by Pratt and Frederick W. Allen (1888–1961) through May of 1916,[19] the two years that a student could remain in the Department of Modeling without special permission.[20] He was rewarded in his career at the Museum School when he received one of the Kimball Prizes for modeling.[21] But De Lue continued

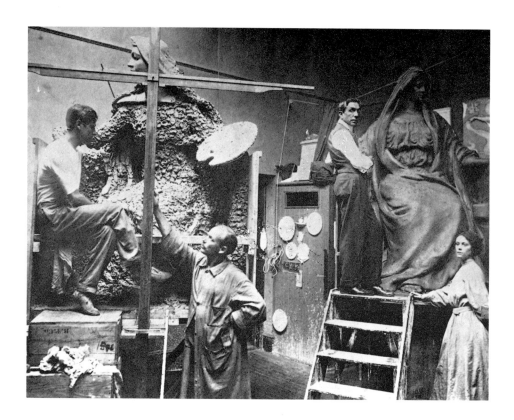

Bela Lyon Pratt in his studio working on the full-sized clays of *Art* and *Science*, 1911.

Pratt is on the ladder, Recchia is to the left and the assistant in the center is George Guest; Miss Nash, Pratt's favorite model, is on the right. De Lue assisted in the Pratt studio as these were being modeled and saw them set in front of the Boston Public Library.

Donald De Lue at 16, drawing by Richard Recchia made on June 11, 1914, eight days after the death of De Lue's father.

in the 1915 letter to Pratt, "I work day and evening at copying my left hand as close as possible as it is the only thing I can model from life. Next term I intend to have my work at the school from 7 a.m. to 8:30, then model afternoons after class and draw from life at the Normal Art till ten p.m."[22] Despite his diligent studies, De Lue was looking for inspiration and a larger vision.

Robert Baker

De Lue later recalled:

It was rather an interesting experience to me. I was working for Recchia and was still in short pants. One day there was a knock at the door and I went to the door and there were two strange looking gentlemen. They

Interior of Richard Recchia's St. Botolph Studio, 1917.

This is where De Lue began to learn the craft of sculpture as Recchia's young apprentice.

OPPOSITE:

The Soul's Struggle by Robert Baker, 1915–1917.

This twelve-foot high plaster monument was De Lue's first major modeling job. Robert Baker designed the work, but De Lue did the largest part of the execution. The figures, which rely heavily on both Michelangelo and Rodin for their inspiration, set a standard for De Lue which continued to his last works.

were young, maybe twenty-five years of age. They were dressed in white linen and carrying canes, which was not usual for Americans. I said to Richard Recchia that there were two gentlemen at the door that looked a little different to me. They said that they would like to come in and that they had not been in a sculptor's studio for many months. Recchia said invite them on in.[23]

Robert Peter Baker (1886–1940), a successful young English sculptor, and his companion, James H. Worthington, had been traveling in Germany when World War I began. Rather than enlisting in the British army, they had gone to the United States, where they visited the Panama-Pacific Exposition in San Francisco in 1915. They traveled east by way of Tucson, Arizona, where a Bostonian, Percival Lowell, had established his observatory. Worthington was a dedicated amateur astronomer, who had supported with his own observations Lowell's theory of canals and life on Mars. It was probably Recchia's medal-winning sculpture at the Panama-Pacific Exposition, which they may have seen and admired, that led them to his Boston studio. By late 1915 they had settled in Boston and Baker had set up a studio at 26 St. Botolph Street. Worthington, a member of a prominent and wealthy British family, had lent money to Baker to set up the studio. Recchia lent him De Lue.[24]

De Lue never regretted his unorthodox teens:

I learned more with Richard Recchia and with Robert Baker and Jim Worthington than I ever could have in school. Jim Worthington was an English Lord and a very nice person, a highly intelligent man who wrote the most beautiful poetry as well as articles on astronomy.[25] Baker was a medalist at the Royal Academy in London and was just as familiar with Rome and Paris as he was with London. I immediately came into a European environment, rather than the Bostonian one that surrounded me. Baker said before that first day was over, "Would you release Donald De Lue to me as an assistant?" I think that this meeting-up with Robert Baker and Jim Worthington did more for me than anything else I could have done.[26]

De Lue was hired at the grand sum of six dollars per week. Baker was twenty-nine when the impressionable seventeen-year-old De Lue met him. He and his brother Bryant came from a family of sculptors and stone-carvers. Robert was a prodigy. He had exhibited at the Crystal Palace Exhibitions when he was eight and received special mention. At ten he was drawing from life; at fifteen he won scholarships to art school and a year later was designing stained glass with Kemp of London. Shortly thereafter he turned to sculpture full time. He had studied at the Lambeth School of Art, at the South London Technical Art School with William S. Frith (1850–1924), at the City and Guild Technical Institute, and at the Royal Academy. In 1911 he won first medal for both *Figure From Life* and *Portrait Bust from Life* at the Royal Academy and held the Landseer scholarship in sculpture.[27] He had assisted Adrian Jones on the *Quadriga* for the Inigo Jones Arch at Hyde Park Corner and had executed many works in the Gothic style in British churches.[28] Baker's training came at a transitional moment in the teaching of sculpture in England, a moment that is only now being studied and appreciated. Frith, among others, set up a program that amalgamated French ideas into a new teaching system in the London technical schools.[29]

"World War I was on; Baker and Worthington used to read the casualty lists in the papers. They would say, 'There's three Robert Bakers in today's casualty list. There were four yesterday. What do they want another one for?' They both began to drink quite a bit. Baker would say, 'Donald, I will design the work and you go ahead and do it.' It was the best thing that ever happened to me!"[30] Working from Baker's designs, De Lue set to work modeling one of his master's best-known Boston works, *The Soul's Struggle*. De Lue, according to his own recollection, created all of the figures except the one in the extreme lower right.

The ambiance of the studio where De Lue was apprenticed is evoked in an article on Baker published in the *International Studio* in October of 1917. The author, W. H. DeB. Nelson, waxes effusive over Baker's work:

> In the completed model soon to be converted into marble and styled as a sop to the catalogues *The Soul's Struggle*, the artist tells just enough to interest his audience and start them on the journey of metaphysical reflection. . . . The most cursory examination of this monumental slab of irregular profile, about twelve feet high and eight across, weighing in the neighborhood of twenty tons, cannot fail to draw the mind to at least two conclusions:
>
> Firstly, one notes that the artist is a cosmic dreamer, if we may be permitted the expression, that though doomed to exist on this little planet he projects his mind continually on others. . . . His leanings to astronomy and years-long association with Mr. James H. Worthington, traveller, poet, scientist, scholar and astronomist, has excited and aided an intellect already matured by ceaseless work and stimulus of travel which has led him over mountains and deserts, tropical lands and polar snows. . . .
>
> Secondly, one recognizes his impeccable draughtsmanship. There is no suspicion of the posed model, and indeed, how could any model fall into such positions as Baker loves to draw or model. He uses the model, how-

ever, so much that the resultant knowledge permits him to express the human form in any attitude with anatomical correctness.

For two years in his Boston studio this exceptional sculptor has been modelling the *The Soul's Struggle*, which is undoubtedly the subconscious outcome of the Great War. It is not an epic of pessimism, as many conceive, but suggests rather the hope of the race. . . . The principal figures in the composition are well over life-size and with Michelangelesque precedent are part and parcel of the earth. . . . Robert P. Baker is fortunate in his ability to devote himself entirely to idealistic sculpture. All true sculptors would do the same if it were feasible.[31]

It is difficult to overestimate the impact that Baker and Worthington and the studio at 26 St. Botolph Street had on De Lue. During his apprenticeship on *The Soul's Struggle* he formed many of the ideals that remained with him until his death. Baker's invocation of Phidias, Michelangelo, and Rodin, his attitude as a cosmic dreamer and dweller on life from the cosmos, his exquisite draughtsmanship proceeding from a thorough understanding of anatomy, and his embarkation on heroic, greater than life-sized, spiritual and idealistic sculpture all seem to have been transferred to his impressionable assistant. De Lue also admired Baker's cosmopolitan ease and his familiarity with Europe and the great sculpture of the Old World. But while he admired Robert Baker's talent, De Lue recognized his weaknesses. He once said, "Robert Baker at this time I adored. He was everything I thought was manly and great. He was really quite a person. He drank too much, but he was brilliant."[32] De Lue also stated that Robert Baker was the most talented man that he had ever met.[33]

It was in this studio on St. Botolph Street in Boston that Donald De Lue practiced and perfected drawing and modeling. He drew constantly, as he had since his very youngest days; when he was a child he had gone to the Boston Public Library to read books on drawing. Under Baker he learned to draw with discipline, first from the live model and later from memory. The same was true of modeling in clay. De Lue later recounted, "In the middle of *The Soul's Struggle* was a female figure. I told Robert Baker that I wanted to model it from life. He got a nice model and I modeled it pretty carefully. Two or three days later, when he came into the studio he said, 'Donald, you did the wrong thing! You copied the damn model. It looks like a person; it looks like you copied it from a model. Destroy it, and do it again—but from memory.' So, I did it again from memory and it *was* better. After that I began to work from my own imagination."[34] De Lue also began to work from a precept that he had heard was a maxim of Michelangelo: train your memory so that you can remember what you are doing and can do it over and over. De Lue continued to work from memory and imagination throughout his career. Years later he said, "I won't ever use a model any more. I draw from what I think it should be. A model can't give you anything, it hasn't got any meaning, there is no energy to it. A model is a placid thing that stands still and has no movement. When I draw a figure it has activity and movement."[35]

Figure drawing by Robert Baker from "Sketches for Poetry, Prose, Paint and Pencil," by James H. Worthington and Robert Baker, 1917.

De Lue learned to draw under the tutelage of Robert Baker; he learned the craft of drawing and the themes, subjects, and expressiveness that would be the mark of his drawings for the rest of his life.

Toward the end of the war, Worthington's money from England was cut off and the studio was closed. Some of the better works that had been cast into plaster were put into storage. Most of them had been heavily modeled by De Lue and some of them were almost entirely his.

In 1916,[36] Robert Baker's brother, Bryant Baker (1881–1970)[37] arrived in Boston and set up a studio at 100 Chestnut Street. He was a sculptor as well, having also been recommended to the Royal Academy by W. S. Frith and having taken prizes there in sculpture in 1908.[38] He had already established a reputation in London for bust portraits of crowned heads and aristocracy, and therefore was in immediate demand in Boston. De Lue met him as soon as he arrived at his brother's St. Botolph Street studio. He worked for Bryant Baker there as well as in the studio on Chestnut Street, but he felt strongly that Robert Baker was much the greater talent.[39]

In 1917 De Lue's gentle mentor and guide, Bela Pratt, died. By 1918, with the closing of both Baker studios in Boston and with Pratt's death, there was little to hold De Lue to Boston. He had been friends for some time with Joseph Pollia (1893–1954), another young Boston sculptor who had studied at the Museum School. They went to New York to see if there was any work for sculptors and took a studio together near 57th Street and 6th Avenue. De Lue was naturally disappointed when they went to architectural carvers in New York and Pollia was immediately introduced around by the Italian workers as a countryman and given work, but De Lue was not.[40]

Robert Baker was also in New York for the Armistice, but he had no studio and decided to visit his brother in Washington. Bryant Baker had enlisted in the American Army shortly before the Armistice and had been assigned to the Army Medical Museum in Washington, where he was making plaster casts for the medical collection. He used this opportunity to model busts of many of the most famous generals and politicians in Washington and to form connections that would profit him the rest of his life.

Years in Europe

De Lue, however, was left alone in New York without job or money. He had thought since meeting the Bakers and Worthington that he needed to have a "European" experience. Since he had no obligations, he signed up as a merchant sailor on the "S.S. Minnesota," a munitions ship leaving for Marseille.[41] A Boston acquaintance and fellow sculptor, George Aarons (1896–1980), joined him.[42] They were at sea by December 1918. De Lue jumped ship at Marseille with thirty-five dollars in his pocket and boarded a train for Paris. Aarons later reported that the captain had had every whorehouse in Marseille searched, but to no avail.[43]

De Lue was appalled at the devastation, disruption, and bleakness of wartorn France, but he was equally excited at the prospect of getting to Paris. He may have taken to heart the advice of Daniel Chester French, which Bela Pratt had related by letter to Richard Recchia from the St. Botolph Studio six years earlier, "He feels, and I quite agree with him, that the live atmosphere of Paris would really be of more benefit to you than the more or less classic and dead atmosphere of Rome and Italy."[44] De Lue arrived there in time for Christmas; however, he was too late to realize his dreams of meeting Rodin, who had died in 1917. He soon made a pilgrimage to the Paris suburb of Meudon and saw Rodin's closed studio and grave. Peering through the windows he could see the great Balzac statue. Behind the house he found a small dump where workers had thrown out fragments of Rodin's work—clay hands and arms and other broken bits. De Lue gathered up several as mementos and kept them with him as he traveled in France. But, as he said, "I had no permanent residence; I had to move a lot to keep ahead of the landlord, so I lost them all eventually."

Paris in the first year after the war was not an easy place for a sculptor—American or French—to get work. De Lue got a job inventorying cigarettes in an American military commissary. It was a job, it paid well, and he began to eat better. He met many French sculptors and found that most of them did not have much work. At the Ecole des Beaux Arts, where he went to see if he might want to enroll in classes, he met a young American soldier in the halls. Edmund Amateis (1897–1981) was De Lue's exact contemporary and had been called in the draft to serve in France. The American military paid for his classes at the Ecole des Beaux Arts, but De Lue did not have the money to attend. Many years later they would recall this irony as they worked on the Philadelphia Court House together.

De Lue did take some drawing classes at the Academie Julian, Colarossi, and the Academie de la Grande Chaumiere.[45] Some of the models there had posed for Rodin and spoke of his work to the students.[46] Schools, however, never appealed to De Lue; studios did. He had met the American sculptor Frederick MacMonnies (1863–1937) in New York. When he got to Paris he found MacMonnies there working on the monument to the Battle of the Marne. Although he went back to the studio several times and was treated very graciously, De Lue could see that MacMonnies had many French assistants and had no need of another.[47]

He also did the rounds of the studios of the French sculptors; that of Paul Maximilien Landowski (1875–1961) was one of the first that he visited. Landowski was working on a nude of Georges Carpentier, the French boxer, at the time. Talking to De Lue and showing him around the studio, he became aware of De Lue's modeling abilities. De Lue later recounted, "I think he realized that I could be very helpful, but he said, 'I have French people to take care of that need more help than you do. You come from a rich country.' "[48]

Finally he landed some work with a decorative, ornamental, and architectural sculptor named DeBert, who sometimes had need of an assistant. De Lue's facility at modeling pleased DeBert, and he would often say, *"Donald, vous êtes trés habille."* DeBert would do whatever the architect called for, whether a Gothic piece or a more modern one. "I might model a Madonna one day and a baby with a bottle of champagne the next; sometimes it was something nice to do, but often it had an element of cheapness . . . I modeled in clay, they would put it into plaster and then they would have it carved in stone. Very seldom would it go into bronze." DeBert suggested that De Lue model a group for a monument and try to get a commission. De Lue made a model of three American soldiers going into battle, which DeBert liked tremendously. He sent him to try to get funds from a French industrialist who was an armaments manufacturer, but to no avail.[49]

Alfredo Pina in his Studio, *circa* 1917.

This was the atmosphere that surrounded De Lue in Paris on the Impasse du Maine in Montparnasse during 1919 and 1920. Pina's work with Rodin fitted perfectly with the aesthetic that Robert Baker had encouraged in the young De Lue.

Alfredo Pina and Antoine Bourdelle

De Lue also met the Italian sculptor, Alfredo Pina (b. 1883). As he later said, "He had a studio at Impasse Du Maine in Montparnasse; Emile-Antoine Bourdelle (1861–1929) had a studio there as well. [Both had studied with Rodin.] Alfredo Pina was about five feet high, a dynamic little man. He created huge female torsos in French clay. He made me his assistant and we made very voluptuous torsos. By working together we could do them rapidly. They were fun to do because the more voluptuous they were the better. French clay is a wonderful clay to work in. You set it up and put a couple of sticks in it and it will harden and

stay hard. You keep the surface wet and it will remain soft enough to work, but the inside is like a rock. So, you don't need a lot of armatures like you do in the United States. We would do these lovely busts one after another, and then Lord Derby would come from England. He would come with a party of ten or fifteen young friends. I don't think he was any more than thirty-five. They used to come to Paris for a good time. There were plenty of girls and plenty of champagne and everyone seemed to have a glorious time. Pina would have some money when they left. Derby and his friends seemed to have a passion for enormous female torsos."[50] Lord Derby was so impressed with Pina that he bought him a quarry with beautiful pink limestone that was perfect for carving torsos. Reviewers attributed to Pina "the true sculptor's feeling for beauty in every inch of his material. He clothes its final expression in plastic values that reveal the essential integrity of technical discipline and a sensitive eye."[51] Pina, at thirty-six, was already being viewed as one of the foremost young Italian sculptors. His eight years with Rodin, up to the latter's death, were cherished in France and forgiven in Italy.[52] For De Lue, who had missed the opportunity to study with Rodin himself, the daily routine of working for one of Rodin's protégés and being across the street from another was sufficient justification for his European odyssey.

De Lue would also remember the custom of elegantly dressed connoisseurs visiting Pina's studio to view work in progress. De Lue recounted, "The visitor would often say, 'Don't let this one go. I'll take this one. This is sold!' " These were collectors who were uncommon at the time in America, and equally uncommon a decade or two later in Paris, for whom quality, not price, was the issue.[53]

De Lue was aware of other Americans in Paris, artists and writers and literati who centered about the Café du Dôme, but he was too driven by the calling of a career in sculpture to be much diverted by the pleasures of the moment. He later remarked, "The Café du Dôme — that's where Hemingway was, and the so-called 'lost generation.' The reason they were lost was because they were drinking so much they didn't know where they were."[54]

Of Bourdelle, De Lue would remember, "I met him and saw him almost every day. When I worked with Pina his studio was exactly across from Bourdelle and neither Pina nor Bourdelle would speak to each other. I was in between. Bourdelle was surrounded mostly by American women; he wasn't doing much of any work at this time. He loved adoration, and he would go out and walk down the Avenue Du Maine with his head up in the air and say things like 'Si glorieux, comme il est glorieux.' People would walk by and say, 'Voilà, le grand sculpteur!' He loved this sort of thing. Since he and Pina did not speak, Bourdelle was not too friendly with me. But he did invite me in one time to see if I would like to look around. I told him I was happy to look around and that I thought he was a great master. He said, 'Well, that is quite a concession.' "[55] Perhaps their both being assistants to Rodin set up an inevitable rivalry. Presumably Pina would have been even more distressed had he known that the Impasse du Maine, on which he had his atelier, would become the Rue Antoine Bourdelle.

The work he did for Pina and for DeBert provided De Lue with the funds to get to Versailles, Fontainebleau, and all the museums of Paris. Postwar France was beginning to right herself. The initial shortages and rationing were becoming less severe.

A Year in Lyon

In 1920 De Lue left Paris for Lyon. The torsos had been both fun and profitable, but it was time to move on. Word had it that there were sculptors needed for the restoration of the Cathedral of Lyon, and De Lue got off the train with great enthusiasm but with little money; however, there was no sign of work on the cathedral. Again the American military came to the rescue with a cot and board for a little while. As De Lue got his bearings in Lyon he began to walk the town. One day as he was on a high road above the city, in the little town of St. Just, he thought that he could see an artist's skylight above the wall that hid the houses from the road. He stopped at 25 Chemin de Francheville. As De Lue told it, "There was a big bell out front. I pulled the bell and the door opened, revealing a portly guy with a big leather apron on. I said, 'Would you have any use for a sculptor?' He invited me in. It was a very nice place and belonged to the man who had a contract to repair the sculpture for the cathedrals. He asked if I could model Madonnas and Josephs, etc. I said, yes. So, I began modeling the saints."[56]

The "portly guy" De Lue had met was Emile Vermare, the brother of André César Vermare, a well-known Lyon sculptor who maintained a Paris studio. The Lyon-based brother had contracts for the embellishment and restoration of ecclesiastical buildings in the Lyon area, as had his father Pierre before him.[57]

> He had plaster casters who would cast them; and limestone carvers who would carve them. All of them were pretty much in the Gothic style, trying to keep the character of the Gothic. I did a statue of a seated Madonna. Her head was down a bit with a bambino in her arms. I modeled it in clay and then another man carved it in beautiful limestone. Although the war was just over, they had sent to Germany for a polychromer who carefully colored the carved stone of the Madonna: blue for her drapery and gold for her halo. Apparently the German did it better than they did; there was no hostility, and I was surprised. We were all journeymen working together.[58]

The expressiveness of the French sculptors that De Lue chose to work with was a reflection of French trends and of the legacy of Rodin. The spirituality and power with which they invested their work perfectly complemented De Lue's growing aesthetic. Pina, Bourdelle, and André Vermare all reinforced the taste established in the young De Lue by Robert Baker. Indeed, Vermare's *Le Rhône et la Saone* bears more than a passing comparison to *The Soul's Struggle* by Baker.

After about a year, De Lue left Lyon. It had been interesting work and had given him a feeling for France and the French countryside, which

9

he valued, but it was not adding much to his career. He went to the famous porcelain works at Limoges to look for work as a modeler, but was turned away because they would not employ Americans. After repeated attempts to find work in the Limoges factories, out of money and with no prospects, De Lue returned to Paris.

There, he got the urgent message that his mother was ill and that he should return to Boston. He rushed to Le Havre and sailed for America, only to find his mother very well in Reading, Massachusetts. After three or four weeks with her, he went to New York and saw James Earle Fraser and other sculptors who said that there was very little going on in New York. He returned to Paris. De Lue later recounted, "Robert Baker was in Paris and he suggested that I come back over. He was living it up fairly well, and I felt that he could pitch in and 'help out' if he had to. Which he did. Ultimately, I found that 'pot luck' in Paris is better than in New York."[59]

Paul Manship

The American sculptor Paul Manship (1885–1966) was working in Paris in 1922. According to De Lue, "He was nice. I needed a job; I don't think he really needed any help, but he asked me to do a little something in plaster and gave me a few dollars for it."[60] He noted also that Manship "was *very* famous by then. I worked as an assistant for a short time. He was doing the portrait of the American ambassador to France, Myron T. Herrick.[61] It was rather interesting to me because it was the first time I'd ever seen a portrait done the way Manship did it. Manship would use French clay, and model a portrait bust very much as any sculptor would model it. Then he let the clay harden and dry, and then he would take small rasps and riffles and work the surface just as if it were plastic; it had already hardened, and that's what gave it that very hard, defined character that went into Manship's work."[62]

De Lue returned to DeBert's atelier to see his *American Soldiers* well tended and cared for, but it was never to become a monument. He received more day work there, but it was never a regular job. Robert Baker left the city. Meanwhile, De Lue had met Bryant Baker several times in Paris, and they continued to correspond. He knew that Baker maintained a studio in London for English commissions and was working there. When De Lue cabled him for money, Baker sent it along with a cable to come to London and assist him with his commissions.

There were a few difficulties in getting De Lue into Britain, but Baker, well connected by way of family and through commissions, got help from the American ambassador, George Harvey, who was currently sitting for his portrait. The ambassador requested that the British Foreign Office look into the problem, and immediately De Lue was admitted to Britain on a six month work visa. He went directly to London. Baker had a very nice studio on the Fulham Road in Chelsea.[63] De Lue lived there while he was in England and assisted Baker on a number of works. When the six-month visa ended, De Lue left for the United States via Scotland as a sailor on another merchant vessel.[64]

Paul Manship working with rasps and riffles on the arm and archaic drapery folds of a nearly completed plaster, *circa* 1920.

De Lue had the opportunity in the spring of 1922 to work with and observe the working methods of this remarkably famous and successful thirty-six year-old American sculptor.

Early New York Years

Donald De Lue was back in the United States by mid-autumn 1922, almost exactly four years after he had left. Bryant Baker was still in London, but Robert Baker was in New York. De Lue's mother, now his only close relative, was ill again in Massachusetts. Robert Baker provided the money to get De Lue from New York to Reading, where his mother died on November 21.[65] The death of his mother cut all ties to Boston for many years. A few weeks later he returned and plunged into the New York City of the 1920s.

At first it looked as if there was little work for him. He was offered a job by Lee Lawrie (1877–1963), who had a tremendous amount of work for architectural sculpture on new building projects in New York. Lawrie was then working on the reredos of St. Thomas.[66] Although it must have been a difficult decision, De Lue declined because he felt that Lawrie's work, with its powerful stylization, and Lawrie, with his dynamic and powerful personality, would so shape De Lue's style that he would not be able to form a distinct one of his own. He saw James Earle Fraser (1876–1953) who asked him why he wanted to be a sculptor when at most fifteen well-known sculptors could earn a decent living in the United States. Fraser noted that a full complement had become well established before the war, and that breaking in in the early 1920s would be a difficult job.[67] For some months, De Lue could find almost no work as a sculptor and refused to take other employment.

In Bryant Baker's New York Studio

After the war, Bryant Baker had reestablished his New York studio at 154 West 55th Street and had no end of portrait commissions, mostly because he had parlayed his contacts in Washington into an exhibition at the Corcoran Gallery in 1919. Baker had chosen his connections in Washington just as well as he had those in Britain and New York. His roommate there had been David Finley (1890–1977). When Baker first met him he was personal secretary to Andrew Mellon, the Secretary of the Treasury. Later Finley became the first Director of the National Gallery of Art in Washington (1938–1956).[68] In May 1923, after his return from London, Baker was given another Corcoran exhibition, which included portraits of Hoover, Roosevelt, Taft, Edward VII, Lloyd George, and General Pershing. This success was followed by a similar exhibition at the Anderson Galleries in New York in October 1923.

Meanwhile, by early 1923, De Lue and Bryant Baker were back together. Donald De Lue was the perfect addition to the Baker studio. His greatest talents lay in the areas where Bryant Baker was weakest. Baker was a highly competent sculptor who had the ability to capture a portrait likeness quickly. His severest critics admitted that while the sculptures might not be artistic, they did look like the subject. He had, however, great difficulty modeling the rest of the anatomy. De Lue's greatest strength was anatomy. Whether working from model, memory, or imagination, his muscles would always connect in the right place and the bone

OPPOSITE:

Icarus, 1934, gilded bronze, 30¼ inches.

There are those that believe that this is De Lue's finest work. He said he modeled it just after his marriage when he was trying to come up with a few important pieces. He did not exhibit it, however, until 1946, when it won the Gold Medal at the Allied Artists of America exhibition in New York. In 1948 a cast was placed in Brookgreen Gardens, S.C. The National Museum of American Art owns the plaster.

Bryant Baker making final modeling corrections on the clay model of *The Pioneer Woman* in the Gainsborough Studio Building studio in New York, 1927.

structure would be accurate. De Lue, therefore, soon had the primary responsibility for all work in the studio except portrait busts. Heads were modeled to Baker's ideal and he often completed the features. It was the perfect arrangement for Baker; it was somewhat less so for De Lue. As Baker's reputation grew, De Lue remained completely unknown except to a small circle of sculptor friends, which included Manship, Herbert Adams, and James Earle Fraser.

It must be said that De Lue's obscurity was not entirely Baker's fault. De Lue perhaps suffered the difficulties of most prodigies. He had begun the life of a sculptor at age twelve. He left formal schooling at fourteen and placed himself in the hands of Pratt, who died, and Recchia, who passed him on to Robert Baker, who vastly disappointed an impressionable twenty-year-old by running out of money. Bryant Baker had been in his life since he was sixteen. Baker was more than sixteen years De Lue's senior; the difference between a thirty-two-year-old and a sixteen-year-old is a generation. This difference may have started the relationship of both admiration and dependence that lasted until the late 1930s. De Lue was in contact with Baker during his sojourn in France, and when he needed help and money, Baker was the first person to come to mind. Baker came through with money, work, and powerful friends. It is difficult to tell when prodigies are no longer prodigies, but mature artists. Nevertheless, while he was Baker's assistant, De Lue could not form an independent identity as a sculptor.

De Lue was a good worker, journeyman, and assistant. He was affable and good-natured. Almost everybody in the New York community of sculptors knew that De Lue was Bryant Baker's assistant. And they knew that Bryant Baker did not have the ability to make a good, fully modeled full-figure statue, but that De Lue did. Once or twice Manship offered De Lue a similar position in his studio, but De Lue felt he was pretty well off where he was. He was happy working as a sculptor in New York and living at 4 West 40th Street across from the New York Public Library. He helped Baker model *Chief Justice White* (1923), *The Pioneer Woman, John M. Clayton* (1932) and *Abraham Lincoln* (1935). In early 1926 De Lue helped Baker move to larger and better accommodations at the Gainsborough Studio building at 222 West 59th Street.[69] He fell into the daily routine here for twelve years.

It was especially on the *The Pioneer Woman* that De Lue manifested his talent. *The Pioneer Woman* won a national competition that had been initiated in October 1926 by oilman-philanthropist Ernest W. Marland. Marland, who was later governor of Oklahoma (1935–1939), conceived a giant monument to the pioneer women of Oklahoma that would be visible for many miles on the open prairies of Ponca City. The maquettes by twelve distinguished sculptors were made at the invitation of Marland. They included models by James Earle Fraser, Jo Davidson, Alexander Stirling Calder, F. Lynn Jenkins, Herman A. MacNeil, Maurice Sterne, Wheeler Williams, John Gregory, Mario Korbel, Arthur Lee, and Mahonri Young, as well as the Bryant Baker entry. Baker claimed that the conception and movement of the final monument was developed in an eight- or ten-inch sketch model made by him in a few hours after he learned about the competition.[70] De Lue executed the thirty-three-inch competition model for the sculpture in 1927, with Baker supervising and completing the face. *The Pioneer Woman* may have been one of the truly populist commissions in the history of sculpture; the twelve models began a national tour, during which the public was invited to vote and the total popular vote was to determine the winner. Even in April 1927, at the Reinhardt Gallery in New York, the first stop on the tour, the Baker–De Lue maquette had placed first in the contest.[71] By the end of the fifteen-city tour, the Baker model had won in eleven cities and had beaten John Gregory's model, which won in four cities, by 42,478 to 37,782 votes.[72] The commission for the seventeen-foot sculpture on a thirteen-foot stone base was given to Baker. De Lue set to work in 1928 and 1929 modeling it in Baker's Brooklyn studio, working with Jean La Seure, the enlarger. De Lue later remembered: "One day Bryant decided he would work on it, and did some work. I said, 'Look, Bryant, if I were you I'd get the hell out of here, because you're not helping at all.' He said, 'Thank you very much!' and he went."[73] *The Pioneer Woman* was dedicated April 22, 1930, in Ponca City, Oklahoma, in ceremonies that included a radio address from Washington by President Herbert Hoover and a principal address by Will Rogers.[74]

De Lue also modeled two versions of *L'Apres-midi d'un Faune* for Baker in the late 1920s and early 1930s. The larger of the two, cut in marble by Baker, is now at Brookgreen Gardens, South Carolina. Baker enjoyed the idea of having his name on idealized subject pieces, but, as mentioned, did not model figures well. When work was slow for De Lue in modeling the bodies for portrait sculpture he would work up smaller pieces. Since, unlike some other sculptors of this period, Baker never gave credit to

L'-Apres-midi d'un Faune by Bryant Baker, marble, *circa* 1930.

De Lue, as Baker's assistant, modeled this and other works. Baker did much of the marble cutting himself in transferring the design from plaster to stone.

his assistant, he published this body of work under his name alone. At first De Lue went along because he had been getting about forty dollars a week from Baker throughout the 1920s. He was living well and enjoying himself as work poured into the studio through Baker's connections. But De Lue increasingly realized that a portion of the success of Baker's studio resulted from his own abilities.

The Not-So-Great Depression

According to De Lue, even in the darkest days of the Depression, Baker could bring in work. His recollection was:

> We were very busy during that time. Baker had all the commissions he could do; while everybody was having a bad time, Baker was doing very well, and I was getting forty dollars a week. I know that when I went

Pegasus, 1930, bronze, 21½ inches.

This is one of a group of very early modernized animals that derive from Greek mythology and one of the first of many Pegasuses modeled over a long career. Pegasus was able to give man the god-like power of flight. (see p. 26, *Centaur with Lyre*.)

OPPOSITE:

Jupiter as the Bull, *The Bull*, or *Jupiter*, 1931, bronze, 24 inches.

As with *Pegasus*, De Lue drew on an animal from Greek mythology and gave him supernatural power and a joyous cavorting character. De Lue first patinated the plaster in a pewtery silver and patined the first bronzes to conform. However, he enjoyed with this sculpture, more than almost any other, exploring the range of patinas that would reveal new sensibilities and nuances in the work. The three casts illustrated here suggest the range of possibilities that include black, gold, green, and brown.

(Courtesy of Childs Gallery, Boston)

different places I was assumed to have a lot of money. I had a studio on 40th Street, but I wasn't doing much in the way of work because all my working time went for Baker. I did a lot of drawing for myself, but not much sculpture at this time.

This was a period of a good deal of play. A friend and I, Terry Ryan, shared quite a swanky studio together. He ran Terri Cosmetics, and hell, he went broke, and I found on forty dollars a week I was supporting quite a few people before long. How far it would go in those days . . . really, money amounted to something! I went to Bermuda and took very nice trips. Baker made contributions to things of that kind—a couple of hundred dollars—but, it cost very little to do things in those days. The Depression really didn't hurt us at all. I've learned since then, that when there's a lot of money, very seldom is it seriously felt. If there's a family that has a great deal of money, their funds may be down but they still have money. This ran all through Baker's life; and much of his work was private. And, of course, David Finley was a big help.[75]

As De Lue phrased it:

I did the *Pioneer Woman* and many other statues for him. I was very well engaged, earning a very good living, and quite happy, excepting: It wasn't

Nymph, 1934, bronze, 26½ inches.

This is probably the earliest surviving work in which De Lue reaches for his final form, style and themes. It would be hardly credible that this streamlined *Nymph* could be from the same year as *Seated Woman* were it not for a 1934 drawing that shows a closely related figure. Once again, the title suggests the deep involvement that De Lue felt in the 1930s with classical mythology and writings.

OPPOSITE:

Echo and *Faun*, 1937, bronze, 22 inches.

De Lue exhibited the patinated plaster of *Faun* at the Architectural League of New York in 1938. This was one of the earliest public exhibitions of a work by De Lue under his own name. The beautiful designing of each piece with its sensuously modeled back, complemented by a splendid base design, is characteristic of the perfection that De Lue was trying to bring to his work.

(Courtesy of the Museum of Fine Arts, Boston)

my own work. I still had to find some way to get out for myself; that was the difficult part. It always is. There are all kinds of young sculptors that are quite capable, but they have to find somebody that has enough faith in them to give them a good commission. Once you get some sort of establishment it comes much easier.[76]

De Lue began to take some ideas that he had for sculpture and do them on his own time in a corner of the 40th Street studio. This resulted in *Pegasus* (1930), *The Bull*, *Modern Madonna* (1931), and others. Unfortunately, aside from his close circle of friends, few had any idea that De Lue had done any work. There was no opportunity to show his plaster models and no money to cast them in bronze.

On October 5, 1933, Donald De Lue's thirty-sixth birthday, he married Martha Naomi Cross. He had met her a couple of years before on a blind date and they had begun to see each other regularly. Her mother had wanted them to get married almost from the moment that they met. Naomi taught De Lue to save money and began acting as his business manager. They moved to an apartment at 322 West 72nd Street, a penthouse on the corner of Riverside Drive which De Lue had already set up as a studio. The process of separation from Baker was beginning.

In 1934 De Lue began one of his most famous sculptures, *Icarus*, and modeled *Seated Woman*. He also experimented with etching and drypoint, executing more than a dozen works, mostly single female and male nudes, but some complicated interactive groups that presaged his aspirational human figures of a decade later. He frankly admittted later they were done in the hope that they would sell well and raise money. Also, they did not compete with Bryant Baker's sculpture. The etching project continued at least through 1935, and while some works sold, it was not the commercial success that De Lue had hoped for. A drawing for the print project, dated 1934, shows the close relationship between the drawings of this period and his ideas in sculpture. In particular the female figure at the center seems to be a reverse study for *Nymph* (1934). In this

Figure Composition 1934, pencil drawing, 8 × 10 inches.

This drawing, which is related to De Lue's etching series, shows in the center a female figure with a composition nearly the reverse of *Nymph*.

same period De Lue modeled three of his most beautiful early works—*Echo* and *Faun*, both of which were substantially complete by 1937, and *Sun God*, which De Lue said was the last work that he modeled in French clay and the last that he cast into plaster on his own.   25 30

De Lue was already very good at the craft of sculpture. His experience and advice given to him suggested that he might find commissions in garden sculpture, the male and female figures, and in competitions for architectural sculpture. As evidenced in *Nymph*, he had already developed a style that would stay with him the rest of his life. However, he was also willing to experiment with a "modern" style of bigger, rounder, and more simplified stylizations as seen in *Modern Madonna, Pegasus, Jupiter as the Bull, Icarus,* and *Seated Woman*. This tendency to develop both styles and to shift back and forth between them to some degree continued until about 1950. He was beginning a struggle for stylistic maturity and financial independence.   24   28, 23   22, 19, 2

Donald De Lue in his studio modeling *Centaur*, 1930–1942.

This photograph, which was probably taken in the Lincoln Arcade Studio about 1942, illustrates the difficulties in accurately dating De Lue sculpture that was not a part of a monument or competition. *Centaur* seems to have first been modeled as shown in this photo, then remodeled replacing the lyre with a bow (p. 27) and finally remodeled entirely as *Pegasus* (p. 23). De Lue said that he did *Pegasus* in 1930, and it is entirely possible that he did, but the evidence presented in this photograph argues for a date of 1942 for all three of the modelings and agrees with the date given in the 1955 *Donald De Lue* University of Georgia catalogue.

NOTES

1. Unless otherwise stated, the work of Plato is quoted from *The Dialogues of Plato,* translated by B. Jowett (New York and London: Oxford University Press, 1892).
2. Boston Vital Statistics, 1897; Vol. 468, p.186, line 8357. De Lue was born as Donald H. Quigley at 13 Savin Hill Avenue where his parents, Harry T. Quigley and Ida M. De Lue Quigley, were living with his maternal grandfather, a widower who still made his living as a carpenter and jobber. De Lue lived there most of the time until 1906.

Donald De Lue began changing his name directly after the death of his father (see footnote 10) by inserting de Lue as his middle name. When he left Boston in 1918, he dropped Quigley altogether. One may speculate on many reasons for the name change: his distance from his father or embarassment over his death; his affection for his mother or his maternal grandfather; his belief in the artistic superiority of French culture; or the statement reported by his Boston contemporary, Joseph Pollia, that "De Lue thought that Donald Quigley sounded too much like an Irish cop." "Harcourt" filled in the "H." on his birth certificate. It may have been suggested by Harcourt Street or the Harcourt Studios in Boston. The Anglo-French name appealed to De Lue.

Boston City Directory, 1897–1906.

In the 1900 U.S. Census (Massachusetts, Suffolk County, Vol. 78, ed. 1452, sheet 3, line 26) De Lue's father listed himself as born in Massachusetts, although he was identified in other records, including his death certificate, more authoritatively as born in Amherst, Nova Scotia.
3. In the Boston City Directory, 1907–1914, De Lue's mother is living at 27 Montello Street, Roslindale (in about 1910 the name of the street was changed to Montvale to avoid confusion with another Montello Street in Boston). During this period, De Lue's father often lived elsewhere and his mother has a separate directory listing under her own name.

The 1910 census notes only De Lue and his mother as lodgers. Donald was twelve years old at the time of the census (April 16, 1910). Clarence De Lue and his daughter Bertha (presumably Donald's maternal uncle and cousin) lived next door.
4. Donald H. De Lue to D. Roger Howlett, taped telephone interview, November 13, 1987, hereinafter referred to as "DDL to DRH."
5. Transcript of "Taped Conversation between George Gurney and Donald De Lue" at his home and studio in Leonardo, New Jersey, March 29, 1978, p.13. copyright; hereinafter referred to as "Gurney."

6. Gurney, p. 5.

7. Boston City Directory, 1909–1912.

8. Donald De Lue to Richard Recchia, letter, Jan. 5, 1977. Richard Recchia Collection, Sawyer Library, Gloucester, Massachusetts (hereinafter referred to as "Recchia Collection").

9. Boston City Directory. 1897–1914. De Lue's father was a clerk at Wetherell Brothers (Iron and Steel dealers) at 31 Oliver Street in Boston in 1897. After 1900 he became a salesman for the same firm. In 1907 he became a partner of McMinn & Quigley, which continued until 1913. In 1914 the partnership ended and he became a sales agent at 141 Milk Street.

10. Boston Vital Statistics, 1914. Vol. 13, p. 306. Arlington, Massachusetts, Vital Statistics, 1914. Vol. 2, p. 372. De Lue's father's death may have been related to business reverses. He died June 3, 1914; the cause of death was "crush of skull caused by precipitous ejection from height (window) presumably suicidal." Harry T. Quigley, age 43, was residing in Arlington at the time, separated from his wife and son, despite the 1914 Boston City Directory entry to the contrary.

11. Paula M. Kozol, *American Figurative Sculpture in the Museum of Fine Arts Boston* (Boston: Northeastern University Press, 1986), p. 315 (hereinafter referred to as "MFA Sculpture"). *Science* was dedicated May 20, 1912, and *Art* was dedicated June 6, 1912.

13. DDL to DRH, 1987.

13. MFA Sculpture, p. 416.

14. DDL to DRH, 1987 (Pratt's use of Recchia's studio confirmed by letters from Bela L. Pratt to Richard Recchia dated Feb. 15, 1912, March 12, 1912, and April 15, 1912 in the "Recchia Collection").

15. MFA Sculpture, pp. 310–311.

16. Boston City Directory, 1913–1919.

17. Donald De Lue Quigley to Bela Pratt, letter July 27, 1915; Pratt Family Papers. The letter was brought to the author's attention by Cynthia Pratt Kennedy Sam, granddaughter of Bela Pratt, who is preparing a biography of Bela Pratt. The letter was sent from 118 Ridge Road in Reading, Massachusetts.

18. Register of Pupils — School of the Museum of Fine Arts, Boston, 1914, p. 741. Donald De Lue entered the modeling class of the School of the Museum of Fine Arts as Donald De Lue Quigley. He was registered as living with his mother at 118 Ridge Rd., Reading, Massachusetts. He was granted a "Sp.Sch 1914–1915." The Annual Circular suggests that the value of this special scholarship with registration fee and tuition for the three semesters was $135.00 per year, a sum utterly beyond young De Lue without scholarship.

19. Ibid. Despite claims, made by De Lue over the years, that he attended the School of the Museum of Fine Arts for only a few months, his attendance record was remarkable. Except for the first term, when he entered three weeks late in the program, he missed only ten days of the following five terms, and in three had perfect attendance. In the School of the Museum of Fine Arts, Boston, Annual Circular 1914–1915. Bela L. Pratt is listed as "Instructor in Modelling," Frederick W. Allen as "Assistant in Modelling."

20. Ibid. The modeling courses probably met from 9–1 daily. This afforded 660 hours of instruction per year which was described in the Annual Circular: *The course in modelling, under Mr. Pratt, is open both to those who wish to devote themselves exclusively to this art and to those students of drawing or painting who wish to practice in modelling as a means toward improving their ability to render the human figure. The pupils in this department are taught to model the human figure both singly and in the composition. Regular attendance in these departments is not compulsory, but it is essential for the accomplishment of the required work. Pupils are not allowed to remain in any one class more than two years without special permission of the Faculty.*

   De Lue's attendance record shows that he attended the last class of the spring term of 1916, thus completing two full years of training.

Centaur Archer, 1930–1942.
The clay in the base of the figure in this photograph seems to be substantially the same as the final form of *Pegasus* (p. 23).

Modern Madonna, 1930, plaster.

This sculpture represents De Lue's extreme attempt to modernize, embolden and eliminate detail from the female form. Like *Seated Woman*, it comes from a desire to conform to the then-current trends toward abstraction of the human figure.

21. Ibid. Mrs. David P. Kimball gave $150.00 to be divided into prizes for the pupils in modeling for 1914–1915.

Register, op. cit. De Lue received the Kimball Prize of $10.00 in May of 1915.

22. Donald de Lue Quigley to Bela Pratt July 27, 1915 op. cit. The "Normal Art" referred to in the letter is the Massachusetts Normal School of Art, now called the Massachusetts College of Art.

23. DDL to DRH, 1987.

24. Boston City Directory, 1916–1918.

25. James H. Worthington, "Markings of Mars," *Nature*, Nov. 10, 1910, p. 40.

See also "Planet Mars," *Scientific American*, Oct. 26, 1912, pp. 266–67.

26. DDL to DRH, 1987.

27. Annual Report of the Royal Academy, London, 1911. Enrollment Lists of the Royal Academy, London.

28. *The National Cyclopedia of American Biography*, Vol. 34 (New York: James T. White and Co, 1948).

29. Susan Beattie, *The New Sculpture* (New Haven: Yale University Press, 1983).

30. DDL to DRH, 1987.

31. W. H. DeB. Nelson, "In a Boston Studio," *The International Studio*, Vol. 62, No. 248, October 1917, pp. 81–88.

32. Gurney, p. 11.

33. Michael Lantz, "Reminiscing with Donald De Lue," *National Sculpture Review*, Vol. 23, No. 2, Summer 1974, pp. 26–27, (hereinafter referred to as Lantz).

34. DDL to DRH, Nov. 16, 1987.

35. Ibid.

36. Beatrice Gilman Proske, *Brookgreen Gardens Sculpture* (Murrell's Inlet, South Carolina: Brookgreen Gardens, 1968), p. 236.

37. MFA Sculpture, p. 447.

38. Annual Report of the Royal Academy, London, 1908. Enrollment Lists of the Royal Academy, London.

39. In 1908 (Percy) Bryant Baker took second prize for *Model of a Design* (Orpheus and Euridice) and *Set of Four Models of a Figure from Life*. In 1911, his brother Robert (Peter) Baker took first prize and a silver medal for *Model of a Bust from Life* and *Set of Three Models of a Figure from Life*. In addition he was holder of the Landseer scholarship in sculpture. The relative standings in the awards seem to corroborate De Lue's assessment of the talents of the two brothers.

40. DDL to DRH, Nov. 13, 1987.

41. "The *S.S. Minnesota* entered the Port of New York on November 7, 1918 and departed for Marseille between the Armistice and December 4, (the only ship to do so in this period). "Register of Ships Arriving at New York from foreign ports;" *New York Times*, November 11–December 4, 1918."

42. Gurney, p. 16.

43. DDL to DRH, Nov. 13, 1987.

44. Bela L. Pratt to Richard Recchia, letter, April 15, 1912, "Recchia Collection."

45. Gurney, p. 27.

46. Lantz, p. 26.

47. DDL to DRH, Nov. 13, 1987.

48. DDL to DRH, Nov. 16, 1987.

49. Ibid. De Lue said that DeBert was not Charles Jules DeBert, but a decorative, ornamental and architectural artisan-sculptor. He further stated that the man's name may have been Joubert.

50. DDL to DRH, 1987.

51. "Alfredo Pina / Fifty-Sixth Street Galleries," *Art News*, January 31, 1931, p. 10.

52. "Alfredo Pina, Friend of Rodin Exhibits," *Art Digest*, February 1, 1931, p. 16.

53. DDL to DRH, Nov. 16, 1987.

54. Gurney, p. 28.

55. DDL to DRH, Jan. 20, 1987. *See also* Gurney, p. 25

56. DDL to DRH, 1987.

57. Gurney, p. 66. *See also* Edouard-Joseph, *Dictionnaire Biographique des Artistes Contemporaines* (Paris, 1934).
58. DDL to DRH, 1987. *See also* Gurney, pp. 22–23.
59. DDL to DRH, Nov. 16, 1987.
60. DDL to DRH, Jan. 20, 1987.
61. Edwin Murtha, *Paul Manship* catalogue 159, figure 24, (New York: MacMillan Co., 1957). Manship was in Paris from 1922–1926. His portrait of Myron T. Herrick was made during the spring and fall of 1922.
62. Gurney, pp. 28–29.
63. The Royal Academy of the Arts, *Royal Academy Exhibitors: 1905–1970* (London: E. P. Publishing, Ltd., 1973). From 1911–1923 Bryant Baker maintained Studio B at 404 Fulham Road, S.W.6 London. In 1923 he exhibited the bronze bust of "H.E. George Harvey, the American Ambassador."
64. *Boston Transcript*, July 15, 1921.
65. Massachusetts Vital Statistics, 1922, Reading, Vol. 67., p. 411. Ida M. De Lue Quigley died of a heart attack at 257 Main Street, Reading, Massachusetts, on Nov. 21, 1922. She was born in South Boston. Both her parents were from New Brunswick; both her husband's parents were from Nova Scotia. All four of Donald De Lue's grandparents were from the maritime provinces of Canada.
66. Gurney, pp. 73–74.
67. Gurney, p. 33.
68. Gurney, pp. 14–15, 36.
69. New York City and Brooklyn telephone directory, 1925–1926.
70. Letter from Baker to Ponca City News, 1968.
71. *Literary Digest*, April 9, 1927.
72. Unidentified newspaper clipping circa 1928 in Bryant Baker file, Fine Arts Reference, Boston Public Library.
73. DDL to DRH, Nov. 13, 1987.
74. Unidentified newspaper clipping, April 12, 1930, in Bryant Baker file, Fine Arts Reference, Boston Public Library.
75. Gurney, pp. 34–35.
76. DDL to DRH, 1987.

Secrets, 1933–1934, drypoint, 7¾ x 8¾ inches.

This is one of a series of about a dozen drypoints made by De Lue in an effort to raise additional money without directly competing with Bryant Baker. Only a small number of each were printed.

And if you were resolved to go to Polycleitus the Argive, or Pheidias the Athenian, and were intending to give them money, and some one had asked you: What are Polycleitus and Pheidias? and why do you give them this money? — how would you have answered? I should have answered, that they were statuaries. And what will they make of you?

A statuary, of course.

PLATO   *PROTAGORAS*

II

AN INDEPENDENT CAREER BEGINS

Opportunities for Exhibition and Competition

B Y 1937, DE LUE HAD BEGUN TO BUILD A SMALL BODY OF FINE WORK THAT no one had yet seen publicly. That year he exhibited *Sun God* and *Allegorical Figure* at the Architectural League in New York and showed *Faun* there the following year. He was beginning to emerge as an independent sculptor.

De Lue had had great success with the competition for the *Pioneer Woman*, for although Bryant Baker had won the contract, De Lue had won the competition. In mid-April 1935 Bryant Baker decided to accept an invitation to compete for the contract for the niche figures for the interior of the Department of the Post Office Building in Washington. He turned the project over to De Lue. Although De Lue and Baker did not win the *Colonial Foot Postman*, no doubt it planted the idea in De Lue's mind that he could compete on his own.[1] De Lue's career was taking shape. He took the step that was to be his "way to get out," although it would be two years before it had any effect on his life.

The Apex Competition

In 1937, De Lue entered a competition for sculpture on the new Federal Trade Commission Building in Washington, known as the Apex building. It was an open competition, judged without the sculptor's name on the work, and attracting 247 sculptors. The Apex building was the last of the buildings to be constructed in the Federal Triangle in Washington, the largest federal construction project in Washington's history. Although the thought and planning of the project antedated the Public Buildings Act of 1926, it was Andrew Mellon, secretary of the treasury, who took firm control, with congressional approval, and began to make the giant project a reality. The arrival of Franklin Delano Roosevelt and the New Deal began to put a new face on the project after 1933. The Apex building was the only building in the complex to be constructed entirely in the new administration and with the advice of the Section of Painting and Sculpture. The section, a part of the treasury, had been created through the efforts of Edward Bruce in 1934. Bruce had had an interesting career that had led him into art, trade, and finance. He developed a specific

Donald De Lue sculpture INC., circa 1940, crayon drawing on paper.

This drawing is certainly a result of De Lue's growing consciousness of the need to promote his career in a business-like way and of the importance of architectural commissions.

OPPOSITE:

Sun God (Helios), 1937, bronze, 33 inches.

Like Apollo, Helios drove across the sky daily in his four-horse chariot and was known as "untiring," "all-seeing," and "he who makes mortals rejoice." This work seems to be De Lue's first publicly exhibited sculpture and was well chosen to exhibit both a theme and a style that would characterize a lifetime of exuberant and optimistic work.

(Courtesy of Osuna Gallery, Washington, D.C.)

31

Clay Model for the *Apex Competition (Trade on Land)*, 1937.

In this early stage of the model the clay is cut out of the block as De Lue described, and major modifications were made before it was submitted to the competition.

program that used federal commissions to help young painters and sculptors and to improve the taste of the public. He felt that the best way to discover talent and to award work was through open, anonymous competition. The Apex was the section's most important national competition. It was to be for two monumental stone sculptures to sit on either side of the building facing Sixth Street, each to be mounted on granite plinths seventeen feet three inches long by seven feet wide.

In January 1938 Michael Lantz was announced as the winner. Although De Lue did not win the Federal Trade Commission Building Competition, he had succeeded, for his models had impressed the judges—Paul Manship, Lee Lawrie, and Adolph Weinman. Twenty-six sculptors received commendations, but only four—Henry Kreis of Essex, Connecticut; Edmond Amateis of Brewster, New York; and Benjamin Hawkins and Donald De Lue of New York City—received honorable mentions.

Of De Lue's models George Gurney, curator of sculpture at the National Museum of American Art, says:

> The models exhibited many of the stylized characteristics that were to be embodied in De Lue's later works. Both groups convey a sense of bold energy through tightly packed masses of forms, curvilinear movements, and the extended gestures of the figures. The rather masculine treatment of the female forms and the pronounced musculature of the male figures were inspired more by Michelangelo than by classical prototypes. Although he was a facile modeler, De Lue decided in executing his groups to employ a different technique because he was not accustomed to doing monumental work. In his words, "in this case I put up a block of clay, thinking of a block of stone, and I cut these figures out of it instead of adding to it. But I tried to keep some sort of monolithic block here. I realized it was a carving job, so that's one of the reasons I sort of carved these groups out of a block

of clay." A generally rectangular shape was preserved in the two groups. In contrast to most of the other competition models, De Lue's sketches are not oriented toward a single viewpoint, but rather conceived to be explored in three dimensions from all perspectives.[2]

Apex Competition Models (*Trade on Land* and *Trade on Sea*), 1937, bronze, 15½ and 16 inches.

These models for the Federal Trade Commission Building in Washington received one of four honorable mentions and gained for De Lue the Philadelphia Court House commission.

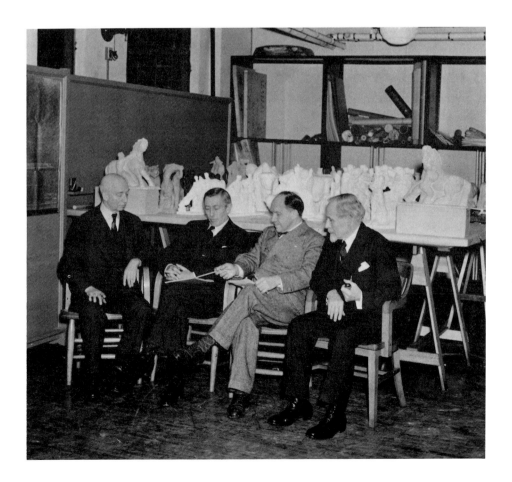

Jury for the Apex Competition, January 1938.

From left to right: William E. Parsons, representing the architects of the building, and the distinguished sculptors Lee O. Lawrie, Paul Manship, and Adolph A. Weinman. Michael Lantz's winning models are elevated on the far right and left; De Lue's models are in the foreground directly to the left of the Lantz model on the right and over the head and shoulder of Weinman. The sculptors on the jury were selected by a vote of the competing artists.

Lafayette, 1938, bronze, 22 inches.

This highly stylized sculpture was created as a model for a competition in Philadelphia. It is the first of De Lue's many American heroes.

Family Group, 1938.

The plaster model for the Metropolitan Life competition shows the heavily stylized, simplified and rounded forms that were sought in the 1930s and 1940s as appropriate to modern public sculpture. The head types, particularly of the standing male figure, are De Lue ideals that continued throughout his life. The disembodied hands are the first appearance of a symbol of spiritual uplift and protection that similarly reappeared through De Lue's career.

Metropolitan Life Competition

De Lue was elected to membership in the National Sculpture Society in 1938. He would never again be without his own studio. That year he modeled *Lafayette* to try to get his first commission in Philadelphia and *Family Group* for a competition for the Metropolitan Life Insurance Company. The contest, which was worth an $8,000 commission, was open to all sculptors who had completed at least one professional piece of statuary. The winner's work was to be exhibited at the center of the Metropolitan Life Insurance Company's exhibit at the 1939 World's Fair in New York. Thomas G. LoMedico was selected by the jury for first place, and Willem Van Beek and Albert Wein received honorable mention out of a field of 257 entries. All the models were shown in a grand display open to the public on April 28 and 29, 1938. If the loss of this competition distressed De Lue, he did not show it, for he wrote to the company, "As a contestant . . . I wish to congratulate you on the manner in which the exhibits were handled. The number of models submitted was amazing and must have presented quite a problem. They were displayed with excellent taste and would do credit to a professional gallery."[3] Four prominent contemporary sculptors, William Zorach, Mahonri Young, Robert Laurent, and Maurice Sterne, had been invited to make models for the contest, but their entries did not receive even a mention when the winner was announced. The solicitation of these four sculptors and the final choices of the judges suggest that the company was looking for a modernist solution to their need for a sculpture.[4] Other sculptors that entered were De Lue's old friends George Aarons and Joseph Pollia, as well as Henry Kreis, Wheeler Williams, Chaim Gross, Isamu Noguchi, Avard Fairbanks, Marshall Fredericks, and Louis Milione. Some of the competition clay models, including De Lue's, were later exhibited at the Clay Club in New York in January and February 1939.[5] De Lue's Apex competition models were also exhibited. The exhibition was especially designed to put before the public the difficulty that competitions caused sculptors. De Lue's *Family Group* was described as "suggesting a scale of monumental proportions. . . . De Lue, along with the other three contestants whose family groups are in the show, turned out a competent piece of work which, after the close of the contest, is of use neither to the artist nor the public."[6] To be sure, certain younger sculptors on their way to a successful career gained attention and contracts through these contests; but, as the exhibition showed, of the thirty-six models exhibited by twenty-one sculptors, only two were winners. The balance were carefully made maquettes cast into plaster that could be retired to the top shelf of the sculptor's studio where they might gather dust. Few if any of these models had another use.[7] De Lue's emergence came just too late for him to be considered for any of the many sculptural commissions for the 1939 World's Fair. All, however, was not lost.

Encouragement of Colleagues

In 1938, as one of his first commissions, De Lue was asked by the sculptor Eleanor Mellon (1894–1979) to model a five-foot five-inch high *Saint John the Baptist*, to be carved in stone for the Church of the Epiphany on York Avenue at 67th Street. De Lue first completed a working model, twenty and three-quarters inches high, in plastiline,[8] which was cast into plaster and then enlarged to the full size.[9] The carving, done in Italy, was arranged by René Lavaggi, whose father was a stone carver. The church was grateful, but it was several years before they mounted it in the interior. Eleanor Mellon, like Anna Hyatt Huntington, believed in encouraging young sculptors through commissions and introductions.

As secretary of the National Sculpture Society, Eleanor Mellon often played hostess to Donald and Naomi De Lue and would invite them to dine with other sculptors at her apartment. She introduced the De Lues

St. John the Baptist, 1938, bronze, 20¾ inches.

This is the study maquette that De Lue presented to Eleanor Mellon for the St. John statue for the Church of the Epiphany in New York. St. John, attenuated but vigorous and clothed in a hair shirt, turns his head as he listens to the word of the Holy Spirit.

to Malvina Hoffman (1887–1966) and to Edward McCartan (1879–1947). Hoffman also made introductions for the De Lues and would entertain them at her New York studio and townhouse. De Lue's notes during this period indicate that he often had lunch with Hoffman. Both Hoffman and Mellon encouraged him, and De Lue's rise in success and prominence in the next few years may have been a result partially of their sponsorship, as well as that of Anna Hyatt Huntington (1876–1973) and Margaret French Cresson (1889–1973), daughter of Daniel Chester French (1850–1931).

McCartan gave De Lue some advice that he took to heart. He said: "If you want to develop into an important sculptor in the United States, forget the female figure. It's all right for fun but isn't going to get you anywhere. Think about architecture and think about monumental sculpture. That's the place for you to go."

James Earle Fraser gave him similar advice: "My advice to you would be to start thinking about monumental sculpture, especially related to the male figure. We all like doing female figures, but if you want to become a sculptor and earn your living at it, think about it in monumental terms. The male figure: it's the males that rule the world. So, do the best male figure that you can."[10]

St. John the Baptist, 1938, pencil drawing, 33½ x 22 inches.

De Lue was aware of the Gothic architectural niche that he was required to fill and drew many studies showing the proposed statue in place. He may have recalled his earlier figures for the Gothic churches of Lyon, for this is the most medievalized of his commissioned works.

St. John the Baptist, 1938–45, stone, 65 inches.

The finished sculpture is mounted over the door in the interior of the Church of the Epiphany on York Avenue at 67th Street in New York. This is probably De Lue's first independent commission. The stone was carved in Italy and the delay in the installation in the Church may have been the result of World War II.

Malvina Hoffman (right) with Naomi and Donald De Lue, summer, 1948, at Bedford, N.Y.

Hoffman admired De Lue's ability and aided his career. De Lue returned the admiration. He recounted that he and Naomi were often her guests both in New York City and at Bedford, where she rented a farm in 1948. He referred to her as the "most famous American woman sculptor."

De Lue further developed these precepts. He felt that a good male figure took much more knowledge on the part of a sculptor than a female figure, that the power of architectural sculpture was better served by male figures and that the male symbolized "dynamic power."

Philadelphia Court House Commission

De Lue got a telephone call in New York one day late in 1938 asking him if he could be in Washington at ten o'clock the next morning to meet with the chairman of a committee to approve sculpture for the new Federal Court House in Philadelphia. When he arrived the aide who greeted him said, "You know Mr. De Lue, you were the runner-up on the Apex competition."[11] The judges had recommended him for a major federal project on the strength of his entry in the Federal Trade Commission Building Competition. The chief of the Section of Fine Arts, Edward Bruce, said to him, "We didn't contact you because we thought you were not in sympathy with what we were doing."

De Lue replied, "Well, I'm not entirely in sympathy with you even now. I don't approve of a lot of people competing in something just because they think they're sculptors. Democracy works everywhere except in art. Art is a thing of achievement and perfection. Many of these people have not had any experience in it. I think what you're doing is all right but the way that you're doing it is wrong. Of course I'm in sympathy with giving sculptors work, but over half of the people that competed had no experience in sculpture."[12]

Despite some philosophical differences, he got on well with the committee and was hired. He received $2,000 each for *Law* and *Justice* and $1,000 for the model of the eagle to be placed over the elevator doors of the Federal Court House in Philadelphia. This combined fee represented

Justice, 1939–40, finished plaster model for the Philadelphia Court House granite relief carvings.

In this, De Lue's first government commission, he was encouraged by the architect to unleash his proclivity for Michelangelesque power. The resulting sculpture also shows the required "modernizing" and simplification of the new federal style.

by far the largest commission or remuneration that De Lue had received to date. The government then cleverly had each duplicated so that they had four granite panels and two eagles. Edmond R. Amateis (1897–1981) did the four other panels on the building. All were carved by Ugo Lavaggi, the father of Rene Lavaggi, who had arranged for the carving of De Lue's *St. John the Baptist* at the church of the Epiphany. According to the *Art Digest*, the project was one of the largest sculpture commissions issued by the government's Section of Fine Arts.[13]

36

The Section versus the Architect

For many months there had been wrangling in Washington between Harry Sternfeld (1888–1976), the architect of the court house, and the administrators of the Section of Fine Arts over who had the right and responsibility to choose the sculptors for the building. Philosophically, the architect was unalterably opposed to an open competition, and the section was equally adamantly for it. The controversy came to a head the very month that the Apex competition was awarded. Since a major federal competition had just been held, and a stated intention of that competition was that those sculptors who had received honorable mentions should receive commissions, the mechanism was in place to award direct commissions and still adhere to the spirit of competition.[14]

Law, 1939–40, finished plaster model for the Philadelphia Court House granite relief carvings.

Sternfeld, however, had a list of eight sculptors that he wanted the section to choose from: Edmund Amateis, Gaetano Cecere, Walker Hancock, Benjamin Hawkins, Paul Jennewein, Louis Milione, Albert Stewart, and Lee Lawrie.[15] Amateis was on the section's list from the Apex competition. This formed a compromise of sorts. De Lue became the section's other choice. In a letter of April 19, 1938, Edward Rowan wrote to Sternfeld, "You will notice . . . a photograph of the two entries of Mr. De Lue in the recent competition here for the sculpture of the Federal Trade Commission Building (the Apex competition). The jury, consisting of Mr. Lee Lawrie, Mr. Paul Manship and Mr. Adolph Weinman, considered Mr. De Lue's work entirely outstanding and rated his entries among the first five chosen. It is my feeling that Mr. De Lue's entries, though presented as figures in the round, are actually designs in high relief and it is for this reason that he is recommended to you for your consideration as one of the artists to be considered for the proposed reliefs on the Philadelphia, Pennsylvania, Post Office and Court House. I can further assure you from my contacts with the artist, that he is easy to work with and amenable to suggestions." The Section further recommended that De Lue do the *Justice* panels.

On January 7, 1939, De Lue was mailed his formal request by Inslee Hopper, consultant to the chief, Section of Fine Arts, Procurement Division of the Treasury Department; it read in part: "The Section of Fine

Designs for U. S. Post Office, circa 1940, plaster.

De Lue submitted a design for the Post Office, Forest Hills Station, in Flushing, New York. These may be related to that project. As with the Philadelphia Court House they are strong, simplified, and somewhat abstracted.

Arts invites you to submit designs for three sculpture reliefs for the Philadelphia, Pennsylvania, Post Office and Court House, on the basis of the merit of the model submitted by you in the competition for the decoration of the Federal Trade Commission Building, Washington, D.C. The submission of designs for this decoration is not competitive. Upon the approval of sketch models by the Director of Procurement, a contract for the execution of the reliefs will be drawn up for your signature."

In a letter dated January 9, 1939, De Lue wrote to Inslee A. Hopper, "I am delighted with the job. I feel that if I were a sculptor of outstanding reputation, I could not have received a more important commission. When Mr. Sternfeld (the architect) showed me the rendering of the building and let it be known that Washington had insisted that I do the two main panels, I was most pleasantly surprised and fully realized that I had been very highly favored to be given a position of such importance on my first public job. I am also delighted to get the eagle to do, as I feel doing a good eagle is the outstanding achievement of architectural sculpture. . . . I found Mr. Sternfeld a little difficult at first, but feel that we shall get along very well."

On February 6, he again wrote to Hopper, "I have been down to see the building and have made a number of small sketches. I find I am in the dark concerning elevation and profiles of the building and even on these preliminary sketches a blue-print or a rendering would help me in my conception of the problem. If for some reason or other it is not convenient to let me have the blue-prints just now, I will manage to work these sketches just as compositions."

The blueprints had not arrived in De Lue's studio before he set out for a conference with Sternfeld in Philadelphia. On February 18, Sternfeld wrote, "The conference was of value because it cleared up many questions and gave Mr. De Lue the direction in which he may proceed with his sketches . . . . We have not yet heard from Mr. Amateis, who we understand has been selected for other sculptural models. We understand that the [stone] panels for the sculptural work have arrived in Philadelphia and will shortly be set in place. We beg to point out, that during the past year, we have repeatedly asked that the models for this work be prepared in order that there be no delay. Unless intensive work is now done on them, we feel that a serious delay will be incurred."[16]

De Lue was modeling clay sketches rapidly. On March 6 he wrote to Hopper:

In regard to the sketches, I would like to say that I have been very busy with them. I have done about fifteen interpretations of the subject and about ten of them are pretty well carried out. These sketches, however, are only one inch to the foot scale; three or four of them are a little larger. I believe that they are large enough and carried far enough along to be looked at.

I felt for my own sake that I wanted to try every conceivable arrangement I could. Also I wanted Mr. Sternfeld to see them and realize that I have given the subject and composition a great deal of thought. Until Mr. Sternfeld approved these small sketches, it seemed unwise for me to start the two inch to the foot size.

I plan to take about six of them to Philadelphia this coming Wednesday for Mr. Sternfeld to see and discuss. If he passes any of these sketches that I have done, I will be ready to start making the two inch sketch models and would have them ready in four weeks' time.

I would say that up to the present I have looked on my work as preliminary study and that I am now ready to start the real sketches for approval by your department. I had planned to have them finished by the middle of April. Then I would be free to settle down on the large panels.

De Lue presented his finished sketch models, in one-and-one-half inch scale, of *Law* and *Justice* on April 27 to Sternfeld in his offices in Philadelphia. The next day Sternfeld wrote to Hopper, "We are pleased to advise that we found his work very satisfactory, and that, with minor corrections and suggestions made by the writer, we feel he should now be free to proceed to the next size model. We understand that he wishes to go to an intermediate scale before proceeding to the full size model . . . We feel that his models promise a fine finished result." On the basis of the finished sketch models the Section of Fine Arts awarded De Lue a contract on May 1, 1939.

Toward a "Federal" Style

The Section of Fine Arts was very much involved with the aesthetics of the commission, and sometimes it seemed as if the architect and the section were jousting to see who would have the final word with De Lue. Hopper wrote to De Lue on May 9, "Our general feeling is that working within the restrictions of the designs required by the architect you have achieved two successful sketches. It was thought, however, that in developing the models, a greater refinement of form with less exaggeration of proportions and muscles is necessary. An exaggeration of the size of the hands and arms, particularly of the male figure, was thought to be unfortunate. It was thought much greater simplification of form, particularly in the legs of the eagles, is desirable. It was also thought that the figures would be less static if more variety in the pose of the legs was achieved by advancing or bringing back one of the legs of the figure in each case."

De Lue replied on May 11, "I shall certainly keep [your suggestions] in mind on the next models. I think up to the present I have had in mind mostly architectural qualities: massiveness, weight, dignity and a wish to convey a primitive power." On the same date, Sternfeld wrote to Hopper, "We are in accord with your thought on exaggeration of proportions and muscles. We are not clear on the idea of greater simplification of form (at least at this stage) since we thought it had been carried out to a marked degree. The sculptor and the architects have striven for this in the design. We disagree on the thought that the figures should be less static—feeling that this quality is equally important with simplification. It is possible, of course, that a more agreeable arrangement of the legs could be worked out—our ¼ scale drawings showing an arrangement as you have suggested. The sculptor, however, chose another direction, and we feel his solution is superior to our original indication."

Within a few days De Lue was enlarging *Law* and *Justice* and had nearly completed the sketch model of the *Eagle*. As the enlargements went along he ran into an unexpected problem. By June the higher summer sun had invaded his studio with direct light destroying the steady diffuse light that he needed to model the exacting requirements of the reliefs. In order to complete the reliefs, he would have to rent a small studio or a loft elsewhere for the duration of the job. By the end of the summer he had found a studio at the Lincoln Arcade Building at 1947 Broadway, which provided both the size and the light needed to finish the court house commission.

Most of the problems of the two main reliefs seem to have been solved in a meeting in De Lue's studio on July 11. Sternfeld wrote to Hopper, "The conferences continued after you left at 1:30 P.M. until 10:00 P.M. Mr. De Lue carried out in the clay the various suggestions offered by you and Mr. Sternfeld; and when he finished at approximately 7:00 P.M. the model on which he worked seemed greatly improved (even though it was satisfactory to begin with)." Another meeting took place in De Lue's studio on August 4 and still another on October 8 and 9. Prior to this the *Eagle* sketch model had been accepted. De Lue later remembered

Eagle, 1939–40, 44 × 17½" finished plaster model for the Philadelphia Court House interior reliefs.

the October meetings: "Sternfeld came up into my studio. I had the two panels done, I think, in half size at this time. He looked at it and said he liked it very much. And then he said, 'You know, I always had a desire to take part in some sculpture myself.' He went into one panel and began to mark it all up with different things. He cut pieces off and I was heartbroken to see all of this work of months going away. He was a very odd man, a very conceited man. He said, 'I'll be back tomorrow morning and you be here at eight o'clock so we can get working.' The following morning I said, 'Harry, if you put your hands on this panel I'm going to throw you right through that window over there.' So he put his hands in his pockets and didn't have much to say after that. He said, 'I always wanted to be a sculptor.' I said, 'You ruined about six months' work.' He said, 'I didn't mean to do that, I thought I was just being sort of picky.'"[17]

Of the latter meeting Sternfeld said, "The various suggestions advanced were immediately carried out by the sculptor, and complete agreement was finally reached between the sculptor and the architect . . . . Mr. Sternfeld was greatly impressed with the fine quality of Mr. De Lue's work, and the successful way in which he had carried his work to this stage."[18]

Not everyone felt this way, however. Sternfeld's nemesis, W. E. Reynolds, commissioner of public buildings, was concerned with the photographs he had received of the panels of *Justice* and *Law*. He suggested in a memorandum of November 6 to Edward B. Rowan that the De Lue panels were overforceful and brutish. Interestingly, the Section of Fine Arts rallied to defend the work and methodology. Hopper wrote on November 27:

> De Lue has been working steadily all the daylight hours every day, including Sundays, since mid-summer and has resolved the difficult problem of prescribed subject matter and frequent criticisms from the architect with his own personal style. His sculpture is of course influenced by the Academy at Rome and the Michelangelo tradition which is very much in favor with many of the architects. The character of the reliefs reminds me of John Gregory on the Folger Library and also the sculpture on Paul Cret's Court House in Philadelphia. The latter has obviously influenced Sternfeld in his use of sculpture on this building, that is, large rectangular reliefs flanking the entrance doors.
>
> It is difficult to judge the scale of the sculptures from photographs. They are to be quite large and I believe the mass of figures is necessary considering their size and importance on the building. The female figure is treated "architecturally" and De Lue agreed that the head should be softened by a different treatment of the hair. The forms of the figure will be developed in the half size model which is his next stage and could then be softened by surface treatment as the fundamental forms have been properly worked out.[19]

Reynolds replied:

> No question has been raised as to the artistic ability of Mr. De Lue or the selection of him for this commission. My chief concern has been in relation to the attitude of the public to the finished work. The exaggerations of the modeling under Mr. Sternfeld's direction have been carried to such an extreme that I anticipate unfavorable reaction if the work proceeds as indicated in the photographs submitted to me . . . I have decided to sign the approval for payment at this stage but with the understanding that the work will be modified in its further progress insofar as the heavy exaggerations are concerned . . . . I wish to emphasize that I have confidence that the Fine Arts Section can secure work of merit. They must accept this responsibility and not permit undue dictation by the local architect. In the last analysis, the Public Buildings Administration is responsible to the public and cannot escape that responsibility.[20]

De Lue recalled that when the section under Reynolds, Hopper, Rowan, and Bruce came to the fore of the federal sculpture projects, the new administration called, subtly, for a new federal style. There was, among the sculptors, a common understanding that the Roosevelt era was to have "modern" sculpture. That did not mean abstract sculpture, which was unheard of except as surrounding "art deco" motifs. It meant simplification and bigness, rounded forms and softening of lines and elimination of detail. De Lue said of the sculptors, "We all felt we had to get Modern, or as Modern as we could get." De Lue noted that it was absolutely conscious that on the court house figures, "the drapery does not buckle around in the natural way". The style was international rather than American; it was seen as proper for public monuments and public architecture in the 1930s and 1940s. The relationship between the federal projects of this period and public projects in Germany, Italy, and Russia points to a worldwide sentiment in government as to what the public wanted and needed.[21]

Reynolds's sensibilities about what the public wanted or needed may have been too acute. On November 30 De Lue wrote Hopper, "I know it is very difficult to please everyone and there is no sense in trying to do so. However, most laymen and artists who have seen these panels seem to think well of them." With very few changes, De Lue proceeded to finish the intermediate models. On December 13, Sternfeld wrote to Hopper that *Law, Justice,* and the *Eagle* were all satisfactory. "We believe that Mr. De Lue has achieved a signal success, and recommend that he be permitted to proceed to the final stage." He was granted an extension until April 30, 1940, in which to complete the contract. He also had the responsibility of recommending a carver and chose Ugo Lavaggi.

De Lue created the court house reliefs in the new federal modern style. As he noted, totally abstract sculpture was unknown in government projects in those years, but there was a shared understanding that a strong, simplified, modern, and somewhat abstracted style was what the section wanted. Although there was not an official style, there was a shared attitude on federal projects that resulted in these works, which stand nearly alone in De Lue's public oeuvre.[22] The *Art Digest* approved; in September 1941 they said of *Law* and *Justice,* "In both works, forms are monumental in feeling, and though naturalistic, are overlaid with a crisp stylization that both clarifies and sharpens. Design is simple, bold and rhythmic, admirably adapted to the specific requirements of facade decoration."[23] In 1974 a critic noted that Sternfeld got what he wanted, an austere confrontation "between a blindfoldless Justice and a figure of Law of Mosaic sternness. The ritual nature of the judicial process is indicated by the stars and bars, and by the presence of eagles of Michelangelesque force unequaled in American sculpture."[24]

The public reaction to the works was very favorable. De Lue received excellent critical reviews and compliments from his peers. More important, this was De Lue's opportunity to meet the French-American architect, Paul Cret (1875–1945). Cret was at this moment engaged on the Federal Reserve Bank Building in Philadelphia on a site adjoining the Federal Court House and Post Office. While De Lue was working on the court house panels, he sought out Cret as he had been told to years earlier by a French architect in Lyon who had been Cret's schoolmate. The architect liked the sculptor's work. De Lue's reliefs on the court house had already been compared to John Gregory's work on the Folger Shakespeare Library which Cret had designed in 1932. Cret introduced him to his younger partners at the firm of Paul Phillippe Cret, where De

Lue established a close relationship that continued beyond Cret's death from cancer. Cret was, in 1940, the firm's senior partner; after Cret's death it became known as Harbeson, Hough, Livingston and Larson. They were one of the most prestigious firms in Philadelphia and had federal commissions and contracts for architectural work at the University of Pennsylvania; the firm's new senior partner was consulting architect to the American Battle Monuments Commission.

Alchemist, 1940, limestone, 65 inches, Chemistry Building at the University of Pennsylvania, Philadelphia.

Paul Cret, the architect of the building, must have had a sense of humor to have commissioned De Lue to have the fun of modeling this sour gargoyle to preside over its entry. One engineer remarked shortly after its installation, " This work is highly symbolic of chemistry's dubious beginnings. . . . [Nevertheless,] many of our highly efficient tools and materials for turning out today's power at greatly lower rates had beginnings about as discouraging as the alchemist's experiments. But like the alchemist, there always were men who didn't know when they were licked."

De Lue later said, "His firm became my sole support for a number of years. After I did *Law* and *Justice* [1939] and *Eagles* for the Federal Court House in Philadelphia, Cret arranged for me to do *The Alchemist* [1940] for the chemistry building at the University of Pennsylvania and *Triton* [1940] for the gardens of the Federal Reserve Bank in Philadelphia. Later I got sculpture commissions for the Chapel at Virginia Polytechnic Institute [1946–1960]. *The Boy Scout Group* in Washington was through [the firm's] influence. Eventually, I did the *Spirit of American Youth* and other work for them at the Omaha Beach Cemetery in Normandy."[25]

46

134

56

Iconography and Symbolism

Throughout his career as a sculptor, Donald De Lue chose to give his work a depth of meaning beyond the literal through his use of patriotic symbols, classical mythology, and the personification of spiritual emotions. De Lue's first major commission, the reliefs for the Federal Court House in Philadelphia, required adept use of the traditional symbols of government. The *Eagle* representing America was executed in a somewhat less traditional way than might have been done, and *Justice* was treated with neither the traditional blindfold nor scales. The Mosaic *Law* allowed more leeway and, with Harry Sternfeld's able assistance, broke some new ground in federal imagery. *Triton*, for the Federal Reserve Bank, used classical Greek symbolism. He had already chosen in his work — *Pegasus, Jupiter as the Bull, Icarus, Nymph, Echo,* and *Faun* — to portray images from Greek and Roman mythology. He was thoroughly familiar with Judeo-Christian iconography from his work rebuilding the ecclesiastical monuments in the Lyon area; he had already chosen to do *Modern Madonna* in his own work and had completed a commissioned *St. John the Baptist*. De Lue's work was already developing the individual iconography that was to become a personal pantheon.

De Lue was deeply impressed with Socrates's comments on the nature

42
38
39

23, 22,
19, 24,
25

28
35, 36

Early Study for Triton Fountain, 1940, plastiline.

This is one of at least four models that De Lue put into plastiline as trials for the fountain. All of them employ archaic style and enormously powerful musculature.

Triton Fountain, 1940, marble, Federal Reserve Bank (now PMA Building), Philadelphia.

In a more serious vein, Paul Cret commissioned De Lue to create the courtyard fountain for the new bank building. *Triton* shows in an exuberant form the archaic patterns which the sculptor used in the Philadelphia Court House.

of the soul, and his use of Pegasus and other winged figures may be read as direct sculptural portrayals of the Socratic imagery in the *Phaedrus*. Socrates says:

> Of the nature of the soul let me speak briefly and in a figure. And let the figure be composite—a pair of winged horses and a charioteer. Now the winged horses and the charioteers of the gods are all of them noble and of noble descent, but those of other races are mixed; the human charioteer drives his in a pair; and one of them is noble and of noble breed, and the other is ignoble and of ignoble breed; and the driving of them of necessity gives a great deal of trouble to him. . . .
>
> The wing is the corporeal element which is most akin to the divine, and which by nature tends to soar aloft and carry that which gravitates downward into the upper region, which is the habitation of the gods. The divine is beauty, wisdom, goodness and the like; and by these the wing of the soul is nourished, and grows apace; but when fed upon evil and foulness and the opposite of good, wastes and falls away.

In his sculpture, medals, and drawings De Lue reinforces the imagery of the winged figure and the winged horse, both rising and falling. It is no accident that at age ninety he chose to portray himself in his only *Self Portrait* wearing the National Academy of Design 150th Anniversary Medal turned to the side representing a man soaring aloft on a Pegasus. Plato intimated the lure of the heavens when he wrote:

> . . . For every one, as I think, must see that astronomy compels the soul to look upwards and leads us from this world to another . . . . The spangled heavens should be used as a pattern and with a view to that higher knowledge; their beauty is like the beauty of figures wrought by the hand of Daedalus, or some other great artist.[26]

Sun God (Helios), 1937, is not Apollo, although the sculpture could be used to represent him. De Lue's etchings and drawings of the 1930s show a preoccupation with cosmic beings and their effect on the human spirit. Perhaps the single most powerful image, and one that repeatedly occupied his thoughts, was *Cosmic Head*. This disembodied visage recurs in large and small drawings from the beginning of the 1930s, often repeated three or four times on a single sheet, always drawn with dramatic intensity, until it culminated in the monumental *Cosmic Head* in 1943. This may be De Lue's single most intense work in a lifetime of intensity. Standing before it at the Canton Art Institute in April of 1987, the designer and sculptor Viktor Schreckengost said that he expected lightning bolts to leap from its eyes. He then went on to say that he thought that it was one of the single most powerful pieces of sculpture of the twentieth century.[27] Of it De Lue said, "It is the kind of being that might come out of the cosmos to visit the earth."[28]

As Plato encouraged his followers to do, De Lue looked to the "spangled heavens" for patterns and inspiration to people his personal pantheon. Preoccupation with man's aspirations toward the stars and the possibilities of godlike cosmic or astral beings influencing the human

181

30

48

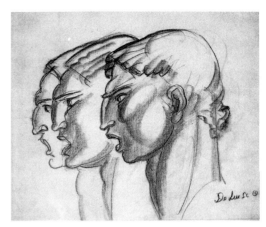

Cosmic Heads, circa 1935, pencil drawing.
De Lue drew hundreds of similar drawings in the period 1933–1943 in both large and small sizes.

Early stage of *Cosmic Head*, 1943, plastiline.
De Lue had been obsessed with this theme; when he came to execute it in a monumental head he tried various combinations of male and female figures that gave the head the sense of enormous size. In earlier stages it also sported wings, spikes and thunderbolts. In a note on the back of one of the photos he writes: "I am enclosing this photo of Cosmic Head as just one of many arrangements I am trying." In the end however, De Lue opted for the simplest form, which resulted in the greatest power.

47

condition spanned De Lue's life. He recapitulated this theme in one of his last works, *Cosmic Being* (1988). Did James Worthington and Robert Baker's speculations on life in the universe and more particularly on Mars find a receptive hearing in the young De Lue that later manifested itself in these works?

To De Lue, the power of the atom seemed both a gift from the gods and an escapee from Pandora's box. In either case, the detonations at Hiroshima and Nagasaki inspired another god in the De Lue pantheon, *The Mighty Atom* (1945). *Airborne* (1948) and *Right Over Evil* (1972) relate to images of St. Michael, but clearly have become forces of good in the service of mankind, which descend from the heavens above to fight the evils of the world.

The spiritual aspiration of man is one of the most recurrent themes in De Lue's work. The aspirations of mankind were, in a sense, the subject of *The Soul's Struggle* (1917) by Robert Baker. De Lue worked with intensity modeling this work for nearly three years. The *Spirit of American Youth Rising From the Waves* uses this theme in memorializing war dead; *Spirit Triumphant* represents the survival of the spirit after physical death; *Quest Eternal* "symbolizes man's endeavor and aspiration for the better things of life and spirit as well as recognizing the future frontiers of space."[29] The *Rocket Thrower* is a less spiritual being and a more dynamic one. He symbolizes man's struggle to reach for the stars. He is De Lue's *Icarus*, striving but not defeated.

"Man in the hand of God" was a recurrent theme for De Lue in both public and personal projects. It was carried out within traditional Judeo-Christian reference, but it has a universality for the spiritual condition of man that transcends sectarian differences. De Lue's Creator as shown in his 1954 *The Creation* for a Queens, New York, school is a cosmic force; the hand of God gently enfolds man, as in De Lue's Virginia Polytechnic reliefs; and man struggles to grow from the tips of his Creator's fingers in *Hand of God* (1969).

De Lue's father was not at all religious; but his mother, although not demonstrating outward signs of religion, held deep spiritual convictions. While he was working with Bela Pratt, he had many conversations with George Guest, who was an assistant to Pratt. Guest was a confirmed atheist who would hold forth on the evils of religion at great length. De Lue went home and told his mother of Guest's opinion that there was no God. "She was shocked as she could be to hear me talking like this, but I thought it was kind of smart."[30] Not surprisingly, De Lue was very interested in ancient Greece and read Plato extensively. He was particularly impressed with Socrates's comments on the nature of the soul in the *Phaedo* and *Phaedrus*. De Lue noted, "As time went on I felt very differently about things. There was so much beauty in the world that there had to be some great force behind it. I still feel that way. I now know that life is forever."[31]

Even in his treatment of historical figures, De Lue often showed his subjects as spiritual (*Washington at Prayer*, 1968) or dynamically striding (*Jefferson*, 1975). It is not surprising, therefore, that he invested his religious figures with such convincing spiritual power. *Moses* and *Isaiah*, the *Stations of the Cross* and *Job*, all have an excess of spirituality and power.

OPPOSITE:

Cosmic Head, 1943, gilded bronze, 32 inches.

The "Cosmic Head" was a recurrent theme in De Lue's drawing and modeling from the early 1930s until this work was completed. Cosmic figures continued throughout his career. This may be De Lue's single most intense work.

170

61, 65,
144

9

56

130

127

102

19

91

184

155

147

52, 51

It is figures of action, "do-ers" as De Lue called them, that interested him. De Lue combined several cosmologies and made them his own, and for the same end: to show those who have affected the upward struggle of mankind or who have had the potential to do so. Through proportioning and modeling, he gave these figures the requisite power to accomplish their very worthwhile goals.

Search For Style

The Archaic and the Michelangelesque

The earliest De Lue works known to survive, those of the early 1930s, are the works of a mature, worldly and traveled sculptor. De Lue knew the sculpture in the museums and on the public buildings in Boston and New York, Paris, and London. Through photographs, books, and discussions with other sculptors he knew works in Italy, Greece, Egypt, and beyond into Mesopotamia and Crete and the civilizations of prehistory.

De Lue was aware of a line of sculptors that stretched from master to pupil in America: St. Gaudens to Pratt to De Lue's own training at the School of the Museum of Fine Arts. He knew, too, the wellspring of the French beaux-arts tradition that culminated in Rodin and led De Lue through Robert Baker's direction to Paris where he was able directly to observe the tradition as practiced by Alfredo Pina and Antoine Bourdelle. In training, practice and methodology, De Lue was the direct heir of the beaux-arts tradition in America and France; but in influence he looked back to Michelangelo in the Renaissance, and to ancient Greece.

Michelangelo was De Lue's acknowledged master and the most persistent and pervasive influence in his life and work. De Lue was perhaps the most Michelangelesque of all twentieth-century sculptors. Rodin, who was himself influenced by Michelangelo, was De Lue's second most admired sculptor. And yet there are qualities in De Lue's work from the beginning that cannot be ascribed to either of these men. De Lue reached further back into the sculpture of ancient Greece and did not stop at the perfection of fifth century B.C. Classicism, but continued back further in the history of sculpture to tap the power of archaic Greek and Minoan art.

De Lue was not the first to explore archaism in sculpture. Indeed, there are archaistic works from the Roman period of the first and second centuries. Two things converged, however, in the early twentieth century to give rise to a union of archaism and beaux-arts tradition in modern sculpture. The nineteenth century's technical mastery of technique, materials, and form was becoming worldwide in Western culture. The academic tradition of ever more polished perfection was losing its ability to command attention from younger sculptors and connoisseurs. Rodin found a way to put power back into the tradition by applying impressionist techniques to three dimensions, and hundreds of sculptors followed his lead. At the same time, however, excavations in Greece, Turkey, and Crete were showing the world an older tradition that carried the same force in sculpture and appealed to many of the younger sculptors. Bourdelle, Rodin's own assistant, incorporated many of the features of

OPPOSITE:

Isaiah, 1972, bronze, 16½ inches.

De Lue pictures the prophet receiving the word of God through a messenger angel. Despite the repose of the figure there is an extraordinary latent power in the sculpture.

archaic Greek sculpture into his later work. Paul Manship may have been the first American to discover the decorative and design possibilities that existed in archaic sculpture, relief, goldwork, and vase and wall painting. In one of the great ironies of art, critics of Elie Nadelman called his archaic horses "modern." Carl Milles employed archaism as well. Whether sixth century B. C. Kuros or prehistoric cycladian figures, twentieth-century American sculpture has drawn on the increasingly available examples of archaic work in museums and publications.

De Lue was sufficiently impressed with Manship's *Flight of Europa* (1925) to have made a drawing of it, and both sculpture and drawing have clear antecedents in archaic works. De Lue regularly used a Kuros-type head on his works of the 1930s and 1940s including *Icarus, Sun God, Triton,* and *Jason.* He readily admitted the archaic quality of the Philadelphia Court House relief panels. His archaism may have been encouraged by the federal modern style and his own desire to achieve "massiveness, weight, dignity, and primitive power." De Lue was no archeologist, however. While his work shows influences of early Greek sculpture, it is by no means a modern copy. Perhaps because of the external factor of World War II De Lue created many of his works with the greatest raw power in the early 1940s.

Ivan Meštrović (1883–1962) was another sculptor greatly admired by De Lue. De Lue might have seen the Meštrović exhibition held at the Petit Palais in Paris in 1919;[32] and he might have been writing of himself in 1962 when he wrote an appreciation for Meštrović that began: "[The] master sculptor of our time has joined the great masters of the past. To those who worked in the tradition of Western Humanism starting with the Great Greeks, followed by the Renaissance and the massive genius of that time, Michelangelo, more recently by Rodin and Bourdelle, can now be added the name of Ivan Meštrović."[33] De Lue certainly became aquainted with Meštrović after the latter came to Syracuse University from Europe in 1946. According to De Lue, it was Malvina Hoffman who introduced Meštrović to Syracuse University; she probably introduced him to De Lue as well. De Lue especially admired Meštrović's relief wood carvings on religious subjects, and De Lue's religious works of the 1950s show some of that admiration; Meštrović, like De Lue, would employ conscious archaism when it increased the power and the meaning of the subject. Each of them could blend and select from parts of the long sculptural tradition cited by De Lue, and for each of them it reached back to the ancients.

In the 1950s the influence of Michelangelo on De Lue, always present, grew stronger. The attenuated figures, contraposto and graceful bodily forms, replaced the more stolid designs completed for the public commissions of the late 1930s and 1940s. The archaic continued, however, in such works as "Courage and Honor" on *Urn Fragment.* By the late 1960s and early 1970s, with *Hand of God* and *Leda and the Swan,* the Michelangelesque had fully asserted itself and could be melded with the most powerful traditions of sculpture to yield all the power and dynamism that De Lue could gain to create such quintessential De Luian works as *Right Over Evil.*

19, 30
46, 67

94, 98

76

184, 187

144

OPPOSITE:

Moses, 1970, bronze, 17 inches.

Moses is shown selecting an unblemished lamb for the Passover.

And the Lord said to Moses . . . every man is to take a lamb, by the number of their fathers' families, a lamb for every family.

Exodus 12:1-3

Moses is presented as one of the great prophet-heroes in one of the key acts of his life, saving the children of Israel from bondage in Egypt and protecting them from the death of every male first child.

Horse and Figure, circa 1940, plastiline model.

This is one of many De Lue figure groups of the 1940s that probably were never cast in plaster or saved but that demonstrate great design movement and an awareness of archaism, classicism, and the simplifications entering figurative sculpture during the Roosevelt years.

1. Gurney, pp. 65–66. *See also* George Gurney, *Sculpture and the Federal Triangle*, Chapter 12. (Washington, D.C.: Smithsonian Institution Press, 1985). Text hereinafter referred to as *Federal Triangle*.

2. *Federal Triangle*, Chapters 13 and 14. George Gurney gives a full discussion of this important competition and elucidates the change that occurred between the Hoover and Roosevelt administrations in philosophy regarding public sculpture policy.

3. *The Home Office*, a monthly publication of the Metropolitan Life Insurance Company, Vol. 19, No. 12, p. 244.

4. Ibid. A. Conger Goodyear, president of the Museum of Modern Art, was the only art professional on the jury of award.

5. Metropolitan Life Archives, James Mann, archivist.

6. "Have You a Little, Orphan Model Gathering Dust in Your Studio?" *The Art Digest*, Vol. 13, No. 9, January 15, 1939.

7. Ibid.

8. A brief note is indicated here on the word "plastiline." As used in this book, it refers to the traditional green artificial clay that was made in Italy before World War Two. It is also known as "plastilina" and should not be confused with either "plasticine," which is generally regarded by sculptors as children's artificial modeling clay, or with the post-war "plastiline" in which the nineteenth-century formula was changed. Since the original formula does not dry out or harden, and has working qualities that are greatly admired by the sculptors that use it, plastiline is in great demand by working sculptors. The only available source is from other sculptors, their widows and heirs, which has given rise to the nickname "dead man's clay." Sculptors like De Lue speak of the history of their plastiline (owned by St. Gaudens and used in the *Sherman Monument*) and of the need to keep track of the likely availability of another ton of it through the closing of a fellow sculptor's studio.

9. The full-sized plaster survives in a private collection in New York City and is dated in the plaster "1938."

10. Donald H. De Lue to D. Roger Howlett, taped interview, 1987, hereinafter referred to as "DDL to DRH."

11. Ibid. *See also* Gurney, pp. 64–65.

12. Ibid.

13. Ibid. *See also* "Amateis and De Lue Do Government Reliefs," *The Art Digest*, Vol. 15, No. 8, September 1941.

14. The following section is documented in part by more than two hundred pages of correspondence available from the National Archives in Washington on the construction of the Philadelphia, Pennsylvania, Post Office and Court House. Correspondence will be referred to as "NA" followed by the sender, receiver, and date, if known. Where the chapter text indicates the above information, additional footnotes have not been provided. NA. Edward B. Rowan to Mr. Bruce, Mr. Watson, Miss Ealand, Nov. 17, 1937: "I found that he had a list of suggested sculptors, see attached, from which he proposed to select one or several to prepare the sculpture models. I was familiar with the work of all but Louis Milione. I told him I could supply a list three times this size of sculptors doing equally good work if not better. He wishes to see such a list and it will be prepared for him. I tried to persuade him to consent to a limited competition in which as many as four or six artists were invited to do a particular subject but did not get anywhere with that suggestion. He regards competition as complete waste of money. NA. Edward B. Rowan to the Director of Procurement through the Supervising Architect. December 29, 1937. Rowan states, "Mr. Sternfeld submitted a list of eight sculptors from which he suggests that one be chosen and given the work. This is a violation of the democratic policies adhered to by Procurement to date in giving out commissions for art work". The impasse that is suggested by this letter was solved by the late January 1938 awards of the Apex competition.

15. NA. "Philadelphia, Pa. Courthouse / Suggested Invited List of Sculptors from Which One Is To Be Selected . . . ," presumably prepared by Harry Sternfeld October 1937 and the "list of suggested sculptors" referred to by Rowan in note 14. The notes scribbled in hand by Rowan or someone else in the section are revealing: "Dividing Work / Democratic Way," "Our list / Carl Schmitz / Archibald Garner / Ralph Stackpole / Henry Kreiss," and "(a) Limited comp. would bring out able sculpture (b) Price: Time element imp."

16. NA. Harry Sternfeld to Inslee Hopper, Feb. 18, 1939.

17. DDL to DRH, 1987.

18. NA. Harry Sternfeld to Inslee Hopper, Oct. 10, 1939.

19. NA. Inslee Hopper to Edward Bruce, Nov. 27, 1939.

20. NA. W. E. Reynolds to Edward Bruce, Dec. 1, 1939.

21. Gurney, pp. 106–110.

22. Ibid., pp. 106–118.

23. "Amateis and De Lue Do Government Reliefs," *Art Digest*, Vol. 15, No. 8, September 1941.

24. George Thomas, "Art Deco Architecture and Sculpture," *Sculpture of a City: Philadelphia's Treasures in Bronze and Stone* (New York: Fairmont Park Art Association, Walker Publishing Co., 1974).

25. DDL to DRH, 1987.

26. Plato, *Phaedrus*, from *The Dialogues of Plato*, translated by B. Jowett (New York and London: Oxford University Press, 1892).

27. Viktor Schreckengost to D. Roger Howlett, conversation, March 1987.

28. DDL to DRH, 1987.

29. Donald H. De Lue as quoted by Caron LeBrun in the *Boston Sunday Herald*, April 30, 1967.

30. DDL to DRH, Nov. 13, 1987

31. Ibid.

32. Laurence Schmeckebier *Ivan Meštrović: Sculptor and Patriot* (Syracuse, New York: Syracuse University Press, 1959). De Lue wrote a review of this book in which he praised Meštrović and commented on the state of scholarship on sculptors of his generation. See note 33.

33. Donald De Lue, "Meštrović," *National Sculpture Review*, Vol. 10, No. 4, Winter 1961–1962, p. 5.

When a man dies gloriously in war shall we not say, in the first place, that he is of the golden race? . . . Have we not the authority of Hesiod for affirming that when they are dead "They are holy angels upon the earth, authors of good, averters of evil, the guardians of speech-gifted men"? We must learn of the god how we are to order the sepulture of divine and heroic personages, and what is to be their special distinction; . . . And in ages to come we will reverence them and kneel before their sepulchres as at the graves of heroes.

PLATO   *THE REPUBLIC V*

WAR MEMORIALS

The War Years

B Y THE TIME HE WAS FORTY-ONE, IN 1938, DE LUE'S CAREER WAS FINALLY OFF and running, and he never again worked as assistant to a sculptor. In 1940 he was elected a fellow of the National Sculpture Society, and in 1945 he was elected president, succeeding Paul Manship.[1] He began exhibiting regularly with the National Sculpture Society and showed his Apex group *Trade on Sea* and *Pegasus Panel*, both in plaster, at the Whitney Museum in April and May 1940.[2] Royal Cortissoz said of his *Triton*, exhibited at the Metropolitan Museum in December 1942, "One piece which I would not neglect is *Triton* by Donald De Lue. Yes there are rewarding objects here displayed, but they have to be hunted down."[3] Adolph Weinman proposed De Lue as an associate of the National Academy of Design and he was elected in February 1941. In April 1943 he was elected to full academician. His diploma work, *Penelope*, was delayed until October 1946. The academy required that it be submitted in "permanent material," and the war years prohibited the use of bronze. De Lue's final selection of terra cotta for *Penelope* is nearly unique in his work; the sculpture was also the first by De Lue to enter a public collection.

Further honors, commissions, and awards began to flow: the National Sculpture Society's Lindsay Morris Memorial Prize (1942) for the reliefs entitled *Free Man at Bay from Thermopylae to Bataan*; the Architectural League of New York's Henry O. Avery Prize (1942) for his small *Lafayette*; the commission for the National Sculpture Society's Fiftieth Anniversary Medal (1943); a Guggenheim Fellowship to work with the architect Eric Gugler; a grant from the American Academy of Arts and Letters; and election to membership in the National Institute of Arts and Letters (1945–1946).[4]

The war years produced some powerful new pieces of sculpture: six *Trophies* for the War Department competition in 1942; *Cosmic Head* (1942–1943); and, under the auspices of the Citizens Committee for the Army and Navy, he designed reliefs of *St. Michael in Armor* (1943), which was adopted by the Army Commandos as their emblem, and *A Knight Crusader* (1943).[5] Each of these designs was replicated as the center for

32–33

46

74

34

48

58

Pegasus Panel, 1940, bronze, 10 inches.
This is one of a series of small relief panels which earned De Lue the title in the mid-1940s of "specialist in bas-relief sculpture." It may have been intended for a larger panel on a government building.

OPPOSITE:
Spirit of American Youth, 1951–1952.
This eleven-foot, half-size, bronze cast of the Omaha Beach Memorial which soars above the entrance to the visitors pavilion at Brookgreen Gardens, S.C. A similar cast honors the men of the First Infantry Division of the U.S. Army at the McCormick Museum at Cantigny in Wheaton, Illinois.

[Vulcan], circa 1942, plastiline.

A powerful, almost brutish figure with a body that reflects simplification and a head that shows archaizing. This figure may be related to *Power* which De Lue exhibited in 1947.

Knight Crusader, 1944, plastiline.

This is the clay model for the carved wood sculpture made for both the West Point and Arlington, Virginia, chapels.

St. Michael, 1942–1943, gold leafed wood.

This was the design of a portable battlefield triptych that was used for religious services. De Lue was one of a number of artists who worked for the Citizens Committee for the Army and Navy during the war. This design was adopted by the Army Commandos as their emblem.

Woman Bearing Light, [Hestia], circa 1944, plaster, 19 inches.

Light is a great gift for good in De Lue's mythology. This compact female figure is less heroic than some of De Lue's figures. She bears the light and eternal fire of home and hearth. This figure was shown at the Philadelphia Art Alliance in 1945.

War Department Competition Model, 1942, plastiline, 12 inches.

The trophy was designed for the War Department in Washington. These competition models are the most machine-like of all De Lue's designs.

North Wind, 1945, plaster.

Of the four winds, it is not surprising that De Lue chose North; in Greek myth, Boreas or Aquilo is the fastest and most powerful. De Lue has given him streamlining worthy of transcontinental train or airplane design of the 1940s. *North Wind* was exhibited at the National Institute of Arts and Letters in May 1945 and at the Philadelphia Art Alliance in November-December.

Benjamin Franklin, 1949, limestone.
De Lue became known early in his career
as a specialist in bas-relief. His APEX
models were "relief in the round," *Law*
and *Justice* were in high relief, but *Franklin*
and *Joseph Willard* for the Science and
Engineering Building at Carnegie Mellon
University in Pittsburgh were designed in
a very low relief reminiscent of ancient
Egyptian carving. De Lue's skill is
apparent in his ability to create
foreshortening and other naturalistic effects
on the figure while stylizing the
composition and overall effect of the panel.

twenty triptychs that were sent to American military forces around the world; further work for the committee included *St. Michael* and *A Knight Crusader* (1944) for the West Point and Arlington, Virginia, chapels. He began his Guggenheim Fellowship May 1, 1944, in order to "do a monumental work of unusual scope conceived by Mr. Eric Gugler, the architect, about three or four months so consumed; the remaining time put to carrying out ideas in sculpture for which up to the present I have had neither the time nor the money."[6] In 1945 he modeled *The Mighty Atom* as his response to the dramatic debut of the atomic age. At the time of the awarding of the grant from the National Institute of Arts and Letters in May 1945 De Lue was given an exhibition of seven of his works at the institute headquarters, which included both of the triptych reliefs and the *North Wind, Icarus, Reclining Nude, Lafayette,* and *Pegasus*.[7] Later that year, from November 27 to December 23, De Lue exhibited a similar group of sculpture in a one-man show at the Philadelphia Art Alliance. In addition to the pieces named above he showed *Woman Bearing Light* and *Cosmic Head*.[8] The exhibitions showed that he had yet to develop models for war memorials.

58

59, 19,
34, 23

59

48

Post-War Artistic Climate

The *New York Times* described De Lue in 1945 as a Boston-born specialist in bas-relief sculpture who had won various prizes and a Guggenheim Fellowship.[9] Edward Bruce, who had interviewed him in Washington in 1938 when he had received the Philadelphia Court House commission, had been troubled, because, as he had put it, "We can't find out anything about you. You are not anyone of importance."[10] Only seven years later he was president of the National Sculpture Society, a National Academician, and the recipient of some of the most prestigious awards in America.

The level of power and prestige that De Lue had achieved is illustrated by an incident that took place in the awarding of the Prix de Rome in 1947. Paul Manship, perhaps the most powerful and well-known of De Lue's peers, was on the committee for the prize along with De Lue. When the applicants were evaluated, Manship put forth Mitzi Solomon (b. 1918), whose work De Lue felt was not worthy of this important fellowship. De Lue backed Albert Wein (b. 1915), a young sculptor who had begun to enter competitions and work professionally about the same time as De Lue. Wein had entered the Metropolitan Life competition in 1938 and received one of two honorable mentions. De Lue spoke forcefully for Wein and swayed the jury, which awarded Wein the Prix de Rome for two years of study at the American Academy. Manship was angry, hurt, and perhaps embarrassed. That De Lue should be able to confront Manship on an award as prestigous as the Prix de Rome (which Manship had won in 1909) and win was a measure of his new standing.

In 1946 De Lue won the Mrs. Louis Bennett prize and the gold medal for sculpture at the Allied Artists of America for *Icarus*.[11] The beautifully finished plaster model that he exhibited attracted the attention of Archer M. Huntington, co-founder of Brookgreen Gardens. Huntington offered to have the sculpture cast and to buy it for the growing sculpture col-

19

The Mighty Atom, 1945, bronze, 47 inches.

De Lue responded to the dawn of the atomic age by creating this powerful new god. As with other work, the figure remained in clay for years and De Lue even experimented with him as an alternative to the *Rocket Thrower* for the 1964 World's Fair. A bronze cast was shown at Lever House at the National Sculpture Society's annual exhibition in 1967. De Lue inscribed a later drawing which presented the *Mighty Atom* as an alternative for the Prudential monument in Boston: "Looking to the future—Man utilizes the elements of the Universe and harnesses them for the good of all mankind."

(Courtesy of John P. Axelrod, private collection)

Victory, Freedom with Wings, 1947–48, pencil drawing, 17 x 23 ½ inches.

The drawing shows the heroic scale in which De Lue conceived his war memorials. For De Lue monumental sculpture meant *monumental*; the drawing shows the figure before wings were added and the sword was removed. On these drawings De Lue wrote, "Design for huge monument at Corregador—Philippines larger than Statue of Liberty," and projected it 240 feet high on a 100 foot base.

OPPOSITE:

Victory, Freedom with Wings, 1948, bronze, 32 inches.

De Lue has imbued his Nike with American attributes. The Greek goddess of victory was not invested with attributes of either freedom or liberty, yet De Lue has his Nike breaking the manacles of slavery and wearing the cap of liberty. This design was conceived as a monument to the battle of Corregador to be erected at Manilla in the Philippines.

lection at Brookgreen Gardens. *Icarus* became De Lue's second work in a major sculpture collection. ¹⁹

De Lue continued to exhibit. In 1947 he showed *Eve* and *Power* at the 121st exhibition of the National Academy of Design. At that time De Lue was having trouble with his landlord at the Lincoln Arcade Building, where he had had his studio since 1939. Edward McCartan (1879–1947), a fellow sculptor and friend of De Lue's, was very sick. He had suggested that, if he died, De Lue should take over his studio at 225 East 67th Street. Directly after his death in September, McCartan's heirs and his landlady carried out his wishes, and De Lue took possession of the studio that he was to maintain for almost thirty years.[12]

In 1948 Jacques Schnier (1898–1988) published his pioneering book *Sculpture in Modern America*. Unlike many writers on art history, Schnier was a working sculptor and an exact contemporary of De Lue. In the book De Lue was ranked with the sculptors following in Manship's path, a group in which Schnier included himself. He wrote:

> Among present day American sculptors whose work, though highly representational, is nevertheless notably expressive [is] Donald De Lue. Some of them, like De Lue, occasionally explore the realm of less representational expression, but generally speaking, subject matter in the work of these artists, though certainly not literal, departs little from impressions made on our eyes by the shapes in nature. De Lue's sculpture, irrespective of its degree of representation, always possesses emotional quality, achieved through the use of effective pose, strong accents and details, and pronounced distortion of form. His fresh, youthful *Cosmic Head*, his agitated *Pegasus* and his aroused *Triton* carved on a monumental urn for the Federal Reserve Bank in Philadelphia, are characteristic of this phase of his work.[13]

In 1948 De Lue completed *Family Group*, a relief of a mother and two children, for the Christian Herald House in New York City. The following year he did very low-cut, incised reliefs of *Benjamin Franklin* and *Joseph Willard* for the Science and Engineering Building (now Doherty Hall) at Carnegie Mellon University in Pittsburgh. The architect, Francis Keally of New York, often incorporated relief sculpture in his designs. But the tradition of architects working closely with sculptors to embellish the surfaces of buildings was coming to an end. In the next forty years figurative sculptors were to find their major commissions in monuments and memorials, and De Lue was no exception.

War Memorials: Worthy of Their High Mission

As early as 1944, Fiske Kimball, director of the Philadelphia Museum of Art, worried that in the plethora of memorials already being proposed to honor those who fought in the war, few would be worthy of their purpose. He noted that:

> The Greeks personified Victory as a goddess, embodied in sculptural figures like the Victory of Samothrace . . . It has seemed difficult to add to the number of such basic types thus become traditional in Western civilization:

19

58

48

23, 46

65

60

the cairn, the mound — or tumulus; the pyramid, the pylon and the obelisk; the tombstone or stele, the tomb chamber or mausoleum, given all the form of the temple; the sarcophagus and the urn; the tablet, with relief or inscription; the trophy, the arch and the column; the statue on foot or on horseback; the cross, the altar, perhaps with a canopy, the tower. Many of the finest memorials of modern times follow traditional types, revivified by the power of the artist.

He noted the precedent of World War I battlefield cemeteries in Europe and continued:

The treatment of the battlefields and cemeteries of our troops in France was entrusted to the American Battle Monuments Commission under General Pershing, with Paul Cret as consulting architect. The individual designs, predominently architectural with symbolic sculpture, were well varied within traditional limits, the sites were admirably chosen and treated and the result was one of measured dignity and solemnity.[14]

As consulting architect for the American Battle Monuments Commission, Paul Cret expressed his philosophy.

In a memorial the end to be achieved, primarily, is the perpetuation of the memory of a great man or a great event to future generations. This object being granted, it follows that permanency and a clear and arresting expres-

God's High Altar, 1947, bronze, 23 ½ inches.

References to Renaissance and Baroque depictions of the descent from the cross and the entombment of Christ in *God's High Altar* are unmistakable. Perhaps De Lue had taken fully to heart John Harbeson's thought that the memorials to World War II ought to embody the "sacrifice motive" and not the "glory motive" of war. The sculpture casts the bodies and rock together into a bold and poignant statement of sacrifice.

LEFT:

Airborne, 1948, bronze, 28 inches.

This is one of the earliest of De Lue's aspirational male figures freed from gravity's grasp. The design was a proposal for a monument to the 101st Airborne Division in World War II. The base has beautiful sketch studies for four relief panels: Justice; Honor—Integrity; Protector of the Family; and Freedom.

BELOW:

Family Group, 1948, limestone relief.

This is the design for the relief sculpture over the door of the Christian Herald House in New York City. The relief was removed. De Lue reused ideas in this design for his medal for the American Mothers Committee Badge in 1950.

Honor — Integrity, Protector of the Family, Freedom, 1948, black conté on paper, 14 x 17 inches.

Studies for the base reliefs on *Airborne.*

sion of the commemorative idea are essentials of the program; and that the most appropriate memorial is that which may best withstand the changes of centuries, and by the beauty and dignity of its design arouse to attention and respect the heedless mind of the wayfarer and that of the wayfarer still to come.[15]

Fiske Kimball, Paul Cret, Robert Moses, and Margaret French Cresson were responding to a growing notion, in the latter years of World War II, that memorials to this war should be practical. At a dinner forum on the subject "War memorials: should they be purely memorial in character or designed primarily for use?" held at the Architectural League of New York on November 16, 1944, Moses made a statement in which he said, "I can sympathize with people who believe that some war memorials should be in the form of endowments — chairs in colleges, beds in hospitals, prizes, research foundations, etc. Certainly these laudable objectives should be encouraged, but they are no substitute for the conventional monumental memorials if these are properly located and designed."[16] The other side of the issue was articulated at the same forum by Dean Joseph Hudnut of Harvard University. As a university dean, Hudnut may have had an interest as vested as any monumental sculptor. Speaking of Grant's Tomb in New York and the Jefferson Memorial in Washington, he opined, "Do not imagine that these things are harmless. Monuments act; they exert a force; and their malice is unpitying. General Grant gallantly overcame his enemies, but he will never overcome his monument; and the renown of Jefferson will be forever imprisoned in that round appallingly permanent banality." Polemics, already beginning to appear in the mid–1940s to advance causes and shout down tradition, would become standard a decade later and by the 1960s would be universal. Hudnut continued that soldiers should be consulted about what they would like to have built in their honor, and then he suggested "A green park, perhaps, in a neighborhood now a waste of asphalt and brick; a playground where children now have only the streets; a schoolhouse to replace one long overtaken by the progress of the art and science of teaching."[17]

Cresson wrote in July 1945, "Ohio, for instance, has launched a nationwide campaign and put out a large and handsome brochure, called 'Memorials that Live,' advocating community centers, gymnasiums, recreation parks. Periodicals are singing the same tune. I cannot feel that calling a community house or swimming pool a war memorial can actually make it a war memorial."[18] The Ohio sculptor Erwin Frey (1892–1968) replied to the state brochure, "The implication in 'Memorials That Live' is, of course, that other memorials do not live. One might ask that you have a look at other periods and civilizations. It happens that the only memorials that survive are the ones that you condemn."[19] Paul Cret continued, "A characteristic of many 'Living Memorials' is that they die young."[20] Utility did become the centerpiece of many memorial projects in the next decade, as hundreds of memorial auditoriums, halls, parks and bridges testify, but some superb works of art were produced as well. The architect, Ralph Adams Cram, may have put forth the case for the appropriateness of beauty and dignity when he stated that, "The utility test, when it comes to celebrating heroes, is like giving rubbers as a Christmas present to a child."[21]

Donald De Lue was a believer in beauty and dignity in art, but had not yet had the opportunity to work on his first memorial commission. The aftermath of World War II suggested themes that would be appropriate to monuments to honor those who had fought and died in the war. De Lue modeled *Jason* in the act of sowing the dragon's teeth, one hand in the ground and one raised in victory over dissension and war. In 1947 he had developed *God's High Altar* as a potential monument to the infantrymen of the war and, in 1948, he modeled *Airborne* specifically as a memorial for the dead of the 101st Airborne Division. The same year he created *Victory* or *Freedom with Wings* as a proposal for a memorial for the Battle of Corregador. There were many other ideas for war memorials that De Lue drew and modeled in plastiline in those years, but most were not cast into plaster and saved.

The War Memorial Chapel

Virginia Polytechnic Institute, Blacksburg, Virginia

When Fiske Kimball had mused about what form war memorials ought to take in a country without an established religion he rightly noted, "Only at colleges and universities, mostly nonsectarian, can we expect local memorials to take the form of chapels."[22] The alumni of the Virginia Polytechnic Institute had approached De Lue as early as 1946 to create the sculptures for a memorial chapel to the war dead of V.P.I., a commission that would proceed over the next fifteen years.[23] The architect of the project was Roy Larson (1893–1973) of Harbeson, Hough, Livingston and Larson, who had suggested De Lue and who began conferring with him and the V.P.I. committee as to the proper interpretation of the themes. De Lue drew dozens of possible arrangements for the sculpture of the chapel walls. As with most of his commissions, De Lue offered a program that was much more fully developed in iconography and symbolism, size and cost than his clients were prepared to build. In the early stages of the chapel project De Lue set forth designs with a score of figures representing "man's growth in knowledge inspired by the Holy Spirit" and "man's growth in ethics and understanding." The architect and committee pared De Lue down to three themes. The most difficult of the themes selected was *The Right Hand of the Lord*, placing man on earth. De Lue then designed *Man Seeks God Through Work* to flank it to the left and *Man Seeks God Through Prayer* to flank it on the right. Clay models were then developed from drawings to one-eighth scale and, with architects and committee approving, enlarged to one-quarter scale. As De Lue noted, models at one-half scale could have been used by the craftsmen to carve the designs into stone, but the sculptor felt that a more accurate reproduction would be obtained if the carvers worked from full scale models, thus achieving a complete and absolute copy. The project stopped and came to life again many times between 1945 and the dedication in May 1960. Just as De Lue was certain that it was another project that he had designed that was to be abandoned, it went forward. He visited the site in 1959 to oversee the carving of the Indiana limestone

Jason, Triumph over Tyranny, 1948, gilded bronze, 18 ½ inches.

The figure is pressing a giant tooth into the earth and raising a hand in victory over war. Although De Lue called this figure Jason, and recounted the tale of the sowing of the dragon's teeth, he was more likely referring to Cadmus, who also planted dragon's teeth which sprouted into soldiers. In the latter case, the soldiers battled each other until only five lived. Then, one cast away his weapons and said, "Brothers, let us live in peace!"

(Courtesy of Lee Fernandez, private collection)

Interior of the Virginia Polytechnic
Institute Chapel, 1946–60, limestone relief.

This project proceeded over nearly fifteen
years through hundreds of drawings and
many changes in clay. From left to right:
Man Seeks God Through Work, *The Right
Hand of the Lord*, and *Man Seeks God
Through Prayer*.

The Right Hand of the Lord, circa 1957,
black conte on paper, 16 ½ x 13 ¾ inches.

This is one of many studies for *The Right
Hand of the Lord*. Man in the hand of God,
or a cosmic or benevolent and protective
hand, is an image that De Lue used as early
as his *Family Group* (1937) and as late as
Hand of God, 1967.

by Bruno Mankowski and Victor Bramante of New York and Joseph
Servos of Washington.[24] Although one of the goals of the design commission was to create a work "without creedal symbolism,"[25] De Lue
felt that he was able in the work to "sound a spiritual note in an age of
materialism."[26]

The Omaha Beach Memorial, St. Laurent, France

De Lue's most important war monument was the Omaha Beach Memorial at the St. Laurent Cemetery in Normandy, France. De Lue was
awarded the work by the American Battle Monuments Commission in
1949. The Commission had been established in 1924 to care for the overseas cemeteries where American soldiers of World War I were buried.
Most of the sculptural embellishments for the monuments of World War
I in France were by French sculptors. General John J. Pershing was the
first head of the presidential commission, and after his death in 1948, he
was succeeded by the equally eminent General George Marshall. After
World War II, John Harbeson (1888-1986), Paul Cret's partner, became
architect-in-chief of the American Battle Monuments Commission; and
De Lue, who had just completed two works for his firm, suggested that
the sculpture for the new cemeteries for World War II be done solely by
American sculptors. When Harbeson proposed the plan in Washington
it was greeted with enthusiasm by other members of the Battle Monuments Commission. By November 4, 1949, the commission had prepared
sufficiently to hold an exhibit at the Philadelphia Art Alliance to show
models, drawings, and plans of fifteen American war memorials to be

constructed over the next few years at permanent United States military cemeteries in Europe, Africa, and the Philippine Republic. These cemeteries were to be combined from sixty-four temporary ones based on the best location and view and on places most easily reached by Americans seeking them. John Harbeson said that in the commission for World War I, "There was a separation of what may be called the glory motive from the sacrifice motive." The commission's goal for the cemeteries of World War II "is somewhat different. We live in a different world—the peoples of our own country and those who were our allies have questioned the expression of military prowess. . . . But there is no wish to lessen the expression of thankfulness to America's soldiery—the soldiers of any rank who did their duty for their country, and sacrificed life itself in doing so. This is no division of opinion as to the appropriateness of making a shrine, a place of beauty, where our soldiers lie buried under the American flag." The exhibition then went to the Architectural League of New York from December 6, 1949, to January 6, 1950, and then to Boston and abroad.[27]

From the massive number of designs that De Lue drew and modeled for the commission project, it is doubtful that his final sculpture was very focused at this point. Modernist criticism, from the *New York Times*, however, was.[28] A serious difficulty was developing both in sculpture in New York and in the organizations that supported it. Professional sculptors in New York could be loosely grouped into the more conservative National Sculpture Society members and those that regularly showed at the Whitney Museum of American Art in the early 1950s. The Museum of Modern Art had long since eliminated the more conservative elements in their exhibitors, and the Whitney, followed by the Metropolitan, was in the process of doing so. Perhaps only José de Creeft successfully navigated between the traditionalist Scylla and the modernist Charybdis as a member and exhibitor at the National Sculpture Society and a regular exhibitor at the more advanced institutions. De Lue showed at the Whit-

Study for the V.P.I. Chapel Interior, *circa* 1956–58, pencil on paper, 13 ¾ x 17 inches.

Among De Lue's many drawings for the relief sculpture for the V.P.I. chapel are iconographic notes which reveal to a large degree his thinking on spiritual matters.

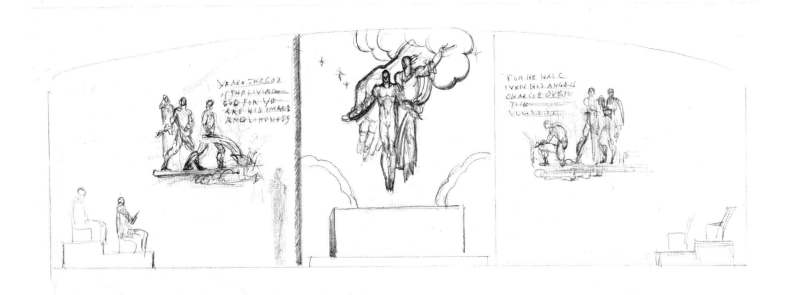

Sketch sheet of ideas for the Omaha Beach
Memorial, *circa* 1949–1950, black conté on
paper, 24 x 18 ¾ inches.

This sheet is one of hundreds of drawings
that helped to develop the project to an
increasingly spiritual and less militant
figure.

Spirit of American Youth, 1950–1952,
bronze, 36 inches.

This is the smallest study size and the
model that met with the approval of the
American Battle Monuments commission
for the Omaha Beach Memorial. In 1951,
José García Mazás wrote: "In the *Spirit of
American Youth*, De Lue was able to lend
eloquence of expression to his masterpiece,
from the feet, which surge from the froth
of a wave, to the moving shape of the head
of the young giant. The arms express the
idea of limitless flight into the blue. This
entire endeavor is a hymn to resurrection,
which is exactly what triumph should
signify to those who died in Normandy."

ney in 1940 and at the Metropolitan in 1942. Shortly after, however, he was exhibiting only with the more conservative National Sculpture Society, the Architectural League, and the National Academy of Design.

Conservatism was the desirable mode for many of the most powerful clients; this was especially true with the American Battle Monuments Commission. They represented a substantial portion of the considerable money that would be spent on sculpture for war memorials in the next two decades. Inevitably, many of the states, cities, towns, and universities that would commission their own works would look to the commission for example. The Modernists and their surrogates were prepared to battle in the press in an attempt to gain a substantial portion of these commissions for practitioners of "the new architecture," abstract sculpture, and abstract painting. After seeing the plans of the commission, Aline B. Louchheim wrote, "These memorials seem to me hardly different from those of World War I. They are based on classical designs, with a deliberate regularity of axial arrangement, with conventionally placed pavilions, staircases and forecourts, and with planting which is equally rigid and symmetrical."[29] Although this may seem a reasonable enough statement today, it was unremittingly damning in the cant of the time. Words that in the early 1990s evoke the essence of Postmodernism, signaled, in the early 1950s, the perceived or hoped-for last gasp of the beaux-arts style. She went on to say, "These are the sculptors . . . whom the architects chose to assist them (and were approved): Wheeler Williams, J. Kiselewski, Carl Milles, Paul Jennewein, Janet deCoux, John Gregory, Louis Iselin, Malvina Hoffman, Lee Lawrie, Donald De Lue, Michael Lantz, Edmund Amateis, Sidney Waugh [and] Paul Manship."[30] Today it is hard to imagine choosing a more august group of architectural

Spirit of American Youth at the pavilion, St. Laurent Cemetery, John Harbeson, architect. (Note De Lue's urns in the colonnade).

sculptors of the time to work on a memorial project, but Ms. Louchheim was in thrall only to "the new." There were more conservative critics, but they did not have column space at the *New York Times*. Thomas Craven, one of the Young Turk critics of the 1920s, found himself in the supremely ironic position of being a conservative critic in the early 1950s. He employed an even more powerful medium than the *New York Times* to bring his criticism and ultimately his positive views on this group of sculptors to the public. In the summer of 1951 he wrote the movie *Uncommon Clay* and filmed it in the studios of Williams, Manship, James Earle Fraser and Laura Gardin Fraser, Cecil Howard, and De Lue. For De Lue, he gives a visual review of the sculptor's career and shows him directly and deeply involved in creating the Omaha Beach Memorial.[31]

The Spirit of American Youth

Harbeson had arranged for De Lue to be the sculptor of the Omaha Beach Memorial, which was, as De Lue later said, "the top one." The main figure was to be twenty-two feet, cast in bronze; it would be by far the largest bronze figure that De Lue had done to date. It was to be flanked by giant bronze urns. "I knew the opportunity would never present itself again and so I put every effort to it I possibly could do."[32] The opportunity was as important as De Lue suspected, but for reasons that he hardly could have anticipated. His largest completed commission was the Philadelphia Court House reliefs. This kind of architectural sculpture was a mainstay of the traditional sculptor when De Lue entered the field on his own in the late 1930s. Commissions were still being awarded for architectural sculpture on buildings across America as he embarked on the Omaha Beach Memorial. Only a few years later, however, architecture would be dominated by unadorned glass boxes and there would be no place for sculpture on major buildings that were built in contemporary styles. The Omaha Beach Memorial established De Lue as one of America's pre-eminent monument makers, an achievement that carried his career forward in the difficult decades of the 1950s and 1960s.

De Lue drew hundreds of studies for the major male figure that was to be the centerpiece of the cemetery, and he modeled 179 plastiline sketches before one was selected by John Harbeson and General Thomas North, who was in day-to-day charge of the Battle Monuments Commission.[33] First a three-foot high model was produced, then it was restudied at five-and-a-half feet. At this point, in June 1951, José García Mazás interviewed De Lue in his studio and wrote:

Penelope, 1946 terra cotta, 11 x 13 x 7 inches.

The reclining *Penelope* is reminiscent of De Lue's early *Seated Woman.* It was De Lue's diploma work for full academician at the National Academy.

> The evolution of the ideas De Lue has developed in his sketches [for the Omaha Beach Memorial] helps us understand the distinct phases of this great sculptor's life. During the first phase the idea of a giant carrying a great sword on its shoulder predominated, symbolizing the great triumph of the Allies over the Nazi aggressor. This is the same De Lue of over twenty years ago when he created the gigantic high-relief structures of the Federal Court House in Philadelphia. He is the main influence behind the "modernist giant" movement, the tendency to exaggerate musculature in sculptures, observed initially during the post-Alexandrian Hellenic era. Eventually, however, the triumph of spirit over brute force becomes evident. De Lue expressed to me that the victorious landing, achieved at the cost of so many lives, should not be remembered as the triumph of brute force, but rather as the resurgence of the free world.[34]

The approved model was enlarged and restudied at eleven feet before the final clay was set up for the twenty-two-foot figure. De Lue's studio was not equipped for such monumental work, so he modeled the final enlargement as a torso and legs in two separate sections. Malvina Hoffman, who had been a good friend for many years, was off to Europe in the summer of 1953 and knew of De Lue's dilemma. She offered him her studio at 159 East 35th Street to help him unify the figure. It was there that the *Spirit of American Youth Rising From the Waves* was completed in August 1953."[35] It was photographed and reported as complete by the *New York Times* on August 6, 1953, and by John Watson in the *New York Journal-American* on September 1. The plaster was then sent off to the Battaglia Foundry in Milan, Italy, for casting."[36]

There had been one slight false start. As De Lue recalled it, "I did the half-size model in plaster. General North was in my studio. He was determined to have everything as 'right' as he could. He was very enthusiastic and said, 'I am heading for the Normandy beachhead within a day or two, and two or three days after I get there I want that statue at the Normandy beachhead.' I said, 'That's going to be a little bit difficult since this statue is only one-half size. The final statue is twice as big as this.' He said, 'I can't wait for that! We'll have to have this carved in marble then.' And I said, 'I think you'll have a little difficulty having this carved in marble, because the marble would never support a figure of this design.' So he reluctantly said, 'All right, we'll have to do it the way you want it.'"

The completed *Spirit of American Youth* pleased the architect. John Harbeson described it as follows: "The figure, balanced in the air with minimum visible means of support, represents a difficult theme nobly done, and promises to be a beautiful and striking work of art, as well as one of deep emotional significance to the relatives of those who died for their country in these great military undertakings."[37]

Urns being uncrated at the Omaha Beach Memorial, May 1955.

"In Memoriam"; "Courage and Honor"; "The Spirit of the Lord Moved Over the Waters"; and "The Angel of the Resurrection." De Lue created an elaborate iconography for each of the designs on the four bronze urns.

Urn Fragment, 1952, bronze, 17 ½ inches.

This redesigning of the study size of the urn bearing "Courage and Honor" created an entirely new work. Of *Urn Fragment* De Lue said, "It is the kind of fragment that might be dug up as a great archeological find." It won the National Sculpture Society's gold medal in 1962.

Memorial Urns

While he was designing and modeling the *Spirit of American Youth*, De Lue was also designing and modeling the urns that were to flank it. One of the urns has a relief entitled "In Memoriam," a kneeling mother with child facing a cross decked with laurel beneath an eight-pointed star; and a second relief, "Courage and Honor," a fallen warrior and his sword being lifted from his rearing steed. The other urn has reliefs of "The Spirit of the Lord Moved Over the Waters" and "The Angel of the Resurrection." Each urn was cast as a pair in bronze by the Marinelli Foundry of Florence, Italy, and one of each is in the loggia on either side of the *Spirit of American Youth*.[38] In late 1952, with the basic design for the urns completed and the half-size plaster in his studio, De Lue was visited by a contingent of Swedish-Americans in New York on their way to Sweden. They asked him if they could have one of the urns, half-size, to present to Stockholm in honor of Swedish-Americans who had taken part in the Normandy invasion. De Lue said that he had no objection, but he would prefer that they have the blessing of the commission in Washington. That given, a *Memorial Urn* in bronze was presented to the city of Stockholm on the occasion of its 700th anniversary, June 7, 1953.

75

Mother and Child, 1952, bronze, 9 inches.

As with *Urn Fragment*, De Lue cut away a portion of the relief of "In Memoriam" and created this new work. In this case it was developed from the full-sized plaster, and the mother now points the child to the open world.

Urn Fragment

The smallest of the models for the urn with "Courage and Honor" provided De Lue with an opportunity to explore a problem of pure design after all of the problems of the official commission had been solved. He took a plaster cast of the urn and began to cut away at it until only a fragment remained around the relief composition and the smooth, curved edge of the base. De Lue said that he wanted to create the kind of bronze fragment that might be dug up as a great archaelogical find: an urn fragment. The shape also suggests a warrior's shield and thereby reinforces the subject of the relief. The transformed *Urn Fragment* won De Lue the National Sculpture Society's Gold Medal at its annual exhibition in 1962.[39]

Mother and Child

Similarly he took the urn relief "In Memoriam" and carved it away until only the closely related heads of the mother and child, the mother's shoulder, drapery, and part of a hand remained. *Mother and Child* is a new work, again a beautiful fragment, that speaks to the dilemmas of motherhood. The close, nurturing care is balanced by the finger pointing the child out into the open world.

For a number of reasons there was considerable delay in the casting and the erection of the *Spirit of American Youth* and the urns. The casting in Italy had to be in manganese bronze to increase its strength. Everything possible was done to make the tall figure secure in the face of the strong winds that blow across the Normandy coast. The monuments were finally installed in 1955 and the Normandy-American Cemetery and Memorial was dedicated on July 19, 1956.[40] Although De Lue received $50,000 for this seven-year project, the largest amount he had ever been paid, it was a vastly larger commission than he had ever undertaken before. He felt undercompensated. Soon, however, the Battle Monuments Commission made partial financial amends.

America and *France*

Visitors to the Omaha Beach Cemetery had noted that the graves that were at the end of the main axis farthest from the *Spirit of American Youth*

America and *France*, bronze, 1955, 32 ½ inches.

These are the study sizes of the emblematic figures of *America* and *France*. The former holds a sword surmounted by an eagle and is draped in the stars and stripes; the latter is an intrepretation of "Marianne" and holds the cockerel of France.

faced an undeveloped facade of the cemetery. The commission suggested monumental figures of *France* and *America* should guard and protect the ends of the monument. De Lue was asked to prepare the models in the mid-1950s. He studied them first as twenty-seven-inch maquettes and then as four-and-one-half-foot models that could be pointed to double size by the stonecarvers. The two completed nine-foot figures were carved in Baveno granite in Italy in 1957–1958 and sent to the U. S. Military Cemetery at St. Laurent. *France*, an interpretation of "Marianne," holds a sword surmounted by a cockerel.[41] *America* holds a sword surmounted by an eagle and is draped with stars and stripes. These figures and some monetary compensation added to the overall scope and concept of the project.

De Lue's figures and urns for the St. Laurent cemetery were the most extensive of any sculptor's work for the American Battle Monuments Commission after World War II. The critic Thomas Craven said that the *Spirit of American Youth Rising From the Waves* "may be the most inspired memorial ever created by an American sculptor."[42]

America and *France*, 1957–1958, Baveno granite, 9 feet each.

The two figures which represent the countries which gained from the victorious assault at Omaha Beach stand guard over the terrace and the allée that leads to the chapel.

1. *New York Times*, January 15, 1948, p. 20, col. 1. De Lue was president from January, 1945, until January, 1948, when he was succeeded by Sidney Waugh.
2. National Sculpture Society and the Whitney Museum of Art exhibition catalogue, April 3–May 2, 1940.
3. *New York Herald Tribune*, December 13, 1942, section VI, p. 5, col. 2.
4. List of honors, commissions, and awards made available through the following sources: Lindsay Morris Memorial—*National Sculpture Society Newsletter*, July 1942. Election to academician at National Academy of Design—*New York Times*, April 30, 1943, p. 24, col. 4. Guggenheim Fellowship—*New York Times*, March 29, 1943, p. 25, col. 7. Grant from American Academy and election to National Institute—*New York Times*, May 18, 1945, p. 17, col. 2, and May 19, 1945, p. 30, col. 5. Also note that the American Academy of Arts and Letters and National Institute met jointly and made stipends together. De Lue received his thousand-dollar grant along with more modern sculptors Peter Dalton and Vincent Glinsky.
5. *Citizens Committee for the Army and Navy, Inc.*, 1943, a pamphlet of twelve leaves.
6. John Simon Guggenheim Foundation application letter as read by Arlene Holden to D. Roger Howlett, July 1988.
7. *The American Academy of Arts and Letters and the National Institute of Arts and Letters Exhibition of Sculpture by Paul Manship, Works by Newly Elected Members of Arts and Letters Grants*, May 19, 1945–June 29, 1945. A copy is at the Frick Art Reference Library.
8. "De Lue Sculpture on Display from November 27th," *Art Alliance Bulletin*, [of the Philadelphia Art Alliance], November 1945, p. 8.
9. *New York Times*, May 3, 1945, p. 21, col. 6.
10. DDL to DRH, 1987.
11. According to records at Brookgreen Gardens, the Mrs. Louis Bennett Award of Honor was given by the Allied Artists of America. In 1946 it was presented to Donald De Lue for *Icarus*.
12. DDL to DRH, April 24, 1987.
13. Jacques Schnier, *Sculpture in Modern America* (Berkeley: University of California Press, 1948).
14. *New York Times*, November 12, 1944, p. 10.
15. Ibid.
16. *New York Times*, November 17, 1944, p. 13, col. 1.
17. Ibid.
18. *New York Times*, July 22, 1945, p. 14.
19. Ibid.
20. Ibid.
21. Ibid.
22. Fiske Kimball, "Worthy of Their High Mission," *New York Times*, November 12, 1944, p. 40.
23. DDL to DRH, April 23, 1987.
24. Edward Hancock, "Sculptor Says Tech Site is Proper for a Memorial," *World News*, undated article, De Lue archives.
25. "Dedication Programme," Virginia Polytechnic Institute, May 29, 1960.
26. *Roanoke Times*, May 29, 1960, section B, p. 5, and *National Sculpture Review*, Summer 1958, p. 8.
27. "U.S. War Memorials Abroad," *Art Alliance Bulletin*, November 1949, pp. 4, 14. *New York Times*, December 18, 1949, p. 19, col. 1.
28. In addition to Aline B. Louchheim, other modernist critics excoriated the traditionalist trend of commissioned war memorials, John Canaday wrote: "How the commissions can have fallen with such dreadful consistency to the least imaginative, most sterile, esthetically most tightly hidebound stone-hackers at work today in this country would be a mystery if the National Sculpture Society were not widely reputed to have one of the most effective lobbies in Washington." John Canaday, *New York Times*, July 25, 1965.

29. Aline B. Louchheim, "Memorials to Our Dead Abroad," *New York Times*, January 15, 1950, section II, p. 10, col. 3.
30. Ibid.
31. *Uncommon Clay* (movie), 1951, produced by and directed by Thomas Craven. Also Thomas Craven, "The Making of an Art Film," *American Artist*, November 1951, p. 51.
32. DDL to DRH, 1987.
33. Thomas Craven, "The Making of An Art Film," op. cit.
34. José García Mazás, "Donald De Lue y su moderno concepto del triunfo," *Temas*, June 1951, as translated by Erik Jarnryd, Harvard University.
35. *New York Times*, August 6, 1953.
36. American Battle Monuments Commission, *Normandy American Cemetery and Memorial* (catalogue), 1987.
37. *National Sculpture Review*, Vol. 2, No. 2, Spring 1953, p. 5.
38. *Normandy American Cemetery and Memorial*. op. cit.
39. *National Sculpture Review*, Vol. 11, No. 1., Spring 1962, p. 4.
40. *New York Times*, June 20, 1956, p. 5, col. 4.
41. *American Artist*, October 1957, Vol. 21, No. 8, Issue 209, p. 49.
42. *Uncommon Clay*, op. cit.

THE 1950s

For an example of how art and architecture have united to produce liveable beauty in structural form we do not have to go back to the days of the great cathedrals. We can find a harmony of the arts in the group of nationally famous office buildings at Rockefeller Center, the first of which was completed twenty-five years ago. Here is a place where fifteen buildings dominate the area completely, and where more than thirty outstanding artists have contributed over one hundred major works to make this one of the most varied and interesting collections of contemporary art in the United States. Here art and architecture are combined to produce a feeling of gracious vitality; where plane surfaces are broken up by paintings and bas-reliefs; and where plazas and courts are lightened and given meaning by the use of sculpture as a focal point.

DONALD DE LUE 1957   *TOWARD A REUNION*

OF ART AND ARCHITECTURE[1]

A Steady Flow of Architect's Commissions

DE LUE HAD BEGUN TO LEARN THAT ARCHITECTS COULD SUPPLY A STEADY flow of commissions. His first major work, the United States Court House in Philadelphia, had shown that he could work with a difficult architect under difficult circumstances. He had met, worked for, and liked Paul Cret; and the relationship had continued with Cret's successors, Roy Larson at the V.P.I. Chapel and John Harbeson at the Omaha Beach Memorial. Cret had been thoroughly trained in the beaux-arts style, first at the Ecole des Beaux-Arts in Lyon and later at the Ecole des Beaux-Arts in Paris. In 1903, Cret had accepted a Professorship of Design at the University of Pennsylvania and began teaching "classic modern" design principles in Philadelphia. Harry Sternfeld, Roy Larson, and John Harbeson were his students.[2]

These more traditional architects working with government, academic, or religious buildings still found sculpture to be integral to the symbolic meaning of their designs. Increasingly, however, architects were the conduit for bringing together clients and sculptors for public monuments and provided their design expertise for the settings and the surrounds. De Lue worked perfectly with architects who were rooted in beaux-arts Classicism pared to its essence. The modified beaux-arts architecture that Cret had inspired competed successfully for commissions throughout the 1950s and 1960s with the "international style." De Lue's sculptural heritage was the same as that of his architect collaborators: Greek and Roman Classicism, the Renaissance, Neo-classicism, and the beaux-arts style that was his direct antecedent. De Lue was taught sculpture by men who had worked with the actual (or spiritual) fathers of the architects who now employed him. These colleagues could advance and modify the traditions

OPPOSITE:

Alexander Astride Bucephalus, 1956–1986, bronze, 31¾ inches.

De Lue hoped for a commission of a monumental equestrian statue of Hernando De Soto in Memphis, Tennessee. He modeled a proposed maquette, but when the project was clearly not proceeding, he changed the subject to *Alexander Astride Bucephalus.* He worked on this sculpture in clay for thirty years.

83

on which they drew; but they could not admit wholesale revolution that turned out and reviled the work of all the immediate history of architecture and sculpture. De Lue had, by the early 1950s, achieved his own modernized classical vocabulary for sculpture. Through his approach, which paralleled that of the architects who commissioned most of his work, he was able to create sculpture that was integrated into the aesthetic of the architecture. He had already worked with the architects Harry Sternfeld, Paul Cret, Roy Larson, John Harbeson, and Francis Keally. With the exception of Cret, who was dead, he would work with all of them again, and add to his list of architect colleagues many others, including Eric Gugler; William Henry Deacy; Vorhees, Walker, Smith and Smith; Carl Braun; Ray Winiger; Charles Luckman; Richard Murphy; and William Heyl Thompson.

De Lue enjoyed his relationship with architects and clients. In 1953 he said:

> Every client I've had since the end of the war has stated in no uncertain terms that the sculpture must be something that he and the public could understand or there just wouldn't be any sculpture. This is not to say that the sculptor is asked to surrender his individuality; that he is denied ample opportunity for the expression of his ideas. After all, exclusion of the unintelligible is not a very serious limitation upon the artist who himself wishes to communicate with his public. When I have once been awarded a commission, I've always been given as much freedom as I could wish for.[3]

The Hall of Our History

While on his Guggenheim fellowship from 1944 to 1945, De Lue had worked with the architect Eric Gugler on a heroic sculpture project to depict the heritage of America.[4] Gugler had conceived a monumental plan for placing the history of America on giant carved stone friezes on the high plateau of Pine Mountain, Georgia. It was planned as a vast court of granite measuring 247 feet wide, 418 feet long, and 90 feet high, to be set in a grove of towering pines and open to the sky.[5] James Earle Fraser, Paul Manship, Cecil Howard, and Donald De Lue had prepared designs according to Gugler's concept to complete the story on four walls of the history of America from the "Age of the Discoverers through World War I."

The announcement of the Hall of Our History was made to the public on August 6, 1953, ten years after the planning had begun. The architect estimated the cost at $25,000,000 with a completion time of ten years. He had a formidable array of trustees and supporters. Among his trustees were the *New York Times*'s Arthur Hays Sulzberger, the president's brother Milton Eisenhower, Eleanor Roosevelt, John L. Lewis, George Meany, Walter Reuther, and the governor of Georgia. Judge Learned Hand wrote an article of support in the *New York Times* in which he said, "It is the purpose of the Hall of Our History to capture in striking form moments in our past that have tellingly embodied this persistent tradition (government of the people, by the people, for the people). We mean to reproduce in picture and in word those occasions that best illustrate our belief that at long last we may safely set no bounds to the vagaries of individual utterance, and trust that particular follies would be cancelled out in the collective judgment of all."[6]

The site had been donated to the Hall Of Our History, Inc. by the State of Georgia, which also approved a $75,000 fund to begin the planning of the granite monolith. By December 1953, the cost was noted as being down to $10,000,000 which was to be sought from subscriptions from individuals across the country.[7] The cost was later further reduced and the proposed site moved to Arlington, Virginia. Yet despite years of work that had gone into planning, designing and sculpting for the Hall of Our History, it failed to spark the imagination of large numbers of the public. Years of sculptors' work, including De Lue's, went to nought. This was probably the first time that he had worked on a grand sculptural project that ended in nothing, but it was by no means to be the only one.

The Harvey Firestone Exedra
Akron, Ohio

In 1950, before the Omaha Beach Memorial was very far along in concept, De Lue was already hard at work on the exedra for the Harvey Firestone Memorial in Akron, Ohio. Eric Gugler, the architect who was already working with De Lue on the Hall of Our History, had received the commission to design the architectural setting for the Firestone Memorial. James Earle Fraser (1876–1953) had been commissioned to sculpt the figure of Harvey Firestone. Gugler, who was a friend of Paul Manship and had often worked with him on monuments and memorials as architect and sculptor, suggested that Manship design the relief panels for the exedra. Fraser, who felt himself in direct competition with Manship, suggested that De Lue was a young sculptor of great promise who ought to be encouraged. Gugler agreed and engaged De Lue.

Donald De Lue seated on the exedra of the Harvey Firestone Memorial, Akron, Ohio, 1950.

Except for the Philadelphia Court House, this proved to be De Lue's largest finished commission to date. He worked up the panels in his studio at 67th Street in New York, but he also traveled to Westport, Connecticut, to Fraser's studio to assist him on the figure of Firestone. Fraser was already showing signs of frailty and needed help in completing the huge seated figure. He had been one of the most successful and prolific of all twentieth-century sculptors, but he was so feeble at the time of the dedication of the Firestone Memorial in 1950 that he was represented by his wife, Laura Gardin Fraser.[8] For the reliefs in the exedra of the Firestone Memorial De Lue was awarded the gold medal of the Architectural League in New York on June 14, 1951.[9] The medal was for "a fine example of Architectural Sculpture fitting to its setting with excellent execution."[10] Ernest W. Watson decried the lack of public attention that monumental sculpture received. He wrote in 1953:

> Strangely enough, the public is scarcely aware of what is going on today in sculpture of this type, that is, monumental sculpture. With what almost seems a conspiracy to keep people in the dark, the press consistently ignores the impressive volume of work running into hundreds of thousands of dollars annually that has been keeping a goodly number of sculptors busy for years. These great monumental works do not rate the space so lavishly give to the cryptic concoctions of neoteric expressionism. *Life* magazine, for example will devote pages to color reproductions of such fantasies, but when it reported the unveiling of the Firestone Monument in Akron, it printed a camera shot which practically ignored this ambitious architectural and sculptural project, focusing upon the Firestone brothers lined up in a row before it. The story never even mentioned architect Eric Gugler and sculptors James Earle Fraser and Donald De Lue, all co-creators of this beautiful memorial.[11]

De Lue must have been pleased to see his shining granite crescent of reliefs in this memorial, and pleased at the successful collaboration with Fraser. He would shortly, however, be preparing the centerpiece for another memorial in another crescent of his granite reliefs.[12]

Edward Hull Crump Memorial
Memphis, Tennessee

Senator Edward Hull Crump (1874–1954) of Memphis and Shelby County, Tennessee, had stood tall in local political affairs for nearly fifty years at the time of his death. He was a prominent U. S. senator during the New Deal and brought many of its blessings to Memphis. De Lue was engaged shortly after the senator's death through the efforts of the architect William Henry Deacy (1889–1967) to create an appropriate nine-foot portrait statue in bronze and a semicircular granite exedra with two symbolic figures. Deacy had founded the American Institute of Commemorative Art, of which he was executive director. The purpose of the organization was to bring together clients, architects, and sculptors of the highest quality. Deacy had also consulted on the Firestone Memorial in Akron. Here, however, De Lue was able to have total artistic control of sculpture very similar in concept to the Harvey Firestone Memorial. As usual, De Lue used his meticulous method of developing each part of the project through extensive drawings and plastiline sketches. Of the male symbolic figure one writer said, "After making trial studies in small scale in clay, De Lue usually reverts to graphic form and produces drawings, especially when the project represents a projection for high bas-relief. High relief is a very difficult problem for it requires artistic distortion to satisfy optical appearance."[13] The $100,000 Crump Memorial was dedicated in Overton Park, Memphis, on Easter Sunday, April 1957.[14]

Edward Hull Crump, 1956, plaster model, 36 inches.

LEFT, ABOVE:

Study for the male figure on the Crump Memorial exedra, 1955–1956, plaster, 10 × 32¼ inches.

LEFT, BELOW:

Edward Hull Crump Memorial, Overton Park, Memphis, Tennessee.

Alexander Astride Bucephalus

Study for *Hernando De Soto*, 1958, pencil on paper, 19 x 19 inches.

There is little question that De Lue was still responding to his first impressions of Donatello's and Verrocchio's equestrian statues when he conceived this design.

De Lue's visits to Memphis led to discussions with some of the local luminaries about the appropriateness of a statue of Hernando De Soto that could overlook the Mississippi River from the bluffs of the city. As he was working out the problems of the Crump project, the sculptor armatured an idea maquette in plastiline of De Soto in armor, mounted on a Spanish horse. As discussions continued on the Crump Memorial, De Lue presented the idea for the De Soto monument to the appropriate officials and found that there was no likelihood of raising the money to proceed with the project. Within a decade, therefore, De Lue altered the concept to suit himself to a nude figure of Alexander the Great astride his favorite horse, Bucephalus. De Lue worked on this equestrian group regularly for thirty years, finally casting it in plaster and making the finishing touches in December 1986. *Alexander Astride Bucephalus* is De Lue's response to his lifelong feeling for great equestrian statues and for the *Gattamelata* and the *Colleoni* that first brought him to sculpture.

104

82

Drawing for the limestone eagle on the Federal Reserve Bank, Boston, 1951, charcoal on paper, 17½ x 23¾ inches.

This eagle for Harbeson, Hough, Livingston and Larson is considerably different in character from the eagle De Lue sculpted for Harry Sternfeld, although each was used on a United States government building.

Federal Reserve Building
Boston, Massachusetts

Harbeson, Hough, Livingston and Larson were becoming very comfortable with De Lue. While he was still at work on the Omaha Beach Memorial they brought him the commission for the Indiana limestone American eagle that was to adorn the new addition to the Federal Reserve Bank building in Boston. The building was described as of classic design, inspired by New England federal architecture of the early nineteenth century. The eagle, eight feet four inches high and very stern and federal, was finished in the summer of 1952. Additionally, he received the contract for the twenty-two-foot high pair of doors for the main entrance to the building, which were to bear De Lue's designs, in bronze, of the six seals of the New England states. They were dedicated May 6, 1953. When the building was demolished, the eagle was destroyed, but the doors were retained and stored by the Federal Reserve.[15]

The newly installed doors of the Federal
Reserve Bank, Boston, dedicated by bank
president Joseph A. Erickson (left) and
board chairman Harold D. Hodgkinson,
May 6, 1953.

Lions of Judah, 1953–1954, Philippine mahogany.

Even in this smaller work, De Lue's ability to adapt his style to the client's demands is evident. The architect, Harry Sternfeld, preferred strong stylization and bold design as well as archaizing, elements that are evident here.

Lions of Judah
Germantown Jewish Center, Philadelphia, Pennsylvania

Harry Sternfeld, De Lue's difficult architect from the Philadelphia Court House Commission, also went back to him for additional work. Sternfeld was the architect in 1953 for the new Jewish Center to be built in Germantown, Pennsylvania. He turned to De Lue to provide a pair of strong and stylized *Lions of Judah* to flank the *Ten Commandments* that were also designed by De Lue. Both were carved in Philippine mahogany and installed in the sanctuary in 1954.

The Creation
Junior High School, P.S. 198, Queens, New York

Francis Keally, of Keally and Patterson, architects in New York City, worked with De Lue in 1954 to bring about the commission for *The Creation*. This ten-foot relief was cast in nickel bronze and set against the black brick facade of the new Junior High School in Queens.[16]

De Lue later recounted that Keally liked to dress up his architectural renderings with drawings of sculpture on the facades. He liked the work of Leo Friedlander (1889–1966) very much, but Friedlander would not embellish Keally's renderings. De Lue had created the relief sculptures for the Science and Engineering Building at Carnegie Mellon University in 1948 for Keally. The architect cajoled De Lue again and again into improving his presentations and then gave the sculptural work to Friedlander. Finally, however, a client liked the De Lue drawing so much, and Keally thought it was time for De Lue to get something out of all of this work, that another commission resulted.[17]

De Lue used variations of the story of the creation to create sculptural works. His relief for the chapel at Virginia Polytechnic Institute, *The Right Hand of the Lord*, shows a man held in the hand of God. The Queens school relief shows Adam and Eve, or man and woman, held at creation in the right hand of God. His *Hand of God* (1967) shows Adam, or man, alone in the hand of the creator. In *The Creation*, Adam and Eve bow their heads and cock their knees in reverence toward the powerful figure of God. In his 1978 figures *Adam* and *Eve*, the physical agony of separation from God is the subject of the work.

68

184

189

The Creation, 1954, plaster detail for facade relief at the Junior High School in Queens, New York.

Collaborating with New York architect Francis Keally, De Lue worked with the classic theme of creation and the birth of mankind.

The Sun As Healer
Abraham Jacobi Hospital, East Bronx, New York

The Sun as Healer, symbolic of the healing power of Mother Nature and the sun, was commissioned in 1954 by the City of New York for the new Abraham Jacobi Hospital. The building was part of a $150,000,000 New York City hospital expansion program. Again, Francis Keally of Keally and Patterson was the architect and Frederick H. Zermuhlen (1897–1961) was the public works commissioner for the city of New York. Not only had he presided over the greatest building program in the history of New York City, but Zurmuhlen had led the drive for the embellishment of its buildings with art.[18] In 1953 he had been awarded the National Sculpture Society's medal of honor for "reintegrating sculpture and mural painting with the civic architecture of today."[19]

Rene Lavaggi, the carver of the relief, remembered one problem. When he was about to carve Zermuhlen's name in the adjoining tablet he noted that it was followed by the initials indicating the commissioner was a

The Sun as Healer, 1954, charcoal on paper, 17½ x 27½ inches.

The Sun as Healer, 1954, marble, 11 x 7 feet.

This relief panel for the Abraham Jacobi Hospital in the East Bronx in New York shows De Lue's belief in the spiritual and healing powers of light.

registered architect and a professional engineer; "R.A.P.E." was rearranged. [20]

The low relief cut into the marble of this sculpture and the poses of the mother and child beneath the sun's rays evoke images of Egyptian reliefs employing similar motifs. De Lue had a precedent within his cosmology for explicating the power of the sun:

> *Noble, then, is the bond which links together sight and visibility, and great beyond other bonds by no small difference of nature; for light is their bond, and light is no ignoble thing . . . And which, I said, of all the gods in heaven would you say was the lord of this element? Whose is that light which makes the eye to see perfectly and the visible to appear? . . .*
>
> *You mean the sun, as you and all mankind say.*
>
> **PLATO   *THE REPUBLIC VI*** [21]

Prometheus, 1978, bronze, 33 inches.

The gifts of power from the sun to mankind were embodied in Prometheus and the legend of his bringing fire to earth. The sun, light, or flame recurs as an image in De Lue's work.

Christ Falls for the Second Time, 1954, charcoal on paper, 17 x 20 inches.

De Lue's preparation for this series for Loyola Seminary involved many drawing studies of each station of the cross.

Donald De Lue with the clay models of the stations of the cross for Loyola Seminary, 1954. De Lue wrote on this photograph, "De Lue with small model of St. Laurent figure—Stations of the Cross in clay and small model of 100 ft figure of Christ." Note the smaller sketch models in the background and the larger final model in plastiline at left. The Loyola Seminary stations of the cross are slightly horizontal. The later Sisters of St. Joseph Chapel stations of the cross are clearly vertical.

Sun God (1937) and "Apollo" (on the obverse of the 1978 *Sculptor's Medal*) radiate power as the embodiment of the sun. *Icarus* (1934) and *Phaeton* (1960 and 1972) illustrate the dangers of that awesome power. *Prometheus,* in both three dimensions (1978) and relief medal (1975), suggests the pragmatic benefits of the sun to man, and the *Portal of Life Eternal* (1969) illustrates the spiritual power of the sun at "high noon." Whether represented by the sun, rays, or flame, light is a recurrent theme that has an obvious intent in this work: "to create a sense of uplifted spirit in those who enter the new hospital."[22]

30, 210

19

123, 191

93

160

Sing to the Lord a New Song

Stations of the Cross
Loyola Seminary, Shrub Oak, New York

De Lue had not worked for the Roman Catholic Church since his year in Lyon in 1920. In 1954 he was approached by the architects Vorhees, Walker, Smith and Smith about a major project for the Jesuit seminary in Shrub Oak, New York. The architects and the Jesuits worked as a team with sculptors Gleb Derujinsky, Joseph Kiselewski, Henry Kreis, Oronzio Maldarelli, Carl L. Schmitz, and Donald De Lue. One of the architects was a priest. When De Lue asked why he, a non–Catholic, had been selected as one of the sculptors on the project, the priest replied that it was because he was the best man for the job. De Lue received the commission for the fourteen stations of the cross, which were carved in white marble and placed on the wall of the Domestic Chapel. The work was completed and installed in June of 1955 and was heralded as a milestone in Roman Catholic and ecclesiastical building in the United States. The building provided an opportunity for a union of sculpture and architecture of the sort that De Lue called for, perhaps inspired by the

success of Loyola Seminary, in his June 1957 article in the *Journal of the American Institute of Architects*, "Toward a Reunion of Art and Architecture."

De Lue and the other sculptors received many commendations and awards for the project, including, in 1957, the prestigious Henry Hering Award for outstanding collaboration among architect, owner, and sculptor. By paring away a plaster cast as he had with *Urn Fragment* and *Mother and Child*, he reduced the motifs in one of the stations to *Three Marys*. This created a new work in very low relief which makes a poignant psychological statement.

76, 77

Three Marys, 1955, bronze, 10 x 22 inches. As he had done in other projects, after the official commission was finished, De Lue trimmed one of the plaster models to create this entirely new work from one of the Loyola Seminary stations of the cross.

Death of St. Joseph
St. Joseph Shrine, Holy Sepulchre Cemetery, Chicago, Illinois

The Loyola Seminary commission was followed by work for two shrines in Illinois. The first was four reliefs in granite on the life of St. Joseph executed in 1960 for the St. Joseph Shrine at the Holy Sepulchre Cemetery in Chicago. The second, executed in 1961, was a series of granite reliefs for the Sacred Heart Shrine in Hillside, Illinois.[23] The architect of the latter project was Carl Braun of Greenwich, Connecticut.

Stations of the Cross
Sisters of St. Joseph Chapel, Willowdale, Toronto, Canada

Ray Winiger of the architectural firm of Morani, Morris and Allan of Toronto, Canada, was the architect for a new chapel for the Sisters of St. Joseph in Toronto. The Sisters of St. Joseph visited the chapel at Shrub Oak, New York, because of the celebrity of the fourteen stations of the cross at Loyola Seminary. They asked De Lue to have an entirely new and larger set of the stations designed and carved in rose marble, and commissioned a corpus in wood to hang over the altar. The project was begun in 1959 and included stations of the cross thirty-six by thirty inches and a twenty-seven-foot cross with a ten-foot lindenwood corpus of the crucified Christ. The stations were installed and dedicated in 1961.[24] The sisters made some suggestions for revisions on the crucifix, which was installed in 1963. The total project cost for De Lue's sculpture was $60,000.[25]

The Eleventh Station of the Cross, circa 1960, charcoal on paper, 23 x 19½ inches.

Although he had recently completed the stations of the cross for the Loyola Seminary, De Lue carefully restudied each of the subjects in more than one hundred drawings such as this one, for the Sisters of St. Joseph Chapel.

Approved drawing for crucifix, Sisters of St. Joseph Chapel, 1960, charcoal on paper, 42 x 28½ inches.

Sister Maura signed this drawing "approved for Carving, Toronto. April 4, 1960."

OPPOSITE:

Chapel interior, Willowdale.

St. Joseph and the Angel, 1960, charcoal on paper, 18½ x 24 inches.

This is a drawing for another sculpture at the St. Joseph Shrine.

Appearance of Christ to St. Margaret Mary, circa 1960, charcoal on paper, 18 x 22 inches.

A preliminary drawing for granite relief at the Sacred Heart Shrine, Hillside, Illinois.

De Lue had been able to give the Church what it needed. In a call in 1961 for increasing use by the Roman Catholic Church of religious sculpture, including De Lue's, Brother Cajetan Baumann wrote, "A work of art always reveals the spiritual state of its creator. When creating religious sculpture the artist's primary aim must be the Glory of God and leading man to God. Here he can reach his highest expression. In glorifying God . . . the artist may compare himself with David the Psalmist and, 'Sing to the Lord a New Song.' "[26]

Hercules as Athlete
United States Naval Academy, Annapolis, Maryland

At the same time that the figures of *America* and *France* were being prepared by De Lue for the American Battle Monuments Commission, he received a commission for a heroic male figure for the new Physical Culture Building at the United States Naval Academy at Annapolis. The architects of the building were, again, Harbeson, Hough, Livingston and Larson. The figure, a granite relief of an athlete, is mounted twenty-three feet above ground level and is ten and one-half feet long and seven feet high.[27] It shows Hercules as athlete and warrior, recumbent with his club, which is draped with the laurel wreath of victory and honor. This relief, carved from Mount Airy, North Carolina, granite, was completed in half-scale plaster models and enlarged in the 1957 carving; it was installed on the building in 1958.[28] The work is reminiscent of his granite reliefs 85 for the Harvey Firestone Memorial exedra (1951) and for the other com-87 mission of this same 1955–1957 period, the Edward Hull Crump Memorial.

The ease and success with which De Lue worked with his architectural colleagues had not gone unnoticed. In 1957, the first year in which they were given, he won both of the National Sculpture Society's Henry Hering Awards for excellence in architecture: the Hering Prize for Out-

Hercules as Athlete, 1957, granite relief, 7 x 10½ feet.

This work was commissioned by Harbeson, Hough, Livingston and Larson for the new physical culture building at the United States Naval Academy at Annapolis. It depicts Hercules as both athlete and warrior, honored in each with the laurel wreath.

standing Collaboration among architect, owner, and sculptor for his work on the Loyola Seminary, and the Hering Prize for Monumental Sculpture in the Round as a collaboration among architect, client, and sculptor for the Omaha Beach Memorial at the St. Laurent Cemetery. He had also won the Avery Prize and later the Gold Medal of the Architectural League of New York. De Lue believed in the synergism which could enhance a project through the collegial cooperation of sculptor, painter, designer, architect, and landscape architect. He expressed his thoughts in 1957 when he wrote:

> I want least of all to deprecate the desire of the architect to view his work as an art. It is this mutual drive toward an esthetic valuation that is bringing the sculptor and the architect together. Architecture is one of the greatest of the arts, with a long history of benefit to the human race. I do not believe that the architect has ever had a greater opportunity than at the present to construct buildings of vibrant beauty. Sculpture and architecture together should make us conscious of our spiritual heritage, and add beauty, imagination and nobility to an otherwise mechanical age.[29]

The Omaha Beach project, together with the Firestone Memorial, Loyola Seminary, and the Crump Memorial, secured De Lue's reputation as an architectural and monumental sculptor. He was now heading for the largest commission for a bronze figure of his career and into the teeth of a controversy.

NOTES

1. Donald De Lue, "Toward a Reunion of Art and Architecture," *Journal of the American Institute of Architects*, Vol. 28, No. 3, July 1957, pp. 200–201.
2. Sandra L. Tatham and Roger W. Moss, *Biographical Dictionary of Philadelphia Architects: 1700–1930* (Boston, 1985).
3. Ernest W. Watson, "Commissioned Sculpture Today," *American Artist*, January 1951, pp. 36–37.
4. *New York Times*, March 29, 1943, p. 25, col. 7.
5. *National Sculpture Review*, Vol. 2, No. 4, Fall 1953, p. 9.
6. Learned Hand, "Hall of Our History," *New York Times*, August 9, 1953, section 6, pp. 8–9.
7. *New York Times*, December 17, 1953, p. 23.
8. After Fraser's death, De Lue acted as artistic executor, and shepherded works by Fraser to Syracuse University and to the Cowboy Hall of Fame.
9. *American Artist*, May 1951, p. 63. *See also National Sculpture Review*, Vol. 1, No. 1, December 1951, p. 5.
10. Ibid.
11. Ernest W. Watson, "Commissioned Sculpture Today," *American Artist*, January 1951, p 37.
12. DDL to DRH, April 24, 1987.
13. "Sculpture by Donald De Lue," *American Artist*, October 1957, p. 50.
14. *National Sculpture Review*, Vol. 1, No. 2, Summer 1957, p. 12. Also, *Memphis Press-Scimitar*, article undated.
15. *National Sculpture Review*, Vol.1, No. 3, June 1952, p. 15. *See also National Sculpture Review*, Vol. 2, No. 4, Fall 1953, p. 12. *New York Times*, May 6, 1953.

16. *National Sculpture Review*, Vol. 3, No. 4, 1954, p. 6.

17. DDL to DRH, November 13, 1987.

18. *New York Times* obituary, January 20, 1961, p. 29, col. 3.

19. *New York Times*, October 14, 1953, p. 27, col. 1.

20. Rene Lavaggi to DRH, telephone interview, May 1989.

21. Plato, *The Republic VI*, from *The Dialogues of Plato*, translated by B. Jowett (New York and London: Oxford University Press, 1892).

22. *National Sculpture Review*, Vol. 4, No. 1, Winter 1954–55.

23. *National Sculpture Review*, Vol. 4, No. 2, Spring 1955, p. 67. *See also* Thomas Lacroft, "Sculpture in Contemporary Catholic Church Architecure," *National Sculpture Review*, Vol. 5, No. 4, Winter 1956–57. *National Sculpture Review*, Vol. 9, No. 4, Winter 1960–61.

24. *National Sculpture Review*, Vol. 11, No. 4, Winter 1962–63. For more information on stations of the cross at Willowdale, refer to *National Sculpture Review*, Vol. 14, No. 4, and Vol. 16, No. 4.

25. Letter to D. Roger Howlett from Sister Mary Trimble, archivist of the Convent of St. Joseph, May 1989.

26. Brother Cajetan J. B. Baumann, O.F.M., "Sermons in Stone," *National Sculpture Review*, Vol. 10, No. 4, Winter 1962–63, p. 13.

27. *American Artist*, October 1957, p. 49.

28. *National Sculpture Review*, Vol. 8, No. 1, Spring 1959, p. 14. *See also National Sculpture Review*, Vol 8, No. 1, Winter 1959–60, p. 4.

29. Donald De Lue, "Toward a Reunion of Art and Architecture," *Journal of the American Institute of Architects*, Vol. 28, No. 3, pp. 200–201.

Wisdom, circa 1942, plaster, 19 inches.

In this design, probably done when De Lue was working with Paul Cret, De Lue shows the massive qualities that are needed for architectural sculpture and, without giving up expressive form, the compactness needed if the model is to be translated into stone.

V

*I*s *the same control to be extended to other artists, and are they also to be prohibited from exhibiting the opposite forms of vice and intemperance and meanness and indecency in sculpture and building and the other creative arts; and is he who cannot conform to this rule of ours to be prevented from practicing his art in our State, lest the taste of our citizens be corrupted by him? We would not have our guardians grow up amid images of moral deformity as in some noxious pasture, and there browse and feed day by day, little by little, until they silently gather a festering mass of corruption in their own soul. Let our artists rather be those who are gifted to discern the true nature of the beautiful and graceful.*

PLATO   *THE REPUBLIC III*

THUNDER OVER OLYMPUS

The Rocket Thrower and the New York World's Fair

ROBERT MOSES (1888–1981) WAS CZAR OF THE 1964 NEW YORK WORLD'S Fair. Whether or not one liked his methods or visions, he was a man with an impressive record of vast accomplishments. Having cut his teeth on the massive engineering projects of the New Deal he had been responsible for the St. Lawrence Power Project; the majority of bridges, tunnels, and parkways surrounding New York City; thousands of units of low-income housing; and New York state and city parks almost without number. He had long had the dream that a final crowning project to his career would be the transformation of the "Valley of Ashes," created by Tammany Hall on the Flushing Meadows, into one of the most beautiful parks in the country. It was Moses who had created the 1939–1940 World's Fair with that end in mind, but the insolvency of the Fair Corporation prevented him from funding his final vision. Great strides had been made, but much more needed to be done. In 1959, when he realized that planning was in progress for another New York World's Fair, he lobbied for a second chance, and he got it. The fair was budgeted at well over one billion dollars.

"Peace Through Understanding" was the slogan for the fair, and "Man's Entry into Space" was its major theme. The central axis was the "Plaza of the Astronauts" and the focus of the plaza was to be a monumental sculpture that reflected the theme of the plaza and the fair.

Gilmore D. Clarke had worked with Moses for years. In 1934, when Clarke was one of the most famous landscape architects in America, Moses had called on him to work on the project of redesigning the New York City Parks system. He continued as one of Moses's close associates and had held many other posts including membership on the Commission of Fine Arts in Washington.[1]

OPPOSITE:

Rocket Thrower, Unisphere and the Court of the Astronauts at night during the 1964 New York World's Fair, 1964–65.

The 45-foot high *Rocket Thrower* was the theme piece for the 1964 Fair, located at its center on the Plaza of the Astronauts; it was conceived as a permanent monument to the fair at Flushing Meadow where it stands today. Man's entry into space was the major theme of the fair.

Four studies on the theme of man's entry into space, *circa* 1957–1958.

The ascension of man into space was a recurrent theme for De Lue and one that made him appealing to the organizers of the New York World's Fair (1964). These studies for the Union Carbide Building anticipated the figures that De Lue was to perfect in *Rocket Thrower* and *Quest Eternal*.

As De Lue later remembered, "I met Gilmore Clarke at the National Academy of Design one evening and I said, 'Gil, do you have anything that a young sculptor like myself might do?' and he said, 'Plenty! I was reading the *New York Times* the other day and found out that Gilmore Clarke has been appointed a director of the New York World's Fair by Robert Moses. This has been a terrible disaster to me, but I have the job and I might as well live up to it. Yes, Donald, I have something for you. If you have something that you think is worthy, just send me the photographs and I'll see that Mr. Moses sees them.' " [2]

At that time, De Lue had just completed study models for a project, never to be realized, for the Union Carbide Building. The executives of Union Carbide had approached De Lue in the late 1950s to make several models four or five feet high on the general theme of man conquering space. One of them was intended to be chosen as the maquette for a huge statue in front of the new headquarters. When the models were finally presented to the architect, Gordon Bunshaft, of Skidmore, Owings and Merrill, it was apparent that he had no intention of using a large piece of sculpture in front of his building because he felt that his building was the sculpture. [3] The theme seemed to De Lue to be very close, however, to what the Fair Commission might want. Photographs of one of the models were sent to Clarke and reviewed by Stuart Constable, Fair Con-

troller Erwin Witt, General Whipple, Clarke, and of course Moses himself, in a meeting on December 18, 1961.[4] The Fair Committee had accepted the work in principle along with work by Paul Manship and José de Rivera. De Lue altered the model so that the figure, which originally had been shooting an arrow into the air, was instead heaving a rocket to the heavens.[5] De Lue then sent a plaster model to the Fair Committee.[6] After some time had elapsed, Clarke announced to De Lue that the fair would want a *Rocket Thrower*, as the proposed statue was called, between forty and fifty feet high. De Lue wrote to Clarke on January 23, 1962, proposing that the five-foot plaster be enlarged to fourteen feet and then to a final enlargement of forty-three feet overall; and estimating that the work would take two years and cost $105,000. In a memo of January 24, 1962, Clarke wrote to Moses proposing that the *Rocket Thrower* be situated on the principal axis of the fair on the site where the *George Washington* statue by James Earle Fraser had been located at the 1939 fair.

Moses was delighted with the figure. Because he wanted it as a permanent fixture of his planned park, he insisted that it be structurally sound and able to withstand high winds and storms. Manship, who had had so much of his work prominently shown in the 1939 fair, was somewhat disappointed, as was Paul Jennewein who had nothing included in

Archer, 1950–58, plaster, 26 inches.

This study was first modeled as an American Indian, but was later remodeled to remove the feathers from the head and a support was added under the calf of the left leg. The revised version was proposed for the Union Carbide Building and became the springboard for the *Rocket Thrower*. *Archer* indicates De Lue's admiration for the treatment of similar subjects by both Bourdelle and Meštrović.

Space Juggler, 1964, plaster, 44 inches.

This work continues the theme of man's eternal fascination with the cosmos. Typical of De Lue, this super-human figure hailing the heavens is conceived as monumental in size, dwarfing the man situated on the base.

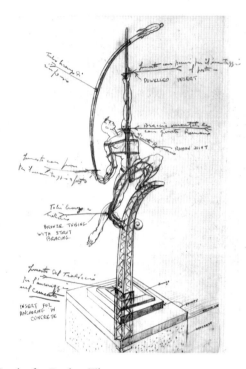

Study for Rocket Thrower, 1962–1963, pencil drawing, 9¾ x 12¼ inches.

One of many drawings for both the form and engineering of the large bronze that De Lue carried out during the course of the commission.

OPPOSITE:

Donald De Lue at work on the full-sized plaster for the *Rocket Thrower*, Spring 1963.

De Lue is shown making final corrections on the full-sized plaster in his Leonardo, New Jersey, studio. The figure, which was to be cast in sections, was sent to Italy later that year. Note the early stage of *Eve* in plastiline, lower left.

the official contracts. De Lue remembered that after a meeting with Moses, Manship said to him, "Donald, you've got it all! I thought somebody like Jennewein would have it. But they've seen fit to give it to you and God bless you!"[7]

De Lue went right to work, since the opening of the fair was only a little more than two years away. He usually worked with contracts, but none was forthcoming from Moses's office. Clarke said to get on with the work and not worry about contracts. De Lue was getting a little nervous as his personal expenses in enlarging the *Rocket Thrower* began to grow. Finally, after some months, Clarke strolled into De Lue's studio and said, "Sign here." The contract had been prepared exactly as agreed upon months before. He had eleven months to complete and fabricate the clay models and the forty-three foot plaster cast and eleven months more to cast the bronze and erect it on the fair site. The stars in the rocket were to be gold leafed. A further stipulation granted De Lue the rights to the five-foot and fourteen-foot models, but enjoined him from creating any other size of the *Rocket Thrower* and especially from erecting another full-sized cast.[8]

As the *Rocket Thrower* grew, De Lue confronted the same problem that he had had with *Spirit of American Youth*: he was outgrowing his studio. In this case, Malvina Hoffman's studio was not available. De Lue's search in 1962 led him to New Jersey. After being turned away by the Rumson zoning board,[9] he settled on remodeling and substantially raising the roof of a house and studio that he purchased in Leonardo. The move to New Jersey, necessitated by the work for the fair, took place in stages; for many years he maintained his New York studio in addition to the larger one in Leonardo. On January 4, 1963, he wrote to David Carruth at Gilmore Clarke's firm, Clarke and Rupuano:

The full size model has been underway for the last four months. The lower part, legs and plinth up to the waist, is almost completed and will be moved into my studio in Leonardo, New Jersey in about two weeks. This piece is quite large and has been quite difficult because of the iron supports and the weight that has to be carried. The upper section, shoulder head and arms, follow very shortly. I expect to work on these two sections in the studio for a month or five or six weeks, put the whole figure together and have it entirely finished by the end of February or the first week in March. A schedule has been worked out carefully and it is as follows: on March 15, the plaster casters move in to make the cast; this will take about six weeks, to the 30th of April. If the figure is cast in Italy it will be crated and shipped, clearing customs and arriving at the foundry during the month of June.[10]

In early deliberations, the Fair Corporation was going to stipulate that the bronze be cast in the United States, but De Lue could not find any American foundry that would guarantee delivery by the required date. He located a representative of Italian foundries in New York, and followed the lead of the *Spirit of American Youth* by having his second major bronze cast in Italy.

Moses wanted to keep everything about the *Rocket Thrower* a secret. By 1961, he was already having difficulty controlling the New York press. Late in the year he stated: "You have no doubt also heard echos of obscure wranglings about art at the fair. We belong to no school at the Fair, subscribe to no thesis, worship at no artistic shrine, advocate no architectural millennium."[11] He and De Lue both knew that the current climate of the New York art world might react negatively to such traditional works at the New York Fair in 1964. Despite the secrecy, a newspaper reporter came to De Lue's studio and said that she knew that De Lue was working on the fair commission and she would like to do a story on it. The sculptor explained Moses's position, but she said she would like him to call Moses and let her ask for permission. De Lue later recounted, "I said, 'If you want to risk it.' She said, 'Okay.' She called Robert Moses and told him what she wanted and he said, 'I can tell you to go straight to hell with my compliments' and hung up on her."[12]

Moses's handling of other members of the press during the fair wasn't much more gracious. By the opening of the fair he was embattled with every paper in New York. Undoubtedly, this adversarial atmosphere contributed to the artistic battle to come. What an unbiased *New York Times* might have reported of the *Rocket Thrower* in 1964 is a matter of conjecture. What John Canaday (1907–1985), the art critic for the *New York Times*, wrote is not. On April 25, 1964, he wrote:

> . . . and the most lamentable monster, making Walt Disney look like Leonardo da Vinci, is Donald De Lue's *Rocket Thrower*, a bronze muscle-man rising forty-five ridiculous feet into the air on the main axis. Since the *Rocket Thrower* is an absurdity that might be a satire of the kind of sculpture already discredited at the time of the 1939 fair, we might get it out of the way, first by describing it as a warmed-over pseudo-Carl Milles and left-over Lee Lawrie. But to get it out of the way physically is going to be impossible, since it was commissioned as a permanent disfigurement to Flushing Meadow Park, one of the fair's residual contributions to culture.
>
> If the jealous heavens do not level the *Rocket Thrower* with a bolt of lightning, a solution would be for some public spirited citizen to pay for melting it down and putting it back into place. Whatever the shape of the resultant lump, it would be better than the shape it is in now.[13]

Of the review De Lue later said:

> I didn't like it, of course. I was rather sensitive at that time. But Robert Moses said, "Look, this is the greatest compliment you could have. This son of a bitch hates everything that is good, so you're highly complimented. Furthermore, if I were you, I would sue the *New York Times* for plenty. I will help you and give you all the support you need." I said, "Look, Mr. Moses, I'm not a rich man, nor am I out to destroy the *Times*. Of course, I don't care for Canaday who likes nothing but abstract art." He said, "If I were you, I would crucify the *Times*." I said, "That's not so easily done." He said, "In my case it would be. If I took on the *Times*, I'd be assured of beating them." I said, "I'm not Robert Moses." He said, "All right, do as you please."[14]

De Lue was probably correct. As long as John Canaday was the art critic for the *New York Times*, no favorable review of any work of any member of the National Sculpture Society appeared in its pages.

> *The love of the beautiful set in order the empire of the gods, for that of deformed things there is no love.*
> PLATO   *THE SYMPOSIUM*

Holding the Fort of Beauty

Art at the 1964 World's Fair

The lines of battle between the traditionalists and the avant-garde were now drawn. In truth, they were forming on the issue of art at the fair as early as 1959. Moses was disposed toward the traditionalists. In an address at Cornell University, which was widely quoted in the press, Moses said, "I believe that public officials charged with building should be conservative, that their oaths of office do not pledge bold experimentation, that they should respect but not be slaves to tradition and that they should keep in mind that the extreme styles, modes and fashions of today may be the bywords of tomorrow."[15]

De Lue wrote a letter in 1959 to Thomas J. Deegan, Jr., president of the corporation sponsoring the World's Fair. In it he summarized his position:

I noticed a statement by you in the *New York World Telegram Sun* hoping that the art in the New York World's Fair would not be of a similar type as shown in Brussels. The directors of the Modern Museum and the Whitney will most likely be heard from. These are the groups that are said to be responsible for the previous debacles at Moscow and Brussels.

If it will be of any service to you in this matter to help protect this Fair from artistic desecration and being an insult to the American people, there are several large and influential groups that can be of great service and strength to buttress your position. One is the National Academy of Design with a large and influential group of sculptors, painters and architects. John Harbeson as President, the distinguished architect, was over-all consultant for the battle monuments erected overseas for our war dead . . . . [There is also] the American Artist Professional League. Mr. Wheeler Williams (sculptor) is President.

There is also the National Sculpture Society, composed of distinguished sculptors. Most of the fine work in this country has been done by members of this oldest sculpture society in the country. Adlai S. Hardin is the present President. Next year Paul Jennewein will be President, a very distinguished sculptor.

Rocket Thrower, 1962, bronze, 58 inches.

This is the study model size that was approved by the Fair Committee in 1961 for enlargement.

Would it be possible for the Presidents of these three societies and one or two members to meet with you and have a little talk about this matter? Judging from an article in the *New York Times,* Mr. Robert Moses is in full agreement with your position, and suggests that the traditional artists make their voices heard.[16]

Paul Manship, Marshall Fredericks, and Theodore Roszak were also represented by commissions at the fair. With the exception of Roszak, who showed at Brussels, all the others, including De Lue, were members of the National Sculpture Society and the traditionalist establishment. The traditional voices were heard at the fair, and the modernist vision was articulated by Canaday.

Robert Weinman, a member of the National Sculpture Society and friend of De Lue's, tried to make peace after Canaday's comments on the *Rocket Thrower* appeared in the *New York Times.* He sent a letter to Canaday and a copy to De Lue. De Lue thanked Weinman for his defense against the vicious attack, but said that he had expected it. Canaday, with his faultless graciousness, replied to Weinman: "Re my 'low-blow' at De Lue's 'Rocket Thrower.' No, I am not anxious about sculpture, muscles or rockets, and least of all about sculpture, which seems to me in a wonderfully healthy state today. That is why a senile and ugly style offends me. If I am 'unkind' it is from the shock of finding so ghastly a work of art as a permanent monument when hundreds of sculptors— literally hundreds—could have done a better job."[17]

The terms of the then current debate on modern art involved not only the works of art themselves, but the criticism of it as well. A critic today would not make a case that the sculpture at the 1939 World's Fair was already discredited; nor would a critic in 1939 have had an easy job of it. But works of art endure, while criticism—which at first is so sharp —becomes dulled with time until it is a harmless curiosity. As Hilton Kramer noted in the *New York Times* in 1975, "Cultural life in the nineteen-sixties, whatever its special merits, was not famous for creating a climate favorable to the disinterested appreciation of tradition."[18] Kramer might well have included the 1950s as well.

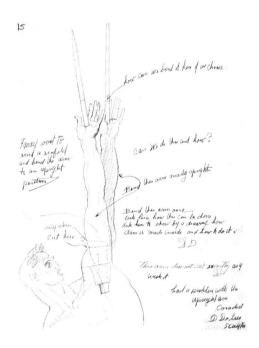

Study for the engineering of the arm and socket of *Rocket Thrower,* 1962–1963, pencil drawing, 10 × 13 inches.

The Moderns in Museums

A careful look at the New York art scene shows that a major change occurred between the exhibitions of 1950 and those of 1951. Both the Metropolitan Museum and the Whitney Museum of American Art changed aesthetic direction within the year. At issue was the question, "What is the real movement in contemporary art?" The problem had been coming for some years. In painting, "modern American art" had been represented from the 1920s through the 1940s by the regionalists, American scene painters, and social realists, all of whom were fulfilling the call of critics such as Thomas Craven to develop an "American" style and to reject European styles and values.[19] At the same time there were painters who were developing a purely abstract form and a political and social theory and style that fitted nicely with the twin mountains of criticism, Clement

Greenberg and Harold Rosenberg, who were at the cutting edge of art journalism in New York. What neither group seemed to understand is that two styles and groups were each claiming to be "modern art." They could not be amalgamated and were so polarized that each sought to discredit the other. Eleanor Jewett, art critic for the *Chicago Tribune*, seemed to understand this better than almost anyone else. She suggested the appointment at the Art Institute of Chicago of a second director so that there would be a modern and a non-modern representation. She opined, "For the first time since 1920 the Chicago Art Institute would admit and support the fact that there are two schools of contemporary art in the United States, one stemming from war-torn Europe, the modern, and one growing out of the courageous and honest soil of America, the non-modern." She suggested that Thomas Craven be appointed and that with him, "we would see sculpture by Wheeler Williams, Donald De Lue, Paul Manship, James Earle Fraser and his wife Laura Gardin Fraser, Cecil Howard and (Albin) Polasek."[20]

At least since Baudelaire and the Paris Salon of 1848, there have been revolutions in styles of art criticism as well as art, and they are often concomitant. In the mid-twentieth century, the same changes that were occurring in the styles of painting and painting criticism were also occurring in sculpture. It is not entirely accidental that Thomas Craven, a writer who had helped to launch and promote many of the American modern realist painters of the 1920s, and who was an early user of the documentary film as a new vehicle for art criticism, chose in 1951 to make a film including six practicing modern realist sculptors: Wheeler Williams, Cecil Howard, Paul Manship, James Earle Fraser, Laura Gardin Fraser, and Donald De Lue.[21] In hindsight, it is also not surprising that the Metropolitan Museum chose to make its first break with the sculpture establishment that year.

De Lue later remembered:

Francis Henry Taylor [director of the Metropolitan Museum] invited Wheeler Williams [president of the National Sculpture Society, 1951–1954] and myself up to the Metropolitan; he wanted to talk to us. We went over to a very nice hotel across the street. He said, "If either of you ever discuss this on the outside, I'll say this meeting never took place."

I said, "That's a rather poor way to start off a nice luncheon."

"Well," he said, "that's the way it's going to be." He told us that there was going to be a sculpture show at the Metropolitan Museum at which no member of the Sculpture Society would have any part. I asked him why. He said, "Well, it's the Moderns, and the Moderns are very noisy, and you people are gentlemen. I don't expect any trouble out of you people. But the modern element comes up to my office and they knock my teeth out and they kick my shins and give me a very bad time. They've made a fuss and I've decided to listen to it and I'm going to give them an all-Moderns show at the Metropolitan. The only person who will in any way represent the Sculpture Society is James Earle Fraser, who will be on the jury."

I said, "Why do you want him on the jury?" He said, "So he'll dress it

Poseidon, 1975, bronze, 36½ inches.
This work was modeled in 1975 and immediately put forth as part of a fountain for a proposed Philadelphia commission. The god of the sea springs from the tails of five diving dolphins.

up. It isn't a question that I don't like to work with the Sculpture Society, but it's over-powerful. Look at Daniel Chester French: he was head of the sculpture department of this museum and look at the sculpture that he bought for the museum. Look at the French sculpture that's up on the sides. I'm going to spend thousands of dollars to get rid of it."[22]

De Lue queried him as to whether he thought he could do any better and Taylor replied that they were living in a changing world and could do a lot better. Although James Earle Fraser declined to be a juror, possibly because of his declining health, De Lue said that he felt similarly that sculpture, like the world, was constantly changing. Fraser said, "We shouldn't be afraid of change. It may have things that are pretty good. Maybe the arts *are* a little stuffy. Maybe they need a change, I'm not to judge that either." Whether they needed it or not the arts were to get the biggest change they had ever seen. The Modernist revolution was in full force, and De Lue was one of a small but powerful band of counterrevolutionaries.

On November 14, 1951 the Metropolitan Museum announced the names of 101 artists that had been chosen for the exhibition *American Sculpture 1951*, which would begin on December 7. The announcement brought about comments that this was, indeed, a reverse twist to the previous year's painting competition, when, it was said, the jury was hostile to advanced art.[23] The subtitling of the exhibition catalogue, "A National Competitive Exhibition," was a cruel hoax perpetrated on traditional sculptors, like De Lue, who were deliberately excluded from the show. In the case of the 1951 sculpture show most traditionalists shunned the show, claiming that the jury had a Modernist viewpoint. Only Gleb Derujinsky, Paul Manship, Adolph Weinman, Peter Dalton, Walker Hancock, Albert Wein, and a few others were represented. Many of the other traditionalists declined to compete. Wheeler Williams said, "You don't enter a German shepherd in the Pekingese class. Judges of the Pekingese class may be excellent judges, no doubt, but not out of their class." De Lue was a bit harsher on the Modernists on the jury, which included David Smith, Hugo Robus, and William Zorach. He said, "We don't like each other. They think we're old hat and we think they're incompetent." Leo Friedlander, also of the National Sculpture Society, said that he was "inclined to progressive art" but deplored the "sick manifestations" of it that were being "promoted" by Metropolitan extremists.[24]

A special committee of the National Sculpture Society, with Donald De Lue as chairman, sent a letter of protest to the Metropolitan, but to little avail. It would be thirty years before one of their members received a one-man exhibition at a series of major American museums, when *Paul Manship: Changing Taste in America* traveled from 1985–1987.[25] The critics for most metropolitan daily newspapers and the directors of the museums closed ranks in what seemed a conspiracy. In truth it was probably the tide of changing taste. In this change, the private collectors and the general public never really got their hearts or their heads into the new forms of

Model for *Poseidon Fountain*, 1975.
This unrealized Philadelphia project incorporated many of the figures De Lue executed as separate sculptures, notably *Orpheus* and *Sun God*.

art. There is a great deal of evidence that artists simply lost the majority of the collecting public for thirty years.[26]

In December 1952 an editorial in the *National Sculpture Review* criticized an exhibition at the Philadelphia Museum of Art, *International Renaissance of Sculpture in Our Century*, organized by Andrew C. Ritchie of the Museum of Modern Art.[27] It said in part,

One concludes very definitely that this is an exhibition put on expressly to further the cause of the extreme modernist of today, while a true twentieth century sculpture exhibition would include the beginnings of that century, as well as some of the better-known traditionalists of the present. Where in this survey of the twentieth century are works by Fraser, French, Haseltine, MacMonnies or Weinman? Where are Donald De Lue, Malvina Hoffman, Lee Lawrie, Mahonri Young? And is it really possible in a supposedly "Twentieth Century" exhibition, to overlook Saint-Gaudens. The exhibition includes, of course, a few fine works, such as those by Rodin and Maillol. Such inclusions seem to have become common practice in exhibitions made up mainly of extreme contemporary modernistic work: bizarre pretzel performances and boresome abstract constructions—designated as sculpture—are associated and displayed with works by the great masters, the intention obviously being to confuse the lay public into thinking that the contorted moderns have won the right to a place on a par with known masterpieces.[28]

Not all critics were afraid to speak out. Margaret French Cresson (1889–1973), daughter of Daniel Chester French and a sculptor and writer herself, became one of the warhorses of the counterrevolution. She wrote in 1952, "Unfortunately, the public has become so intimidated by what he reads in the art magazines and in the art columns of the newspapers that he scarcely dares to call his soul his own. Many of the things he sees around in the galleries are distinctly upsetting to him, many of them revolting and an insult to his intelligence. He realizes that it is high time for much of this art to be put out to pasture. But not for the world would he dare to say so out loud."[29]

Exhibition of American competition models for *The Unknown Political Prisoner* at the Museum of Modern Art, New York, in 1953. A British entry by Reg Butler won the prize in the final judging at the Institute of Contemporary Arts in London.

The two sides were at odds worldwide, as evidenced by another letter of protest, signed by Wheeler Williams as president of the National Sculpture Society, to the Institute of Contemporary Arts, London. This debate concerned the recent winning selection in a competition for a sculpture to commemorate *The Unknown Political Prisoner*. The letter complained that despite the originally stated intention of treating the non-representational entries in the same way as those that were more traditional, the eleven entries sent to London on behalf of the competition by the Museum of Modern Art represented "a small and relatively unimportant phase of sculpture scarcely to be called representative of American sculpture today. The same type of work was selected by the Italian jury; and the English jury chose similar oddities, from among which a strange and contorted mass of wire has now been pronounced winner of the first prize."[30] Sir Jacob Epstein (1880–1959), the British sculptor, wrote a letter of reply from England:

> Naturally a committee that emanated from the Museum of Modern Art and the Institute of Contemporary Arts of London could have only one purpose in view: the encouragement of abstract (so-called) sculpture. The size of the award to my mind constitutes a sort of bribe which can only have a disastrous effect on the minds of the young. The rot in sculpture (as in painting) is today global, and is not confined to any group or nation. It is extremely difficult for sculptors working in the tradition of sculpture to combat a tendency to aberration and eccentricity, as most of the key posts in art today are held by the abstractionists or critics who propagate those ideas. We here know nothing about what is done in America, and your A. Calder has had a most pernicious influence. Likewise you do not know what is going on here, except for this stupid and empty construction in wire, now happily destroyed.[31]

Epstein referred to the strange saga of the winning model by Reg Butler, an erstwhile British blacksmith. "Two days after the opening of an exhibition of the models in London, a spectator named Laslo Szilvassy took action. Szilvassy, a Hungarian whose parents had been killed by the Nazis, grabbed Butler's model from its stand and threw it on the floor explaining, 'I think people have seen enough of this.' He was clapped in jail and placed under medical examination."[32]

Speaking on behalf of the professional artist, Ernest W. Watson, editor of *American Artist*, wrote in March 1954:

> Few intelligent painters and sculptors, I think, deny the privilege, even the obligation, of artists to explore every facet of art expression; nor do they object to seeing new ideas exhibited for all to see and appraise. I am sure they acknowledge and pay tribute to the modern art movement for its emphasis upon freedom and the creative spirit in art. What they justly deplore is the alarming rejection of traditional standards by many museums, critics, professors and schools, an attitude that threatens the professional survival of artists who have not "gone over" to the new cult body and soul. If this seems overstatement, I assure the readers that I could quote testimony of some painters of unquestioned distinction who have said, "I used to be invited to the important national shows."[33]

Orpheus, 1966, bronze, 45½ inches.

Orpheus was modeled as a fountain piece and exhibited in 1966 at the National Sculpture Society's annual exhibition where it won the gold medal. The figure later appears in De Lue's design of a fountain with many classical figures for the civic center in Philadelphia.

The Goodrich Report

For the traditionalist, sculptor or painter, there was much to fear in the advancing cause of the modernists. Only five years earlier they were hardly a factor in the market and were not generally well regarded by the critics. Now, however the ad hoc Goodrich Committee, a self-appointed group formed to consider the United States government's activities in the fine arts, was suggesting that government art contracts should be awarded in a new way. The program of the unofficial Committee on Government and Art (chaired by Lloyd Goodrich, then associate director of the Whitney Museum of American Art) seemed democratic enough. It comprised twelve national organizations: the Artists Equity Association, the National Institute of Arts and Letters, the American Institute of Architects, the National Academy of Design, the American Association of Museums, the American Federation of Arts, the American Institute of Decorators, the Association of Museum Directors, the College Art Association, the National Association of Women Artists, the National Society of Mural Painters, and the Sculptors Guild. As the committee began to draft its report, certain of the participants began to have grave doubts. The Artists Equity Association, the National Institute of Arts and Letters, and the American Institute of Architects had reservations about the report but approved it with those reservations stated. The National Academy of Design declined to approve the report. The others signed.[34]

The *New York Times* reported, "Among the most serious differences between the Academy and the Committee is the point of veto power. The Committee recommended the creation of three advisory commissions with the power of approving or vetoing Federal Art projects. The Academy will not endorse this."[35] The seemingly democratic and public-spirited Goodrich Committee sought more than their stated purpose of differing from the official finding of the Federal Commission of Fine Arts in "Art and Government." The Goodrich Committee said that the official Federal Commission of Fine Arts report, "in our opinion does not propose adequate bodies or procedures to effect any substantial improvement in existing art activities. It does not propose any new advisory bodies, not any which would be genuinely representative of the art world."[36] By "substantial improvement" the Goodrich Committee meant changing the current methods as set by the Commission of Fine Arts in Washington, which had review and advisory status over most federal art projects. In practice, the Commission of Fine Arts, founded in 1910 and headed in 1953 by David Finley (director of the National Gallery of Art), probably rarely disagreed with the direction of the government agencies such as the American Battle Monuments Commission. It was part of the establishment. Rather, they often initiated the course of the architecture or sculpture, and they had distinctly conservative tastes by the standards of the New York art world of the 1950s.

The real agenda of the Goodrich Committee, despite the high-sounding language of the report, was to change completely the direction of the federal commissions. "If The Commission of Fine Arts declines to accept responsibility for suggesting artists, and if there is no artist body connected with the General Services Administration qualified to do so, there can be little hope for improvement in the decoration of Federal buildings. Some agency has to take the responsibility for suggesting artists, and such an agency should be fully qualified to do so."[37] The artists that they had in mind were, in the darkest fears of the traditional sculptors and the brightest hope of the modernists, exactly those that had been shown in the Metropolitan in 1951 and the Philadelphia Museum in 1952, and had controlled the Institute of Contemporary Arts Competition in London in 1953.

De Lue had every right to be fearful. His largest commission to date was from the American Battle Monuments Commission, the sculptures at the Omaha Beach Memorial. He was in the middle of finishing it when the Goodrich Report was made public. It questioned the taste and competency of those in control such as John Harbeson, William Deacy, Eric Gugler, and other architects that had long steered the government to a modernized classicism. These men were the lifeblood of sculptors like De Lue. Margaret French Cresson came to the battlefront again with a "Minority Opinion on the Goodrich Report." She said of the Goodrich Report:

> The real issue, unfortunately, is another battle in the war that has been waging between modern and traditional art for so many years. It is an endeavor by certain forces in the art world to get control of Federal funds in the name of progressive art; to lay down an art program on the ostensible basis of being democratic. It may even be part of a socialist program to tax and spend. Even without too much research it would appear to be a program that is un-American in its challenge of tradition in general and of the Commission of Fine Arts in particular.[38]

Goodrich replied to her article, taking her to task particularly on her suggestions that there was a socialist or communist element associated with the rise of more progressive forms of art. He ridiculed the thought, but one should put her remarks in context and also realize that they were not entirely without foundation. These were years characterized by the deepest chill of the Cold War. The Rosenberg trials had just finished, the McCarthy hearings were to begin shortly. Communists were seen in every corner. There was a distinct association between many of the more modern artists and socialism, and neither the "Red baiters" nor many socialists made very fine distinctions between radical "isms." Goodrich attacked her wariness of museum professionals and art historians.[39]

De Lue replied to Goodrich's criticisms of Cresson:

> If you don't believe that the acceptance of such a plan as the Goodrich report would result in a dictatorship in the arts, please recall this statement (italics mine): "We also recommend that it be *mandatory* that the administrative agency charged with the various activities should consult with these commissions in artistic matters at the beginning of each project and that these commissions should have the power of *veto* in artistic matters."
> Up to now we have not used this language in America.
> I believe that many fine artists in this country will agree that in the arts there is already a dictatorship in effect, that in museums, the art press and

Molly Pitcher, 1966–1981, bronze, 30 inches.

Molly Pitcher, heroine of the battle of Monmouth was modeled shortly after De Lue opened his New Jersey studio. He attempted from that time until his death to interest the state or a civic group in having him do a major monument. The determined Molly Pitcher was his first entry for a monument on a New Jersey subject.

the magazines only those artists who subscribe to the modern cult receive acclaim or win awards. For the most part the awards are derived from funds left to encourage artists who would add to the luster of American art, by art-loving patrons who had no idea that these funds would be used as prizes to art forms that would degrade human thought and portray an impoverished America.

It is the museum director, however, that the practicing artist takes the greatest exception to. Since when has he known anything about art? Most

120

artists regard the museum director as a glorified clerk. If the museum director's taste is reflected by the so-called works of modern art in their museums, the public can readily see what this cult would inflict on them in the realm of federal art. All the great in the public domain has been accomplished since the founding of this country without benefit of museum directors.[40]

As if to ratify De Lue's comments, one of Goodrich's acts on being elevated to the directorship of the Whitney Museum of American Art was to sell the museum's nineteenth-century American painting collection and to sell or give away substantial parts of the collection of early twentieth-century painting that had been formed under Gertrude Vanderbilt Whitney and Juliana Force. But despite the proper fears that the Goodrich Committee had inspired in traditional sculptors, the ad hoc committee did not take control of either the American Battle Monuments Commission or the Commission of Fine Arts. The Goodrich Report, however, may have formed the philosophical basis for the 1963 one-half-of-one-percent Art in Architecture legislation that was placed under the General Services Administration during the Kennedy administration.[41]

Modernist Criticism in the Press

The power base of the traditionalists remained partly hidden from public view in such discreet bodies as the Commission of Fine Arts in Washington and the American Battle Monuments Commission, but they wielded enormous influence through their ability to grant or sway many of the most major commissions for American sculptors. States, cities, towns, and patriotic organizations looked to these conservative commissions for guidance when they had the unenviable task in the 1950s and 1960s of engaging a sculptor for a public monument. The modernists had more obvious power bases from which to launch attacks against the traditionalists. They held at first the modern art museums. In New York they began at the Museum of Modern Art and then took over the Whitney Museum of American Art about 1950–1951. The latter year they began the assault on the Metropolitan Museum, and slowly in the next two decades they achieved aesthetic sway over most of the nation's better-known museums. Similarly, they held the critical high ground among the most influential newspapers and magazines. Critics writing for the *New York Times* and *Art News* found the traditionalists to be an easy target for polemics that enhanced a writer's career.

The modernists' campaign against the classicists was ongoing throughout the 1950s and 1960s. De Lue remembered a telephone call that he received from Sanka Knox of the *New York Times* on March 30, 1955. She said, "Mr. De Lue, we are going to crucify you on the front page of the *New York Times* tomorrow." De Lue asked why and she said, "We don't like your sculpture and we don't like your attitude on communism." De Lue asked what communism had to do with her writings in the *New York Times*. Her reply was, "It has plenty. You don't like communism and you criticize people because of it." De Lue noted that many other people did as well and that the United States government

Phaeton and the Horse of the Sun, 1940, crayon on paper.

This drawing is difficult to orient, since it works nearly equally well in any direction and suggests the disorientation of the falling figures. Phaeton, representing man, reaches for a star even as he falls.

had fought a recent war on that issue. On March 31, the *New York Times* did print a front page, second section article on public sculpture with Sanka Knox's byline.[42] It was a clever column in which Knox was only reporting on an article that was to appear in the April 1955 *Art News*. She, therefore, was able to remove herself from responsibility for any opinion.

Charlotte Devree, the author of the *Art News* piece, had opinions a-plenty. She began, "There is almost no hint in official government sculpture that truly creative sculptors exist in the United States today." Her thesis was that the federal government was wasting the taxpayers' money, that the sculptors were overpaid, and that some sort of conspiracy existed between the National Sculpture Society and the Commission of Fine Arts in Washington. She decried the aesthetics of works by John Gregory, Paul Manship, Edmund Amateis, Malvina Hoffman, Paul Jennewein, Lee Lawrie, Michael Lantz, Wheeler Williams, Carl Milles, Boris Lovet-Lorski, and Sidney Waugh, among others. She especially savaged Felix deWeldon's *Iwo Jima*, which has become something of an American icon, and lumped it with the two pairs of equestrian groups, by Leo Friedlander and James Earle Fraser, on the Arlington Memorial Bridge Plaza in Washington as the three most wasteful new United States monuments. She grudgingly gave De Lue the same sort of compliment (technically proficient) that was regularly used to describe John Singer Sargent during the 1950s and continued:

> Artistically appalling as deWeldon's enormous bronze triumph is in Washington in its stylistic resemblance to sculptural monuments of the Nazis and the Soviets, Donald De Lue's figure commemorating 9,385 Americans who fell in the Normandy invasion and just after is drearier in its funereal implications. At the St. Laurent cemetery, on a stunning bluff overlooking Omaha Beach where Americans landed in June 1944, there now towers De Lue's twenty-two foot bronze male nude, its arms flung gracefully in the air, the figure upward flying from a watery surfaced fish or wave-like form—symbolizing the English Channel. The figure is sleek, wind-tossed, Milles-like. It represents, De Lue says, nothing so banal as victory, but rather the spirit of young American manhood triumphing over the pain and death of battle. At its base bronze letters read: "For mine eyes have seen the glory of the coming of the Lord."
>
> De Lue traces his esthetic line to the Greeks. He feels, however, that in this figure he has not merely copied them but has created in the greatest tradition, a new symbol with modern meaning. He claims kinship proudly with the sculptors of the Parthenon frieze and remarks that Greece was the cradle of Western civilization, and that it is difficult to get out of the cradle. His Renaissance hero is Michelangelo. He is less proud of some intermediate ancestors of nineteenth-century academic Neo-Classicism (Canova) and scorns their slavery to representation. His respect revives for the Dane, Thorvaldsen, and is high for Mestrovic, and he regards his more immediate family—Daniel Chester French and St. Gaudens of a generation ago and Paul Manship, Wheeler Williams and others of his clan today—as an intrepid band holding the fort of beauty against a threatening invasion of "modern" ugliness.
>
> The contemporary statue-maker is technically proficient. De Lue made dozens of maquettes for his St. Laurent figure and worked during three years on the final selection. He regards his fee of $26,500 for the figure and two urns as barely adequate.[43]

Eleanor Roosevelt, a commissioner of the American Battle Monuments Commission, unreservedly praised the sculptors of those monuments for their work. She wrote, "Designed and built by some of our foremost architects and adorned with statues and mosaics by some of our finest sculptors and artists, they are superb as works of art."[44]

John Canaday, perhaps unaware that the *New York Times* had already taken a shot at the American Battle Monuments Commission in 1955, fired a salvo in July of 1965. He had been sent a copy of the Spring 1965 *National Sculpture Review* and wrote in the Sunday *New York Times*, "Any issue of that publication is good for a bitter laugh or two," and continued to decry the magazine's discussion of the World War II memorials:

OPPOSITE:

Phaeton I (Phaeton Falling with the Horse of the Sun), 1960, bronze, 20¼ inches.

It is hardly surprising that during the development of the *Rocket Thrower* De Lue should return to a classical subject which also expresses the striving of mortals to reach to the heavens. Phaeton is a subject that De Lue returned to in drawing and sculpture many times. He was fascinated with the meaning and the formal problems of the figure falling through space with a horse. *Phaeton I* won the Samuel F. B. Morse prize in 1967 at the National Academy of Design's 142nd Annual Exhibition.

It isn't just that the sculpture is just old-fashioned. The trouble is, it's just plain bad. At best innocuous, it becomes offensive when its stale, trite and altogether specious idealism is compared with the bloody tragedy it supposedly commemorates. I am not an unqualified admirer of Richard Stankiewicz, the American leader of the international group of sculptors who weld discarded machine parts and other junk into something like sculpture. But a mammoth tower of wrecked planes, rusted LST's (Landing Ship Tanks, if you have forgotten) and twisted girders rising against the sky, could have a majesty that would evoke the sacrifice. When the first American World War II memorials began to appear in the early 1950s, they were blasted (only verbally, alas) in a way that would have made less atrophied sculptors or a less atrophied American Battle Monuments Commission take a second look at their handiwork. But the most recent monuments follow the same style, a style that was never anything but modish and became demode long before the war opened.[45]

He went on to excoriate individual sculptors and said of De Lue's *Spirit of American Youth*, "Having gotten away with this in 1956, he did it again last year and called it the *Rocket Thrower* for Flushing Meadows."[46] Canaday's suggestion that the sculptures be blown up may have been a subtle reference to the discovery and trial that was current in New York in early 1965 of the Black Liberation Front and the Quebec separatist movement's attempts to blow up the Statue of Liberty, the Washington monument, and the Liberty Bell. Neither those groups nor Canaday held much with diversity of opinion. Canaday should be commended in this article for finally and clearly stating what he really wanted to see in American monumental sculpture, *A Mammoth Tower of Wrecked Planes*. Of Canaday's taste, his fellow critic at the *New York Times*, John Russell, said, "John Canaday had a position peculiar to himself. Though neither scholar nor historian, he had in a high degree the gift of communication. If the art of his own day left him cold, he never hesitated to say so, thereby alienating many living artists, now universally recognized, for whom he could have performed a valuable service." In a much publicized letter to the *New York Times*, fifty of the country's leading art figures said Mr. Canaday's writing "is the activity not of a critic but of an agitator."[47]

Traditionalist Ideals

Donald De Lue was aware of the difficulty of getting good publicity for traditional sculpture or sculptors in the 1950s or 1960s, especially in New York. He knew, however, that the modern art establishment had almost no effect on the availability of public commissions. The American Battle Monuments Commission, with John Harbeson as consulting architect, and the Fine Arts Commission in Washington, headed by David Finley, knew that their constituency wanted more traditional sculpture. They knew that a select group of American sculptors had talent and craft to execute work to the highest standards.[48] Even in 1984, with the general approval by the American public of the aesthetics of the Vietnam Memorial wall in Washington, a more traditional figurative group by Frederick E. Hart was added at the insistence of veterans of the Vietnam

Torso, 1975, glazed ceramic.
This torso, given to John Manship, son of Paul Manship, is unusual in material, glaze and in its reference to a truncated and broken classical Venus.

War.[49] De Lue's greatest worries for today did not concern ascendencies of abstract sculpture, but the appearance of a "new" figurative sculpture without the underpinnings of anatomical knowledge and the craft of sculpture handed down from the Renaissance in a direct line to his generation. He feared the loss of many of the supporting crafts, such as plaster casting and enlarging.

De Lue had spent more than a half-century fighting for the highest standards of aesthetics and craft in all the arts, but particularly in sculpture. He had used the National Sculpture Society as his main platform during that battle. He was comfortable in most ways with Robert Moses's program. Moses also liked to dream and build larger than life, for generations yet unborn. There is no question that the 1964 World's Fair had chosen to ignore the forefront in contemporary sculpture, but Moses had a program that went beyond temporary display.

Indeed, the *Rocket Thrower* was not the only sculpture that De Lue had in the 1964 fair. The Masonic Pavilion had a cast of his *George Washington as Master Mason*. This work, as well as the *Rocket Thrower*, was part of the permanent legacy of the fair to Flushing Meadow. On June 3, 1967, as Robert Moses unveiled the De Lue bronze statue of Washington on its dedication as a permanent addition to the landscape he said:

133

> We have been told by sour, unhappy critics and avant-garde planners that our fair lacked fun in the modern vernacular. It all depends on your definition. The fair had inspiration which will long outlast the cheap, strident ballyhoo and sensationalism which we refused to exploit and accommodate.[50]

Quest Eternal

The Prudential Center, Boston, Massachusetts

At the time of the New York World's Fair De Lue was shaken and hurt by the *New York Times*'s criticisms of the *Rocket Thrower*, but the Canaday review was read favorably by Charles Luckman of Luckman Associates of New York City, the architect of the new Prudential Center in Boston. Luckman called De Lue repeatedly and wrote him letters, but De Lue, knowing of the reputation of his firm for modernism in architecture, concluded that they had nothing to discuss. Finally De Lue consented to a meeting. It seems that the Canaday article had reminded Luckman that every building that the *New York Times* had liked around the United States, he and his partners had hated, and that every building that they liked, including many of their own, the *New York Times* disliked. This polarity prompted Luckman to go to Flushing Meadow to see the *Rocket Thrower*, which he liked. He then said to De Lue that he had a commission of some importance that he would like to give the sculptor for a monument at the new Prudential Building in Boston.[51]

First, however, there were the financial arrangements. Luckman asked how much De Lue had received for his last project, and the sculptor replied that it had been in excess of $150,000. The Prudential, living up to its name, was unwilling to pay that, and they finally settled on a figure

Sketches for *Quest Eternal*, 1965, pencil
drawing, 18 × 24 inches.

Drawing for "Quest Eternal," circa 1965,
pencil on paper, 24 x 19 inches.

This is one of scores of drawings for the
shape and placement of the sculpture in
front of the Prudential building in Boston.

of $75,000 for *Quest Eternal*. The truth may be that the Prudential Build-
ing, which had been beset with construction problems, was vastly over
budget. No building of its dimensions had previously been built in Boston's Back Bay. It was a complex located over the old train yards, and
the digging for footings had gone on well beyond the scheduled deadline.
De Lue's earlier drawings for the monument show it set in a more fully
developed surround, suggesting that the final manifestation was reduced
from a grander scheme.

Quest Eternal symbolizes man's endeavor and aspiration for the better
things of life and spirit as well as recognizing the future frontiers of space.
De Lue said, " I behold this man as the doer, the creator and the builder,
inspired by recognition of eternal values . . . the spiritual idea, the great
truths that have come down to us from the past."[52]

The working model went through an enlargement first to six feet and
to nine feet before the final plaster enlargement was ready at twenty-
seven feet. This was also cast in bronze in Italy. De Lue said that he
trusted the foundry and had every confidence in his agent; nevertheless,
he felt that he ought to go to Italy to inspect the chasing and the cast
before it was shipped to Boston. It was not with dread that De Lue
looked toward a few weeks in Italy as he supervised the finishing of *Quest
Eternal*, but it was with great surprise when he first saw it and realized
that it had been mounted on its support backwards so that the figure
would face the Prudential tower, and the public would view his backside.
The foundry remounted it in short order.[53]

It was unveiled in April 1967, by Thomas Allsopp, Prudential's senior
vice president, and Hans Swarzenski, curator of Decorative Arts and
Sculpture at the Museum of Fine Arts, Boston, with the sculptor standing
by. It was noted in the papers that this was all taking place only a few

Quest Eternal, 1967, bronze, 27 feet.
The sculpture reaches up to the Prudential
Building and the skyline of Boston.

hundred yards from the studios on St. Botolph Street where De Lue had
served his beginning apprenticeships with Recchia, Pratt, and Robert
Baker more than fifty years earlier.[54] He had finally fulfilled the 1912
prophecy of Bela Pratt, that he should erect a monument in Boston. Since
its dedication, *Quest Eternal* has become a Boston icon. It appears on a
daily or weekly basis in the news media; it presided for nearly two decades
over the finish line of the Boston Marathon and reaches up to appear to
touch the official Christmas tree of the City of Boston each December.
The negative criticism of much of the national art press and the inhos-
pitable atmosphere of the largest museums, however, led De Lue to seek
his major commissions and public recognition from the mid-1950s to the
mid-1970s among more conservative patrons. These were often the most
lucrative projects and were unavailable to the more extreme modernists.
Just as architects had provided De Lue with commissions in the earlier
part of his career as an independent sculptor, he relied on conservative
patronage for the latter part of his career as a monumental sculptor.

1. Robert A. Caro, *The Power Broker: Robert Moses and the Fall of New York*, (New York: Random House), 1975.

2. DDL to DRH, 1987.

3. Ibid.

4. Memo from Robert Moses to Mr. Thornton, *circa* 1962, New York Public Library Archives.

5. Gurney pp. 57–59. *See also* DDL to DRH, 1987.

6. *Newark Sunday News*, April 26, 1964.

7. DDL to DRH, 1987.

8. Letter from Robert Moses to Donald De Lue, April 5, 1962, New York Public Library Archives.

9. Unidentified newspaper clipping, May 1962, De Lue archives.

10. Letter from Donald De Lue to Daniel B. Carruth, January 4, 1963, New York Public Library Archives.

11. *National Sculpture Review*, Vol. 10, No. 4, Winter 1961–62, p. 3.

12. *New York Times*, March 10, 1964, p. 34. *See also* DDL to DRH, 1987.

13. John Canaday in the *New York Times*, April 25, 1964.

14. DDL to DRH, 1987.

15. *National Sculpture Review*, Vol 8, No. 1, Spring 1959, p. 16.

16. Letter from Donald De Lue to Thomas Deegan, Jr., November 18, 1959.

17. John Canaday to Robert Weinman, Weinman Papers, Archives of American Art.

18. "National Academy of Design Celebrates its 150th Anniversary," *New York Times*, October 10, 1975, p. 39.

19. D. Roger Howlett, *Molly Luce: Eight Decades of the American Scene*, exhibition catalogue by Childs Gallery, 1980.

20. *National Sculpture Review*, Vol. 1, No. 2, March 1952, p. 5.

21. *Uncommon Clay* (movie), directed by Thomas Craven, 1951.

22. DDL to DRH, 1987.

23. *New York Times*, November 15, 1951, p. 31, col. 5.

24. Ibid.

25. Among other stops, the Manship show traveled to the Currier Gallery, the National Museum of American Art, and the Minnesota Museum.

26. *National Sculpture Review*, Vol. 1, No. 3, June 1952, p. 4.

27. *Art Digest*, October 15, 1952.

28. *National Sculpture Review*, Vol. 2, No. 1, December 1952, p. 7.

29. *National Sculpture Review*, Vol. 1, No. 3, June 1952, p. 5.

30. "Protest on 'Unknown Political Prisoner,'" *National Sculpture Review*, Vol. 2, No. 2, Spring 1953, p. 5.

31. *National Sculpture Review*, Vol. 3, No. 3, June 1953, p. 5.

32. *Life*, Vol. 34, No. 22, June 1, 1953, p. 39.

33. Ernest W. Watson, "More About Standards," *American Artist*, Vol. 18, No. 3, March 1954, p. 3.

34. *National Sculpture Review*, Vol. 3, No. 4, Fall 1954, p. 7.

35. Dorothy Grafly, "Toward a Federal Art Program," *American Artist*, Vol. 18, No. 8, October 1954, No. 8, p. 69.

36. Ibid., p. 32.

37. Ibid.

38. Margaret French Cresson, "A Minority Opinion on the Goodrich Report," *American Artist*, Vol. 18, No. 9, November 1954.

39. *American Artist*, Vol. 19, No. 1, January 1955, p.12.

40. *American Artist*, April 1955, p. 20.

41. Even after a quarter of a century, the General Services Administration still found that provocative or confrontational public art was resisted by the very public that had paid for it. Richard Serra's *Tilted Arc* was removed from Federal Plaza in New York on March 31st, 1989, amid charges that it was " aggressive . . .

intrusive, impersonal [and experienced] as a personal attack." (Michael Brenson, "The Messy Saga of Tilted Arc is Far From Over," *New York Times*, April 2, 1989, Sec.II, p. 33–34). Brenson noted that "when public art is permanent, it is now likely to be far less confrontational than *Tilted Arc*. . . . The G.S.A. now seems to be leaning toward upbeat, nonconfrontational art. . . . Since 1985, the program has changed its procedures. Any artist commissioned by the G.S.A. is now going to be involved with the architect from the beginning." Perhaps the federal officials were learning the wisdom that Robert Moses had expressed in the late 1950s, "that their oaths of office do not pledge bold experimentation, that they should respect but not be slaves to tradition and that they should keep in mind that the extreme styles, modes and fashions of today may be the bywords of tomorrow."

42. *New York Times*, March 31, 1955, p. 29, col 6.
43. Charlotte Devree, "Is This Statuary Worth More Than a Million of Your Money?" *Art News*, Vol. 54, April 1955, pp. 34–37.
44. *National Sculpture Review*, Vol. 5, No. 1, Spring 1956, p. 3.
45. *New York Times*, July 25, 1965, section 2, p. 10.
46. Ibid.
47. *New York Times*, obituary, July 21, 1985.
48. Gurney, pp. 96–101.
49. *National Sculpture Review*, Vol. 33, No. 4, Winter 1984.
50. *New York Times*, June 4, 1967.
51. DDL to DRH, 1987.
52. Caron Le Brun, *Boston Sunday Herald*, April 30, 1967.
53. DDL to DRH, 1987.
54. Caron Le Brun, "Quest Eternal for a Better Life," *Boston Sunday Herald*, April 30, 1967.

Cosmic Quest, 1969, plaster, 23¾ inches.

This soaring figure, executed in plaster only two years after *Quest Eternal* was erected, sustains many qualities of its predecessor. Here, the ideal male nude springs triumphantly into the air, body elongated and jubilant.

VI

Let them fashion the mind with such tales, even more fondly than they mold the body with their hands . . . . You may find a model of the lesser in the greater . . . for they are necessarily of the same type, and there is the same spirit in both of them. . . . A fault which is most serious is committed . . . whenever an erroneous representation is made of the nature of gods and heroes—as when a painter paints a portrait not having the shadow of likeness to the original.

PLATO   *THE REPUBLIC II*

APPRECIATION OF TRADITION

The Iconography of Patriotism and Faith

Commissions in the 1960s and 1970s

IN ADDITION TO THE INSPIRATIONAL AND TRANSCENDENT THEMES THAT were at the core of De Lue's own thought, he was regularly called upon to interpret imagery of patriotism and faith. As the work of architectural embellishment began to disappear in the early 1950s, De Lue took on more and more the role of an interpreter of the iconography of America. He also found that he was called upon by several religious orders to do the same.

Both patriotic and religious groups were more conservative in their artistic doctrines, as well as in other tenets, than many other segments of society. It is not surprising therefore that De Lue was sought out by the Masons, the Boy Scouts of America, the Roman Catholic Church, the Peace Mission Movement, the United States Army Special Forces, the Freedoms Foundation, the Daughters of the Confederacy, and the states of Louisiana and Mississippi. When West Virginia University wanted an institutional symbol and, later, when Brookdale College wanted a memorial to Martin Luther King, they did the same.

De Lue served as chairman of the Fine Arts Committee for the Hall of Fame of Great Americans and as such selected sculptors to memorialize the patriots and leaders of America in every field. He also created medals for the Hall of Fame, the Masons, and the National Medal of Science. De Lue's own conservatism and spirituality as well as his abiding belief in the innate goodness of America allowed him to be carefully attuned to the needs of his more conservative clients.

The states of the Confederacy have long had the reputation for patriotism and conservatism in politics and religion. In the 1960s and 1970s they were the site or the commissioners of *George Washington as Master Mason*, three memorials at the Gettysburg Battlefield, a half-size of *Spirit of American Youth*, the *Special Warfare Soldier (Green Beret)*, *Thomas Jefferson*, and *Leander Perez*. From 1960 to 1976 De Lue saw four dedications of major works in or for the State of Louisiana alone.

133
56
147, 148

OPPOSITE:

Spirit Triumphant, 1971, bronze, 86 inches.
Spirit Triumphant, the one-third size model from the State of Louisiana memorial at the Gettysburg battlefield, symbolizes the survival of the spirit. The laurel tree is in two parts, one representing the South, the other the North; it is united by the dove of peace.

George Washington as Master Mason
New Orleans, Louisiana

George Washington is perhaps the cornerstone in the pantheon of American mythology. In his own lifetime he was elevated in the esteem of his countrymen to only a little less than a god, and immediately following his death paintings and prints depicted his apotheosis. In various forms this recapitulation and enhancement of the mythic status of Washington continues to the present.

Donald De Lue created his first George Washington—his first work for America's Masonic Fraternity and first work in Louisiana—in 1959. A nine-foot statue of *George Washington as Master Mason* was done for the Grand Lodge of Louisiana and erected in front of the Public Library in the New Orleans Civic Center. The full-sized plaster was exhibited at the 1964 New York World's Fair, and at the close of the fair a bronze cast was commissioned by the New York Masons as a permanent reminder of their pavilion at the fair. Three thousand visitors and guests witnessed the dedication at Flushing Meadow in June of 1967.

Washington as Master Mason has an interesting history. In 1948 Bryant Baker was commissioned by the Masons to execute a seventeen-foot three-inch statue of Washington for the George Washington Masonic National Memorial Building in Alexandria, Virginia. It was unveiled and dedicated on February 22, 1950.[1] In 1959, the Grand Lodge of Louisiana wanted a similar statue to be erected in New Orleans. Baker, who had not kept the plaster model of the Alexandria cast, was unable, because of various commitments, to undertake the commission, and so he turned to his former assistant, Donald De Lue. De Lue agreed to take the commission. He used the Baker model as the springboard and design for his own model in exactly the reverse of their relationship of the 1920s. De Lue acknowledged the debt to Baker, but pointed to the great differences in anatomy between the two. It is a fair comment on the close relationship between Baker and De Lue that the Baker work in Alexandria has been constantly attributed to De Lue and that occasionally one of the several casts has been attributed to Baker. It is ironic not only that this sculpture, which is a tribute to the long working relationship between the two sculptors, should be De Lue's most replicated work, but also that it should have been the focus of a misunderstanding that led to a falling-out of the two artists.

Baker apparently thought that De Lue was still willing, twenty-two years later, to work as his assistant, and he believed that the latter was merely again executing his old master's thoughts. De Lue felt that he had agreed, as a professional courtesy, to honor Baker's obligation, but under his own name and terms. The terms used to describe the relationship at the time of the dedication, February 1960,[2] were: "The Sculpture was executed by Donald De Lue of New York employing Baker's research work."[3] The quarrel that arose between the two men over this misunderstanding ended their relationship.

Full-sized replicas of this sculpture stand at the Masonic Hospital, Wallingford, Connecticut; at the Civic Center, Detroit, Michigan; at Flushing Meadow, Queens, New York; and just outside the capitol building in Indianapolis. A cast of the half-sized model is at the Museum of Our National Heritage in Lexington, Massachusetts.

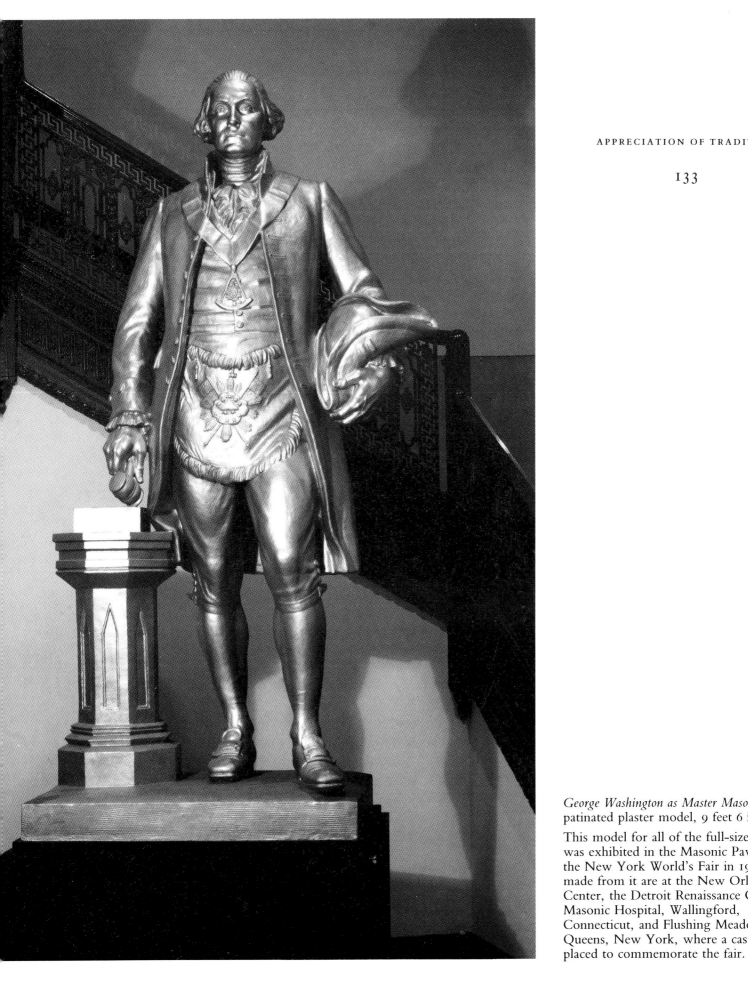

George Washington as Master Mason, 1959, patinated plaster model, 9 feet 6 inches.

This model for all of the full-sized bronzes was exhibited in the Masonic Pavilion at the New York World's Fair in 1964. Casts made from it are at the New Orleans Civic Center, the Detroit Renaissance Center, the Masonic Hospital, Wallingford, Connecticut, and Flushing Meadow in Queens, New York, where a cast was placed to commemorate the fair.

The Highest Ideals
Symbols of Country, State and Patriotism

If Washington was a historical figure who became part of the American iconography, other figures, who may be mythic, also honor the highest ideals of the aspiration of man. In the next several years De Lue was called to embody in clay visual idealizations for the Boy Scouts of America, the United Daughters of the Confederacy, the states of Louisiana and of Mississippi, the mountaineers of the State of West Virginia, the United States Army Special Forces, and the F.B.I.

Head of Patriotism, 1962, bronze, 8½ inches.
This study of the head for the male figure of the *Commemorative Tribute to the Boy Scouts of America* embodies De Lue's ideal male head.

Patriotism, 1962, plaster, 20½ inches.
Preliminary "idea maquettes" such as this one were done for De Lue's clients before enlargement. In the final version the figure became less stern and militant.

Commemorative Tribute to the Boy Scouts of America with Donald De Lue (center) and William Henry Deacy (right), November 1964.

The Commemorative Tribute to the Boy Scouts of America
The Ellipse, Washington, D. C.

During the 1964 World's Fair De Lue had another dedication. On November 7, 1964 he appeared on the Ellipse between the White House and the Washington Monument with Roger S. Firestone, Brigadier General William J. Morgan, U.S. Supreme Court Justice Tom Clark, and Chief Scout Executive Joseph A. Brunton, Jr., to unveil and dedicate *The Commemorative Tribute to the Boy Scouts of America.*

The Boy Scouts of America had been founded in Washington in 1910 and chartered by Congress in 1916; this monument was to commemorate a half-century of scouting in the United States. The project was authorized and the land appropriated by Congress in 1959 through a bill introduced by then Senator Lyndon B. Johnson. Several sculptors, including Avard

Fairbanks, submitted models, but Donald De Lue was chosen. The money for the statue was supposedly raised by contributions of one dime each by thousands of Boy Scouts throughout America, but in actuality any shortfall had been guaranteed by Harvey Firestone, Jr. Indeed, the Firestones' family experience with De Lue on the Firestone monument in Akron may have given him an edge in the competition. The charitable commitment of the Firestone family to the project was kept completely secret, even from many of the committee members.

In De Lue's words, the man and the woman of the monument "represent the sum of the great ideals of past civilizations, developed through the centuries and now at best delivered by American manhood and womanhood to the present generation." These figures come directly from the De Lue pantheon of symbolic heroes. The scout is another matter. De Lue had numerous scouts pose for him and help establish the model for the figure. The committee was strict in requiring anonymity on the part of the scouts and a generalization on the part of the sculptor, so that the resulting figure could not be identified with any particular model. Again, in De Lue's words, "The Boy Scout, aware of his fellowship with scouts around the world and symbolic of all Cub Scouts, Boy Scouts and Explorers striding into the future, represents their hope that all that is fine in our nation's past will continue to live in future generations." The project, as with so many of De Lue's works, engendered many drawings and idea maquettes. Most of the work other than enlargement was completed by 1962. The *Head of Patriotism*, for the male figure, shows the careful study that went into every part of De Lue's work. The idea maquette of *Enlightenment* shows an alternative to the final design. There is a tension that vibrates between the comfortable realism of the scout and the heroic idealism and spirituality of the male and female figures behind. This tension is an uncomfortable reminder that high ideals are more accessible when they are not related directly to daily life.[4]

Enlightenment or *Let There Be Light*, 1962, bronze, 23 inches.

This is an "idea maquette" for the female figure on the *Commemorative Tribute to the Boy Scouts of America*.

The Gettysburg Monuments
The Soldiers and Sailors of the Confederacy

In the late nineteenth and early twentieth centuries most of the Northern states erected monuments to their heroes on sites at Gettysburg where they had fought and died; only later did the Southern states begin to follow with their own monuments. Miss Désirée L. Franklin, who lived in New York City and was obsessed with the history of the Civil War, had visited De Lue many times in his New York studio. She claimed to have walked the battlefield at Gettysburg when the crosses for the fallen soldiers were still on the ground waiting to be erected. She was in charge of the centennial celebration for the United Daughters of the Confederacy and initially proposed erecting a monument to Walter Washington Williams of Texas on the Gettysburg battlefield. Eventually, the United Daughters of the Confederacy generalized the figure to represent all of the soldiers and sailors of the Confederacy. Miss Franklin cajoled De Lue into submitting a design.

Miss Franklin also arranged for each of the legislatures of the eleven states of the Confederacy to vote $3000 and each of the three border

Drawing for *Soldiers and Sailors of the Confederacy*, 1963, pencil on paper, 18 x 24 inches.

Soldiers and Sailors of the Confederacy, 1964, bronze, 14 feet.

This first Gettysburg memorial by De Lue was described by the critic Wayne Craven as a "striding, flag-bearing image of a Southern warrior [that] suggests Michelangelo's awesome Moses; having sprung from his seated position into the dynamic action that always seems his potential."

states to vote $1000 toward the erection of the monument. The design was approved by the Coordinating Committee of the United Daughters of the Confederacy and the Sons of Confederate Veterans on November 10, 1963; the contract was signed on February 1, 1964, and the work was cast at the Fonderia V. Lera in Via Reggio, Italy, that same year. The formal dedication at Gettysburg occurred on August 25, 1965, with representatives of the National Park Service accepting the gift of the statue from the United Daughters of the Confederacy and the Sons of Confederate Veterans.

The design represents the spirit of the military forces of the Confederate States of America. The bronze statue is fourteen feet high; the overall height of the monument, with base, is twenty feet. The fourteen-sided base bears the names of the eleven states of the Confederacy and the three border states. One of the major historians of American sculpture, Wayne Craven, wrote of it: "One stands in awe before the monumental beauty of a great bronze hand or foot, or senses in the twisted positions, or contraposto, of the figures the anguish of the moment represented. De Lue's striding, flag-bearing image of a southern warrior in *Soldiers and Sailors of the Confederacy* suggests Michelangelo's awesome *Moses*, having sprung from his seated position into the dynamic action that always seems his potential."[5]

The State of Louisiana Monument
Peace and Memory

There is little question that the United Daughters of the Confederacy were pleased with the De Lue monument, *The Soldiers and Sailors of the Confederacy*, and that this qualified him for an invitation to participate in the larger competition for the monument to the Louisiana soldiers who fell at the Battle of Gettysburg.[6] The project was initiated by the Louisiana chapter of the United Daughters of the Confederacy and the Sons of Confederate Veterans in May of 1966. By December the initiative had reached the Louisiana legislature and the Louisiana Gettysburg Memorial

LEFT:

Donald and Naomi De Lue with *Peace and Memory* at the Gettysburg Battlefield, circa 1971. According to De Lue, "It flies over the battlefield blowing the long, shrill clarion call on the trumpet over the long forgotten shallow graves of the Confederate dead. It is taps for the heroic dead at Gettysburg."

Peace and Memory, 1968, pencil on paper, 19 x 23½ inches.

Commission was authorized in May of 1967. Governor John McKeithen appointed Katherine V. Letteer chairman. Angela Gregory (b. 1903), a New Orleans sculptor, was appointed as professional consultant and guided the selection of twenty-four qualified sculptors for committee consideration. The design committee chose three sculptors by ballot from that list to submit scale models.

The *New Orleans Times-Picayune* on October 6, 1968, described the three sculptors as follows: "[Jean] Seidenberg, who is a native of New York, has lived in New Orleans for many years, earning a reputation for imaginative art; [James] Rice, who is a Texan by birth, is also an adopted son of Louisiana, working first at Southeastern College of Hammond and then at L.S.U.; De Lue, who is past president and fellow of the National Sculpture Society, is the recipient of many awards of merit."

De Lue's meticulous preparation for each of his monuments, together with the transcendent spiritual quality that they expressed, gave him a great advantage with a thoughtful committee. The committee announced on October 16 that De Lue's *Peace and Memory* was the winner, saying his monument was intended to express the ideals of sacrifice of the past and of hope and peace in the future. Mrs. Letteer said:

> The selection was unanimous and based on what members of the commission felt best conveyed the significance and meaning to the average layman who will comprise the vast majority of the visitors in Gettysburg.
>
> We in all probability, will not have made the proper selection from the viewpoint of the sculptor or a student of art, however, we can only hope that the selection we have made from our conception of the significance of such a monument will appeal to the general public.[7]

Letteer's timidity about the committee's decision-making is a reflection of the time, a distant echo of Canaday's criticisms destabilizing the self-assurance of otherwise formidable Louisianians. De Lue had no such self-doubt. He stated that

> [the] great symbolic figure representing the Spiritual idea of Peace and Memory, also a resurgent Confederacy, strong, confident and prosperous, flies over the battlefield blowing the long, shrill clarion call on the trumpet over the long forgotten shallow graves of the Confederate dead. It is taps for the heroic dead at Gettysburg.
>
> At the base of the bronze figure [of *Spirit Triumphant*], lies a recumbent figure of a young cannoneer from the Washington Artillery, who has paid the full price of his devotion to his cause. A comrade has laid the Confederate battle flag over the prostrate form, who has clutched the flag to his heart. The Memorial monument will be twenty-four feet in height and will proclaim that generations unborn at the time of Gettysburg, 105 years ago, have seen fit not to forget their gallant men; and that their memory shall endure for thousands of years. The base will be of the finest granite, with the Washington Artillery insignia on the back, while the Confederate battle flag denotes a memorial to all Louisiana's Confederate Soldiers.[8]

De Lue's thoughts were immediately reinforced by a New Orleans writer, who mentioned "how appropriate the Washington Artillery was as De Lue's theme. The Washington Artillery fired one of the first shots at the Battle of Manassas and one of the last before Lee's surrender at Appomattox. And at Gettysburg, it fired the signal gun for, and participated in the artillery preparation for Pickett's Charge."[9]

De Lue completed the one-third-size enlargement by July 18, 1969. By then he had expanded his symbolic thinking for the monument. The female figure is "*Spirit Triumphant*, symbolizing the survival of the spirit and ideas of these men . . . that they did not die in vain. The eternal flame, held in the other hand of the female figure, symbolizes the memory of these gallant men. It is the embodiment of the spirit that went into the Battle of Gettysburg with them. The laurel tree which supports this symbolic figure is in two parts. One represents the North; one the South. It is now one tree trunk, united by the dove of Peace which has now come to the Battlefield of Gettysburg and to the Nation."[10]

The monument to the Louisiana soldiers fallen at the Battle of Gettysburg, *Peace and Memory*, was dedicated with great ceremony by the Governor of Louisiana, John J. McKeithen, on June 11, 1971. Of the states that had troops in the Battle of Gettysburg, Louisiana was the next-to-last to erect a monument; Mississippi was the last.

Donald De Lue with the nearly completed full-sized plastiline of the Mississippi Monument, May 24, 1972. De Lue is seen at work in his Leonardo studio with the clay towering above him.

The Mississippi Monument

Not surprisingly, in 1968, only two years after Louisiana, the Mississippi legislature passed a bill authorizing funds to erect a monument to their men who had fought and fallen at the Battle of Gettysburg. A commission was appointed by Governor John Bell Williams, with Dr. M. Ney Williams as chairman. Again, not surprisingly, they turned to Donald De Lue. As early as April 1970 the commission was discussing the final plans for the monument and inspecting the thirty-six-inch model with the sculptor in Jackson, Mississippi. The design showed two soldiers of Barksdale's Mississippi Brigade in the midst of furious battle on July 2, 1863. This, De Lue's third monument at Gettysburg, is possibly his best.[11]

He first enlarged the Mississippi model to approximately five and one-half feet, or about half the height of the finished figures. The full-sized version, in which the main figure is eleven feet high, was enlarged in clay and ready for casting into plaster by June 1972. It was then painstakingly corrected in the plaster before being shipped to the Fonderia V. Lera in Italy, where it was cast into bronze, chased and patinated in the winter of 1972–73, and shipped to Gettysburg. There it was mounted in summer 1973 and dedicated in October 1973. It was at Gettysburg that Sen. James O. Eastland said, "Though fewer in number than their comrades from other states," the Mississippi units "advanced farther than any others in the bloody battle."[12]

As Wayne Craven describes it,

> The design is meant to show the sacrifice and courage of the men that Mississippi sent into battle. One loyal son has already fallen, mortally wounded, while another stands over him, deserting neither his comrade nor his position; he guards his friend and holds the line even though he has no ammunition and has to use his rifle as a club, suggesting the fierceness of the hand-to-hand combat in the area where the Mississippians fought.
>
> To convey such ideas De Lue wrought his design on a truly titanesque scale—that is, he followed the philosophy that to express a monumental idea, a sculptor must use monumental scale as well as monumental forms. As one stands before the group one is impressed by its colossal size; by making these men larger than life he gave them the desired heroic quality, suggesting that their deeds and their courage were also larger than life. There is a quality of dynamic vigor to the figures that reminds one of the work of Michelangelo, and De Lue was in fact very strongly influenced by the art of the great Renaissance master.[13]

The Mountaineer
Morgantown, West Virginia

The mountaineer has long been a symbol of the state of West Virginia, whose nickname is the Mountain State. The mountaineer is also a symbol of West Virginia University. Daniel Boone was one of the early figures in the exploration and settlement of the territory, and the pioneer image of the mountaineer as the first settler in the territory was appropriate to both state and university.

Unfortunately, the image of the mountaineer in the early twentieth century at the university was converted to that of a hillbilly, with all of the potential for embarrassment that could be associated with it for the state and for the university. The students' dress during the annual Fall Mountain Week in the late 1940s and early 1950s was hillbilly costume and the "Mountaineer," mascot of the school's football and basketball teams, dressed and behaved similarly.

"Mountain," the ranking men's honorary society at West Virginia University, sought a role in the new image-making for the University and the "Mountaineer." The idea of a permanent tangible object to be symbolic of West Virginia University was conceived by Arch A. Moore, Summit of Mountain (head of the honorary society), during the academic year 1948–1949. This landmark was to be a statue of a typical mountaineer, located at some appropriate spot on campus, which would serve as a reminder to West Virginians of their famous heritage.[14] Moore started a fund with $100 for a statue to change the image of the "Mountaineer." Eventually, primarily through student fundraising projects, the fund reached $15,000.

In the early 1950s the project was blessed with the approval of the Board of Governors, which appointed three of its members to work with the annually appointed Mountain Committee. In 1953, Rachel Hawkes of Baltimore submitted a model for a ten-foot sculpture. It was estimated to cost $20,000, and critical controversy began. Two major issues evolved: aesthetics and control. The aesthetics issue was essentially the same modernist (abstract) versus traditionalist (figurative) confrontation. Alternatives to the Hawkes model ranged from a barefoot hillbilly to an abstract rendered in glass and steel.[15] On September 21, 1967, an editorial by Jerry Bowles in WVU's *Daily Athenaeum* lamented: "Mountain, men's honorary, has decided to commission Donald De Lue, a commercial sculptor, to do the work. The argument at this stage hinges less on the merit and business perception of choosing a commercial sculptor over a 'fine arts' sculptor, than it does on Mountain's right to make this decision for the university community."[16] De Lue might have been surprised at being described as a commercial sculptor, but after the New York World's Fair no amount of controversy would astonish him.

The project was very much one of remaking an image. The "Mountaineer" was to become a brave, resourceful, strong and confident, buckskin-clad man standing on a mountain peak. De Lue, modeller of "do-ers," was the right choice for the job. He began work on the figure in March 1967. The model was presented to the campus on Homecoming Weekend, October 27–29. A local newspaper writer said on February 14, 1968, "Despite a trickle of dissent over the choice of a mountain man, men of the Mountain will stick with what they believe is the best depiction of a Mountaineer, the bronze statue that will grace the University campus. That statue has created some controversy and snide remarks seemingly projected by proponents of abstract art or those who envision a Mountaineer as a slick-skeletal space dreamer. The Mountain has on hand $18,000 of the necessary $36,000. The honorary [society] will complete contract signing in the near future with Donald De Lue of New Jersey, a Guggenheim fellow whose granite statues adorn the French beaches where Americans landed on D-Day and with Russell Sheidow of Kingwood who will do the bronzing."[17]

As De Lue recalled, Sheidow, president of the Sheidow Bronze Company, wanted to cast the bronze and took responsibility for it, but the cast was actually made at Modern Art Foundry in New York. Fred Aurori, who was employed by the Sheidow Bronze Company, supervised the work, which was cast between March and July 1971. It seems that the long delays between the modeling of the figure and the dedication of the statue on October 30, 1971, were the result both of fundraising and of changing foundries. The 8-foot statue was presented to West Virginia University by Arch A. Moore, who was now the governor of West Virginia, and Tom Tinder on behalf of Mountain.[18] After twenty-two years the mountaineer had come home.

The success of the campaign and the statue is manifest. The new

Mountaineer, 1968, bronze, 8 feet, 6 inches.

De Lue set another precedent in West Virginia as a maker of heroes and icons. The *Mountaineer* has become the informal "coat of arms" of West Virginia University at Morgantown and an unofficial symbol of the state.

The Green Beret, 1969, plaster.

Mountaineer is an official symbol of West Virginia University and an unofficial symbol of the State of West Virginia. It appears on maps of the state, in literature for the school, and in advertisements for both the state and the university. Most tellingly, however, the "Mountaineer" mascot, who fires his rifle at each score made by the West Virginia University basketball and football teams, now dresses to resemble the De Lue *Mountaineer.*

The Green Beret
Special Warfare Memorial Statue, Ft. Bragg, N.C.

In early 1964 the campaign began among soldiers and civilians to erect a statue to honor the memory of special warfare soldiers killed in combat. By 1966 a plot had been chosen at Ft. Bragg opposite John F. Kennedy Hall, headquarters for United States Army Special Warfare Training. The sculptor was not selected until 1968, when, in consultation with the National Sculpture Society, several sculptors were approached. There were concerns that the selection comply with the trust agreement, which required approval by the Commission of Fine Arts in Washington before the memorial statue could be conveyed to the military.

De Lue later remembered that Abram Belskie (b. 1907) called him and said that he had been making designs for the monument and that he hoped that De Lue wouldn't have anything to do with it. The committee felt otherwise. They had not liked Belskie's designs, and possibly through Richard Murphy, the architect of the base, De Lue was invited to Ft. Bragg for more than a week to help him prepare a design for the statue. De Lue was already working with Murphy on the *Portal of Life Eternal* for the shrine at Woodmont, Pennsylvania (see p. 159). He was awarded the commission for *The Green Beret* in the spring of 1968.

America was in the midst of the Vietnam War. The Green Berets as part of the Special Warfare forces were bearing a large portion of the casualties in the war. Therefore, the soldier to be represented would be a Green Beret. Further, at the request of the Special Warfare Memorial Committee, De Lue outfitted the soldier in jungle fatigues and boots, pistol belt, and beret wearing the rank of sergeant first class. He carries an M-16 rifle on his right hip, symbolizing his willingness to defend freedom when necessary, but offers his left hand in friendship, signifying he is willing to help and advise when called upon.[19]

The statue was enlarged in De Lue's Leonardo studio until the figure of *The Green Beret* stood twelve feet from head to heel. The overall height of the monument is twenty-two feet. In spring 1969, one year after the commission was awarded, the plaster was on its way to be cast in Italy. As was his custom at the time, De Lue and his wife went to Italy to the Fonderia Lera in Via Reggio to supervise. De Lue was fond of these trips and the privilege of walking in the steps of Michelangelo at Carrara and Pietrasanta.

The Green Beret, 1969, bronze, 22 feet.

The dedication and unveiling of the statue was particularly sensitive, since feelings ran very high and opinions were polarized during the war. The ceremonies were kept relatively quiet and were attended primarily by the military at Ft. Bragg. The unveiling of the statue took place on November 19, 1969.[20]

Right Over Evil, circa 1972, pencil on paper, 19 x 24 inches.

An early study for *Right Over Evil*, this proposed design depicts the victory of Right as he descends upon a weakened figure of Evil.

RIGHT:

Right Over Evil, 1972–1986, bronze, 49½ inches.

This work occupied De Lue both artistically and politically for fourteen years. The statue was completed two years before the artist's death. It originated as a commission for the J. Edgar Hoover Building in Washington, and was cancelled in the controversy that followed Hoover's death.

(Courtesy of Louis Newman Gallery, Beverly Hills, Ca.)

Right Over Evil
F.B.I. Monument

J. Edgar Hoover (1895–1972) and the Federal Bureau of Investigation were almost synonymous for a half-century. When the new F.B.I. Building in Washington was being planned in the early 1970s, De Lue was invited to design a large sculpture on the theme of *Right Over Evil*. The design had been fully developed in plastiline at 49½ inches when Director Hoover died in May 1972. In January of that year Ada Louis Huxtable of the *New York Times* had approved of the design of the building, in a "Miesian modernist idiom" by C. F. Murphy Associates of Chicago.[21] In October the House of Representatives, in a controversial bill, approved naming the building for J. Edgar Hoover.[22] This was the year that the country was becoming inexorably involved in Watergate. There was increasing scrutiny of the role of the F.B.I. under Hoover in policymaking, as well as policing, at every level in American society. The new director of the bureau, Clarence M. Kelley, noted that the past year had been "one of the most trying eras in the F.B.I. history."[23]

Hoover had made many Washington enemies, and almost immediately upon his death his history was being re-written. Part of that revision was the cancellation of the new F.B.I. statue. Interestingly, it was perhaps exactly what the building needed. Writing about the completed building in October 1975, Paul Goldberger said, "There are white vinyl floor tiles, white ceilings and white walls. The concrete facade is beige, and the paving block in the huge central court is a sort of murky grayish beige. The absence of color would not in itself be so important were it not an indication of the utter banality that pervades every aspect of the design."[24] In the three years since Huxtable had written about the building, praise for Miesian modernism was fading. The building may have needed the focus that this extraordinarily active sculpture would have given it. Unfortunately it was not enlarged. The design may have been inspired and in part derived from De Lue's design for the reverse of the John Adams Medal in 1973. In each he personifies, through St. Michael-like imagery, Justice as a divine attribute.

Fortunately, the sculpture remained in clay until early 1987, when De Lue had it cast into plaster and made the final revisions before a bronze edition was cast. In some ways it embodies better than almost any other of his works De Lue's use of the active male figure and symbols to create a visually successful sculpture that serves both personal and public iconography.

Viet Nam Memorial

De Lue was able to idealize the heroism and sacrifice of the many individuals who fought for the United States in World War II, Korea, and Viet Nam. He was also able to appreciate individual heroism, and through that heroism to extrapolate the collective experience of the soldiers who fought for their country. From 1951 to 1966 De Lue followed the career of James Jabara (1923–1966) with great interest. Jabara was known as America's first jet ace. He had flown in World War II and downed five and one-half planes, was assigned to Korea and downed fifteen MIGs in

208

Jabara Head, 1986, bronze, 8 inches.

James Jabara represented the wartime American hero for De Lue. Jabara was known as America's first jet "ace"; the small "x's" along the base of the bronze symbolize the fighter's victories.

RIGHT:

Viet Nam Memorial, 1975, plaster, each figure between 34 and 36 inches.

Striding together as a united front, De Lue's subjects upheld American ideals during a period of deep unrest. Headed for war, the two soldiers seem fearless, a quality that, for De Lue, merits commemoration.

his F-86 Sabre jet, and was commander of a fighter group during the Viet Nam War when he was killed in a automobile accident in November 1966. For De Lue, Jabara epitomized the heroism of the American fighting man. De Lue appreciated that he was from an Arab-American family and had all of the attributes of patriotism and anti-Communism that De Lue felt were necessary to defend America during the 1950s and 1960s. He created a sketch study eight inches high inscribed "ACE NO 1 / JABARA / 30" on the front and with a series of "X"s on the side indicating enemy planes that he had shot down. Jabara became the symbol for De Lue of the heroism of Americans in two difficult wars, Korea and Viet Nam.

With his experience as a sculptor of monuments and memorials for the soldiers of World War II, it was only reasonable that De Lue should model a monument for the soldiers who had fought in Korea and Viet Nam. In the latter case he chose to portray a group of two soldiers, one a flying ace, the other a footsoldier striding together. The flying ace was developed from the images that De Lue had drawn and modeled of Jabara. Jabara was the "do-er" that De Lue so much admired. De Lue's heroes did not need to be presidents or generals, but they did have to represent action and high ideals. *Viet Nam* was one of several designs for monuments, both built and unbuilt, that De Lue created for a series of men and women of action who had affected the course of America.

Patriots, Politicians and Heroes

Washington was not the only historical figure to merit a monument. Other patriots, politicians, and heroes were proper subjects to be honored. In the 1970s and 1980s De Lue was asked to develop projects to honor Thomas Jefferson, Leander Perez, the heroes of the Alamo, Columbus and Isabella, Molly Pitcher, Martin Luther King, and John F. Kennedy.

Thomas Jefferson
Gretna, Jefferson Parish, Louisiana

The citizens of Jefferson Parish, Louisiana, sought an appropriate way to celebrate the Sesquicentennial of Jefferson Parish, which was created February 11, 1825. They chose to commemorate Thomas Jefferson on the one hundred and seventy-second anniversary of his conclusion of the Louisiana Purchase. It is not entirely surprising that the Jefferson Parish Bicentennial Commission of Louisiana should turn to Donald De Lue. In 1962 the adjoining city of New Orleans had his *George Washington as Master Mason* erected in their Civic Center in front of the new Main Public Library; and the Sons and Daughters of the Confederacy in Louisiana had turned to De Lue in 1968 to provide the monument to the fallen soldiers of Louisiana at the Gettysburg Battlefield.

The Jefferson Parish Sesquicentennial Commission was created in 1973 by Parish Council President Charles J. Eagan, Jr. He named the parish historian, Msgr. Henry C. Bezou, and the editor of the Jefferson Parish Times, Joseph M. Miller, as co-chairmen. They were charged with arranging a year of celebrations in 1975 with a parish budget of $150,000, which included a book and a film but was to culminate in the erection of a permanent monument to Thomas Jefferson. The commission solicited two New Orleans sculptors to submit competition models in January 1975, and at the suggestion of Mrs. Esther L. Eble, a member of the commission, they invited De Lue to compete as well. Esther Eble was a history buff and knew De Lue's monuments on the Gettysburg battlefield. The commission asked representatives from three New Orleans museums to act as judges in the three-way competition. After only fifteen

Thomas Jefferson, 1975, bronze, 22½ inches. De Lue's interpretation of Jefferson, based on the Houdon model of 1785, is imbued with assertive strength and conviction to secure the rights of man.

133

137

Leander Perez, 1976, bronze, 29 inches.

The children of politician Leander Perez commissioned this statue as a memorial to their father to be placed in a newly developed park in Plaquemines Parish, Louisiana. This model was enlarged to nine feet. A second idea maquette for the commission was cast in bronze and titled *A Southern Politician*.

minutes of deliberation behind closed doors they unanimously chose the De Lue *Jefferson*. Msgr. Bezou remembers that both the superb modeling and De Lue's careful thought as to how Jefferson was to be dressed, what he was to carry as attributes, his exact pose, and the orientation of the statue added great weight to the decision of the judges.[25]

The Jefferson Parish Bicentennial Commission did not conclude their arrangements too soon. They approved the contract for De Lue's model of Jefferson early in 1975 with the understanding that it would be enlarged from the 22½-inch plaster study maquette to the eight-foot six-inch plastiline; it would be cast into a full-sized plaster for final corrections; and it would finally be cast into bronze. The cost was to be $60,000, or almost half the money for the Sesquicentennial celebration, and all work was to be completed in time for dedication ceremonies in December 1975.

The study model had taken great thought. De Lue selected Houdon's bust of Jefferson as the model for the sculpture. Jean-Antoine Houdon (1741–1828) had Jefferson sit for him in 1785 and had completed perhaps the truest artistic and sculptural likeness of the president. De Lue's task was now to interpret the likeness and artistry of Houdon and add to it the spirit of the man for the project. De Lue saw Jefferson as a man of action, conviction and progress. He set him actively striding forward with his right foot oversteping the platform and his leg muscles in tension. His left hand holds a quill pen, the Declaration of Independence and the Bill of Rights; his right hand is balled into a gentle fist, slightly forward, to suggest force for freedom and rights. The thirteen stars at the base symbolize both the original thirteen colonies that became the United States and the thirteen states that were made wholly or in part from the Louisiana Purchase.[26]

Two casts of the maquette were made for the two Jefferson Parish courthouses. The parish is divided by the Mississippi into the East Bank and the West Bank, each with a courthouse with council chambers, and each with a small bronze De Lue *Jefferson*. In addition the Sesquicentennial Commission presented a bronze maquette of Jefferson to President Gerald Ford in Washington. Another of the Jefferson bronzes stands on the grounds of Wichita State University, Kansas.

The full-sized clay model was begun in late March or early April and was substantially complete in late June 1975; after the plaster had been made and corrected, it was sent to Modern Art for casting. It was then shipped to Louisiana in November. The statue of Jefferson was placed on a substantial granite base symbolically facing the West, which Jefferson and the Louisiana Purchase had helped to open. The sculpture was dedicated on December 6, 1975, in front of the Gretna Courthouse.[27]

Leander Perez

Judge Leander Perez (1891–1969) of Plaquemines Parish, Louisiana, was one of the legendary figures of politics in a state of larger-than-life politicians. He had advanced and maintained the benefits of the parish to such an extent that the interests of Plaquemines became identified with the interests of the judge. His biographer, Glen Jeansonne, stated, "Leander Perez was so forceful that he managed to stamp his image permanently in the 1960s even after his type of politics, not to mention his political philosophy, had long passed. The rough-and-tumble politics of the Huey Long era, when Perez became a potent force in Louisiana, have largely vanished. Even if such a man as Leander Perez were born today, he could not lead such a career."[28] In 1976, the four Perez children decided to honor their father by carving a park out of the family homestead, which included Judge Perez's birthplace, and deeding it to the parish. As part of the preparations for converting private land to a public park they commissioned a statue of Leander Perez. Angela Gregory, the New Orleans sculptor who had consulted on both the Louisiana Gettysburg Monument and the Jefferson statue for Jefferson Parish, was retained by the Perez family to advise them on the statue of the judge. She strongly suggested that they consider Donald De Lue and recommended that they look at the newly completed *Jefferson* as well as the *Washington* in front of the New Orleans Civic Center. Chalin O. Perez, who led the family committee, agreed that De Lue should come to Louisiana to discuss the project. Contracts were signed and De Lue produced two different idea maquettes for consideration, one with and one without a hat.[29] The one without hat was selected, erected, and dedicated. Four bronze casts were made of the maquette, one for each of the Perez children. De Lue thereinafter referred to the second maquette as *A Southern Politician.*[30]

The Last Heroes of the Alamo

The Alamo in San Antonio, Texas, is the spiritual center of the state and evokes memories of the Republic of Texas. In 1972 the United Charitable Foundation conveyed $50,000 to the Daughters of the Republic of Texas, who administer the Alamo, to acquire sculptures, paintings, or audiovisual equipment through which the history of the Alamo could be better displayed for visitors. By 1974 the Daughters of the Republic of Texas, together with Evander M. Lewis of the foundation, had settled on a sculptural group depicting the last four survivors battling for the Alamo—David Crockett, William Barrett Travis, James Bowie, and James Bonham. They had selected De Lue to do the sculpture after reviewing, with advice, the work of more than ten prominent sculptors.

De Lue completed drawings for the group and was paid for work in progress on July 24, 1974. He next modeled a twenty-one-inch clay sketch model of the four figures, which was approved by the Daughters on September 4, 1974, and cast into bronze. He then produced a thirty-three inch working model, which the Daughters approved on April 17, 1975. On May 15, 1975, the Daughters gathered for their annual convention in Midland, Texas. As part of the procedure toward the acceptance of the finished statue, a motion was made by Mildred Bugg that, if accepted, the statue should be placed on the grounds surrounding the Alamo. Evander Lewis of the United Charitable Foundation felt that this change was adding an unacceptable condition to an established, approved, and ongoing project. Neither Lewis nor the Daughters would budge on the issue of location, although each agreed on the success and appropriateness

Last Heroes of the Alamo, circa 1974, clay model.

De Lue was commissioned in a joint project of Daughters of the Republic of Texas and The United Charitable Foundation to create a memorial to the last four Americans standing at the Alamo. Unfortunately, a battle between the two groups over whether the statue would be inside or outside the building proved fatal to the project.

of the De Lue sculpture. Despite the considerable expenditures of the foundation, the Daughters notified Lewis on September 17, 1975, that the work was disapproved and would proceed no further.

The Daughters of the Republic of Texas, the foundation, and De Lue reached another agreement in 1976 to have De Lue proceed to the full-sized enlargement with a somewhat enhanced payment to De Lue, but they inserted three conditions. The Daughters required: that the placing of the statue cause no structural damage to the building; that the consent of the governor of Texas be obtained if required by law; and that such placement not be in violation of the act by which custody and title were conveyed to the Daughters. Before De Lue could comply, another hurdle was placed in the path of the project.

The Attorney General of Texas, John L. Hill, issued his opinion to the effect that the placing of the statue would violate the empowering act of 1905 because of a hypothetical excavation of four feet to provide a foundation.

Legal action on the part of the foundation against the Daughters of the Republic of Texas did not cause them to relent. The suit was settled in 1982, a decade after the project had begun, and, not surprisingly, the Daughters had prevailed in the suit. Unfortunately, all of the litigation meant that the project would not proceed. In a letter to De Lue sending him a resolution of the Daughters of the Republic of Texas, Mrs. B. F. McKinney said, "It expresses in a small way the appreciation we hold for you and the magnificent Texas heroes statue you created. Each of us enjoyed basking in the warmth of such a wonderful person and talented artist. You probably know the outcome of the litigation by this time, and I want you to know that we are sorry that it could not have been worked out so Texas and the World could enjoy this wonderful work."[31]

Columbus and Isabella

Although Christopher Columbus discovered the Americas in the name of the King and Queen of Spain, he was Italian by birth, and Italian-Americans have long honored him as the first of their countrymen to arrive in the New World. So Mariano A. Lucca, chairman of the National Columbus Day Committee and Son of Italy, set about a grandiose plan to erect statues of Columbus and Isabella in all of the cities that Columbus visited, founded, or influenced that did not already have memorials. He

Columbus, 1979, clay model, 30 inches.

This model, intended to be cast into a ten-foot bronze statue for the five-hundredth anniversary of Columbus's voyage, was modeled in plaster but was never realized in full size.

Isabella, 1979, clay model, 35 inches.

Like *Columbus*, *Isabella* was intended as part of a series of statues to commemorate the five-hundredth anniversary of the first voyage of Chiristopher Columbus and was also not enlarged beyond this model.

planned that large numbers of replicas of the models would be in place by 1992 for the five hundredth anniversary of Columbus's voyage.

To that end, Lucca sought out De Lue and convinced him to make models of *Columbus* and *Isabella*. The clay models were finished in 1979 and cast into plaster. Lucca took several of the plaster models to try to sell his plan for the enlargements to Miami, Bermuda, Cleveland, Niagara Falls, Buffalo, and Concord, New Hampshire. They were intended to be enlarged to heroic size and either cast into bronze or carved into marble, but the project was unrealistic. That there would be reasonable use for many cities seeking public sculpture for such monuments is undoubted, but to try to coordinate the efforts of so many communities concomitantly seems to have been a splendid dream. No enlargements were ever made.[32]

Molly Pitcher

For De Lue, the move to New Jersey in 1964 began a search for appropriate local heroes to realize in clay. He also sought, unsuccessfully, during his nearly quarter-century in New Jersey, a commission in his adopted state. Molly Pitcher seemed the right kind of hero for De Lue.

119

Winston Churchill, circa 1950, plaster, 28¼ inches.

This portrait of Churchill, a history-maker of the twentieth century, suggests that De Lue did not always picture the heroes of our age as soaring mythic figures. Churchill, one of the most significant politicians of American history, is fashioned in a simple suit and hat, respectfully extending his hand in a peaceful but understated gesture.

General Douglas MacArthur, circa 1960, plaster, 35 inches.

Winston Churchill and Douglas MacArthur

In a way these two larger-than-life figures of the 1940s are appropriate as subjects for De Lue's pantheon. Each made a real-life model for the De Lue ideal of a "do-er"; De Lue believed in both the mythic and actual man who can change the course of history. Winston Churchill and Douglas MacArthur challenged their fellow citizens to successful resistance of the Axis menace of the 1930s and 1940s and they were defeated to some extent by the less heroic 1950s.

Martin Luther King

In 1976 students at Brookdale Community College in Lincroft, N.J., were outraged when a memorial to Martin Luther King was vandalized. They worked with faculty and administrators to secure an appropriate

Martin Luther King, 1976, bronze, 20½ inches.

A civically minded De Lue donated hours of time and labor to replace a Martin Luther King memorial which was vandalized at Brookdale Community College in New Jersey. In 1987, Wichita State University in Kansas requested a cast of the same bronze.

replacement to honor the slain civil rights leader. De Lue, as a member of the commmunity, came forth and donated much of his time and talent to the project. With the approval of the King family, he finished the project in January 1977 and a bronze cast of the bust was placed at the college. Another cast stands at Wichita State University in Kansas.[33]

John F. Kennedy

Even noble commissions with powerful backers often go astray. In 1983 the "John F. Kennedy Twentieth Year Anniversary Commemorative Committee," based in Houston, Texas, announced that they were proceeding with a plan to erect a fourteen-foot statue of the late president in both Houston and Dallas. The chairman, Janette Nikolouzos, noted that the committee felt that Texas owed Kennedy a memorial for future generations so that he would never be forgotten. As they organized they contacted Sonny Giddon, a local expert in memorials and monuments, who recommended De Lue as the finest sculptor of a monument or memorial working in the United States. De Lue was selected by the committee and prepared models in clay and plaster, which were approved. The cost of erecting the two monuments, bronze statues, and bases in Houston and Dallas was to be $280,000.

Donald De Lue with the model of *John F. Kennedy*.

The *New York Times* quoted Senator Edward M. Kennedy: "The Statue will enable the memory of my brother to live in this country in future years."[34] The Texas economy had other plans. A precipitous decline in oil prices at exactly the moment that the committee was attempting to raise money for the pair of statues proved to be the key factor that prevented the project from being completed. De Lue tried to tap funds from some of his Texas friends. The group considered cutting the scope of the project back to a single statue in Houston. The committee continued to explore new sources of funding for nearly four years but were, in the end, forced to abandon the project. As Nikolouzos stated, " We had everything: we had the location in Dallas and in Houston; we had top quality people; everything was organized perfectly. The only holdup was the money. I spent three years of my life on the project, yet I still don't regret the time that I spent even though it wasn't completed. With Mr. De Lue, I learned so much!" Nikolouzos said that she thought it was unlikely that this project could go forward at this late date. "Since Mr. De Lue's death — this meant so much to me and Mr. De Lue — I don't think anyone could ever take Mr. De Lue's place."[35]

Sculpture in the Service of Faith

Washington at Prayer
The Congressional Medal of Honor Grove,
Valley Forge, Pennsylvania

De Lue's growing acceptance as a master of patriotic memorials is evidenced by the kind of patrons who were increasingly seeking him out. In *Washington at Prayer*, De Lue had the opportunity to forge patriotism, heroism, and faith. Dr. Kenneth Wells, who was the driving force in the establishment of the Freedoms Foundation at Valley Forge, Pennsylvania, felt that the ideals that had made America great were being eroded in the twentieth century and that the establishment of a patriotic foundation

Washington at Prayer (Valley Forge), 1967, bronze, 10 feet.

George Washington as a larger-than-life hero is emphasized in this giant, public sculpture. Kneeling in prayer, an unusual pose for the subject, Washington has become a symbol for both Valley Forge and the Freedoms Foundation. A bronze cast of the 39-inch mid-sized model of the sculpture was placed on the grounds of the State Capitol Building at Olympia, Washington in September 1987.

De Lue and the clay model for George Washington's head.

could encourage the ideals and practices of good citizenship. He had purchased fifty-three acres of land that had been part of the revolutionary battlefield and was adjacent to Valley Forge Park land, and he had prepared a site for a sculpture of Washington that would overlook the battlefield. De Lue visited Wells, who suggested that the sculptor prepare a small model of *Washington at Prayer* for the site. In 1965, De Lue sent two idea maquettes, one with a sword and one without. He had first modeled Washington kneeling with a sword in his hands, a pose that De Lue felt composed very well, but Wells drew his attention to a letter that describes Washington in a grove of trees, laying down his sword on the snow and then kneeling in prayer. De Lue therefore modeled the second idea maquette, which was eventually selected, based on this letter. Former president Eisenhower was a close friend of Wells; the two of them decided that this second work should be enlarged. First, however, Wells had two problems. He had a close friend who was a sculptor, and he felt that he had to offer him the opportunity to make a model for the Washington statue, but he told De Lue that his first allegiance was to the Freedoms Foundation and to doing what was was best for it. Both sculptors submitted models, and Wells selected an impartial judge —Eisenhower—to decide between them. Eisenhower chose De Lue's. Wells's second problem was funding. But he was very active in the Masonic fraternity in Pennsylvania and so invited the Grand Lodge of Pennsylvania to fund the project, which they did happily. De Lue's plaster studies and maquettes all belong to the Freedoms Foundation or to the Grand Lodge of Pennsylvania, and casts of the smallest working model have gone to each president of the United States since Johnson.

The intermediate working model was enlarged in 1966 to a final height of ten feet.[36] If the heroic Washington stood, he would reach a height of fourteen feet. This monumental representation of the Father of the Country was cast into bronze in the Fonderia Lera in Via Reggio, Italy. The dedication on September 9, 1967, was accompanied by a crowd of 27,000 people; busloads of people as well as unprecedented numbers in private cars poured into Valley Forge State Park. When confronted by an amazed press at the sight of this vast throng appearing to see his statue, De Lue said, with characteristic modesty, "Mr. Washington is rather well known."[37]

The statue has since become the symbol of the Freedoms Foundation and an American icon in its own right. It has been reproduced in miniature at four and one-half inches and six and one-half inches. De Lue, however, had nothing to do with the work at that size. It was a reduction made by the Limited Editions Collectors Society of America and issued January–February 1978.[38] A medal designed by De Lue was issued at the time of the dedication.

At the time of the dedication of the *Washington* statue at Valley Forge, De Lue had three other important commissions in progress in his studio: the Shrine of St. Anthony, the *Mountaineer* for the State of West Virginia, and the doors for the Woodmont Shrine.[39] Each of these works took years of De Lue's time from inception to dedication.

The Shrine of St. Anthony
St. Raymond Cemetery, The Bronx, New York

De Lue was commissioned to create an eight-foot figure of St. Anthony in marble for St. Raymond Cemetery in New York. As with the Crump Memorial, he worked with the architect W. Henry Deacy, who had brought him into the project. Deacy had several commissions for the embellishment of St. Raymond Cemetery. By September 1967, De Lue had armatured a half-sized plastiline undraped version of the figure, allowing him fully to work out the pose and anatomical problems in the sculpture, before adding the saint's robes. De Lue felt strongly that even a fully draped figure like St. Anthony required a modeling of the underlying anatomy before the drapery was added. The resulting finished clay model was cast into plaster and the half-sized model was sent to Italy, where it was carved into marble at full size. The shrine and statue were dedicated and blessed, Msgr. Schultheit officiating, on June 13, 1969, the Feast of the Sacred Heart.

De Lue also did a large head of St. Peter, which he felt was a very beautiful model, for St. Raymond Cemetery. The decision was made to turn it over to a local stone carver at St. Raymond's who "decided to improve the De Lue sculpture," according to Henry Deacy. De Lue said, "They carved it so badly that I was ashamed of it."[40]

St. Peter, circa 1968, charcoal on paper, 19 x 24 inches.

This early study for *St. Peter* was developed in clay by De Lue but was subsequently turned over to a St. Raymond stone carver who decided to "improve" the work.

St. Anthony, circa 1968, plaster, 30 inches.

Photographs of the full-sized version of this work in progress attest to De Lue's method of always modeling his figures in the nude and then clothing them. He believed that only in that way would the underlying anatomical structure of the figure be correct.

 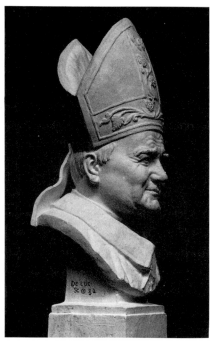

Bust of Dr. Ralph Sockman, circa 1960, plaster, 28 inches.

Bust of Pope John Paul II, circa 1979, plaster, 21½ inches.

De Lue writes on the reverse of this photo, "Pope John Paul before the attempt on his life. His face was a little fuller than it is now." Notes such as these indicate how closely the artist studied his subjects, their lives and careers.

Busts of Dr. Ralph Sockman and Pope John Paul II

In addition to the bust of Martin Luther King, De Lue modeled two other busts of prominent religious leaders. In 1961 he was called upon to model *Dr. Ralph Sockman* for Christ Church Methodist of New York City. It was presented in bronze to the church in late 1961. At this time, Sockman was also director of the Hall of Fame of Great Americans on the Bronx Campus of New York University, where De Lue was chairman of the Fine Arts Committee (see Appendix B).

De Lue began to model the bust of Pope John Paul II on the occasion of his visit to the United States in 1979. De Lue was impressed by the sincere outpouring of sentiment by millions of Americans for this spiritual leader and felt that he could make his own proper memorial to the event. Moreover, he may have intended the *Pope John Paul II* bust to serve as a model for reproduction for Roman Catholic Churches in the United States. Although he had commissions for carefully considered monuments such as the stations of the cross at Shrub Oak, New York, and Willowdale, Ontario, and the two Illinois shrines, as well as the work at St. Raymond Cemetery, he was acutely aware of the difficulty of small parishes having similar access to professional sculptors. In 1945, as president of the National Sculpture Society, he had first addressed this problem as the principal speaker at the annual meeting of the Liturgical Arts Society. The president of the Liturgical Arts Society was Hildreth Meiere, who was one of the co-chairs of Citizens Committee for the Army and Navy—which created triptychs in editions for military chaplains. The same multiplication of original art was the subject of De Lue's talk. In it he noted: "We all realize that much of what passes for religious art today is of very mediocre quality. It is useless to complain of the bad work produced unless we are prepared to offer the prospective client— in most cases this means the clergy —some alternative." De Lue then

94–99

suggested the establishment of a firm underwritten on a business basis. "Then this new firm could commission sculptors to make original models of perhaps twenty subjects from which reproductions could be made." After noting that the National Sculpture Society had just sponsored a competition to generate models for Our Lady of Victory and that other competitions were planned, he concluded, "These reproductions could be of plaster, terracotta, or ceramics."[41] De Lue's *Christ* of the mid–1940s may have been his own entry in the project that he discussed. He succeeded through direct commission in elevating the standard of religious art in the Roman Catholic Church in America, although the program to establish models by major sculptors for reproduction for use in churches met with limited success.

The Portal of Life Eternal
Woodmont, Gladwyne, Pennsylvania

The Reverend Major J. Divine, better known as Father Divine, had founded the Peace Mission Movement in Philadelphia in the first years of the twentieth century. The mission was interracial, interdenominational, nonsectarian, and nonpartisan. Father Divine preached a code of self-reliance, modesty, clean living, fair treatment of all mankind, and universal education. He said he had been sent from God as a coming of

Madonna and Child, circa 1948, plaster, 33 inches.

This work offers a good example of how important a part the medium plays in the ultimate design of a piece. *Madonna and Child*, intended to be completed in stone, had a more compact form than works intended solely for bronze.

Head of Christ, circa 1960, plaster, 28 inches.

Rarely does one find such a vulnerable and anguished expression in the De Lue oeuvre. The thorn-crowned *Christ* is among the most beautiful and sensitive of De Lue's religious work.

St. Francis, 1940s, plaster, 18 x 23½ inches.

159

Exterior of Father Divine's Shrine at
Woodmont, Gladwyne, PA.

OPPOSITE:

Portal of Life Eternal, 1970, bronze, 10 feet
6 inches.

De Lue's doors to the shrine of Father
Divine of the Peace Mission Movement
mark a pinnacle in the development of the
artist's iconography. Deep with meaning
and reverence, *Portal of Life Eternal* was an
important spiritual as well as creative
experience for De Lue. He believed that a
great pair of doors was one of the highest
opportunities for a sculptor and these were
his "Gates of Heaven."

Christ together with his spotless virgin bride, Mother Divine. On September 10, 1965, at an age said to be 100, his mortal remains were set
aside in what his followers call, "The Supreme Sacrifice of Father Divine." William Heyl Thompson, A.I.A., was engaged by Mother Divine
to design and supervise the construction of the Shrine to Life at Woodmont, "the Mount of the House of the Lord," at Gladwyne, Pennsylvania. The shrine was designed to incorporate the symbolism of the
teachings of Father Divine. It fulfilled many of the descriptions of the
Ark of the Covenant of the Old Testament and was surmounted by a
pyramid. The architect and Mother Divine planned the shrine with a
great pair of bronze doors which would have sculpture symbolic of the
ministry of Father Divine.

    De Lue later recalled that he was visited at his studio by Thompson
and his associate, Richard Murphy. Thompson had hired Bruce Moore
(1905–1980) to design bronze doors for the shrine. Thompson and Murphy were both disappointed with what De Lue called a horrible abstract
design. They asked him if he would be willing to make some preliminary

Cherub, at Father Divine's Shrine, 1970, bronze.

One of two cherubim guarding the red granite ark in the shrine, as in the biblical description of the ark of the covenant.

OPPOSITE:

Justice (Libra), 1969, bronze, 9½ inches.

Justice weighing the extremes of good and evil is an appropriate image of the Day of Judgment. A classical figure, she opens her hand to the inspiration of Divine Power.

drawings and then visit the site. De Lue agreed and produced drawings that Thompson liked a great deal. They all went to Woodmont to meet with Mother Divine and to see the location of the shrine. While sitting with Mother Divine, De Lue remarked of the drawing that "the sun was always at high noon." Mother Divine turned to De Lue and said, "That's right out of Father Divine's mouth—you must be listening to him." De Lue had the commission. By September 1967 De Lue was laying up the upper part in clay of what were to be doors ten feet six inches high, six feet six inches wide, and three inches thick.[42]

First, however, he modeled two cherubim to be cast in bronze to sit upon and watch over the red granite ark in the shrine, and a bronze dove of peace that would ascend the wall behind them. These were cast, gilded,

installed, and dedicated with the shrine on September 10, 1968. The shrine was rumored at the time to have cost a half-million dollars.[43]

The doors took shape over the next two years. The many drawings show that revisions were made in iconography and arrangement again and again. The doors were dedicated and unveiled September 10, 1970.

The complicated composition and extensive iconography executed in extremely high relief worked well for both Mother Divine and Donald De Lue. De Lue's innate spirituality was given a great opportunity and his genius for composition and modeling was challenged on the flat open space of the bronze door to bring about a unified artistic composition as well as a spiritually uplifting design. Many of the themes in the door are recurrent in De Lue's work: the spiritual ascension of man, Genesis or creation, liberty, justice, the triumph of right over evil, the sun as a unifying spiritual element, and the builders or do-ers. One notes the close relationship between *Liberty* on the shrine door and *Spirit Triumphant* in the Louisiana Gettysburg monument. As De Lue was laying up the clay for the relief on the door in early autumn 1968, he was sending his plaster model for Gettysburg to Louisiana for approval.

130

From Ghiberti's *Gates of Heaven*, the great doors on the Baptistry of the Duomo in Florence, to Rodin's *Gates of Hell*, sculptors have found the bronze door an appropriate medium to celebrate art in the service of the spirit. De Lue at Woodmont created spiritually sculpted bronze doors worthy to be compared to the greatest in history, and he dealt with relief and composition in new and successful ways. The parts are superb on their own and the composition integrates perfectly as a whole. De Lue had speculated that he would have liked to have the opportunity to rearrange all of the figures from the door in different compositions and photograph them to see what other successful combinations of the parts might be possible. He chose groups from the door to be cast as separate entities that can be enjoyed for their individual meaning. The quality, thought and detail in each of these can be seen in the examples of *The Builders* and *Justice*.[44] The *Portal of Life Eternal* was a great opportunity to break from the staid and workmanlike doors that he created for the Federal Reserve Bank of Boston. However handsomely the bank doors were crafted, the Woodmont doors ascend to an entirely different level of performance.

89

The *Portal of Life Eternal* allowed De Lue not only to build an iconography for the Peace Mission Movement, but to expand iconographically on his own themes of spirituality and patriotism. He was given great freedom on the commission. He said, "I am especially interested in this project, because they are allowing me to do the figures as I want. Most times your design has to conform to the ideas of those who are granting the commission. But this one I can design as I want."[45] De Lue's own deeply held belief in the American Republic and the striving of spiritual man coincided with the major tenets of the Peace Mission Movement. De Lue believed firmly in great men and heroes, but he believed more firmly in the beauty of the individual and collective spirit. The *Portal of Life Eternal* is his essay in bronze on that subject.

OPPOSITE:

The Builders, 1969, bronze, 18 inches.

Including himself as one of the "builders," De Lue idealized the origins of human work. Camaraderie as a tool for political, social, and wartime gains interested De Lue and was symbolic of the togetherness that the *Portal of Life Eternal* project promoted.

(Courtesy of Griffith Menard Gallery, Baton Rouge, La.)

1. *Illustrated London News*, February 19, 1949.
2. *National Sculpture Review*, Vol. 10, No. 1, Spring 1961, p. 20.
3. *New Orleans States Item*, article of 1960.
4. DDL to DRH, April 24, 1987. *See also*: *Scouting Magazine*, February, 1965, and *National Sculpture Review*, Vol. 14, No. 2, Summer 1965, pp. 20–21.
5. Wayne Craven, "The Sculptures at Gettysburg," Gettysburg National Military Park: Eastern Acorn Press, 1982.
6. De Lue was honored at the seventy-third anuual convention of the U.D.C. with a certificate of merit, Richmond, Va., 1966.
7. *Morning Advocate* of Baton Rouge, October 18, 1968, p. 14.
8. *Kentwood News* of Kentwood, Louisiana, October 24, 1968.
9. Pie Dufour as quoted from the *New Orleans States-Item*, October 22, 1968.
10. Letter from Angela Gregory to Lamar Gibson and Mrs. Clarence Letteer, July 24, 1969, Gettysburg Archives.
11. *The Clarion-Ledger–Jackson Daily News*, April 28, 1970, and *Asbury Park Press*, June 4, 1972.
12. James O. Eastland as quoted in *Vicksburg Sunday Post*, October 28, 1973.
13. Wayne Craven, "The Sculptures at Gettysburg," op. cit., p. 90.
14. Preliminary draft of manuscript for *Mountain of West Virginia University: A History*, at West Virginia University, no date.
15. Ibid.
16. Jerry Bowles, "To Be or Not To Be--That's Mountaineer," *Daily Athenaeum*, September 21, 1967.
17. Thais Blatnik, *Morgantown Post*, February 14, 1968.
18. Mildred Lindley, *Morgantown Post*, October 29, 1971. *See also*: Dedication program, October 30, 1971.
19. *Fort Bragg Paraglide*, November 27, 1969.
20. *Fayetteville Observer*, November 27, 1969.
21. "The F.B.I. Building: A Study in Soaring Costs and Capital Views on Beauty," *New York Times*, January 24, 1972, p. 16, col. 2.
22. *New York Times*, October 4, 1972, p. 16, col. 2.
23. *New York Times*, December 16, 1973, p. 77, col. 2.
24. Goldberger, "Building Viewed as Dullest of the Dull Lot," *New York Times*, October 1, 1975, p. 47, col. 1.
25. Telephone conversation between D. Roger Howlett and Msgr. Henry C. Bezou, October 8, 1987.
26. *Daily Register*, Shrewsbury, N.J., June 26, 1975, p. 16. *See also*: *The Courier*, July 3, 1975, p. 14, and *Jefferson Times* (Louisiana), April 11, 1975.
27. Manuscript copy of George C. Shackelford's "Speech Delivered at the Dedication of Monument to Jefferson December 6, 1975," available at Jefferson Parish Library Headquarters (Metairie, Louisiana). *See also*: *East Bank Guide*, December 10, 1975; *Jefferson Parish Times*, December 5, 1975, p. A3; and *New Orleans States Item*, December 6, 1975.
28. Jeansonne Glen, *Leander Perez: Boss of the Delta* (Baton Rouge: Louisiana State University Press, 1977) p. 384.
29. After a client had settled on one or more drawings, of the many that De Lue had made on a commission subject, the sculptor would model two "idea maquettes" and present them to the client in clay in the studio or by photograph. Generally one of the two would then be developed into the final "working model," which was then enlarged. The alternative "ideal maquette" was sometimes cast aside and the clay reused, sometimes left on the armature in clay, and sometimes cast into plaster.
30. Angela Gregory to D. Roger Howlett, 1988.
31. Letter from Mrs. B.F. McKinney to Donald De Lue, October 12, 1982. *See also*: Suit No. 78-cI–9120 District Court, 37th Judicial District, Bexar County, Tex.

32. Buffalo, New York: National Columbus Day Committee, Christopher Columbus Banquet Programme (1979).
33. *News Tribune*, Woodbridge, New Jersey, January 18, 1977.
34. *New York Times*, May 22, 1983, section 11, p. 3, col. 2.
35. Janette Nikolouzos to D. Roger Howlett, April 11, 1989.
36. *Masonic World*, July-August, 1966.
37. *Asbury Park Press*, September 17, 1967, p. 20.
38. *Christian Science Monitor*, January 25, 1978, pp. 14–15.
39. *Asbury Park Sunday Press*, September 17, 1967. *See also*: *Daily Register*, Red Bank, New Jersey, September 14, 1967, p. 14.
40. DDL to DRH, August 2, 1987.
41. "Sculptors and Religious Art: A Symposium," *Liturgical Arts*, Vol.13, No. 4, August 1945, pp. 73–74.
42. *Daily Register*, op. cit.
43. *Main Line Chronicle*, Ardmore, PA. September 5, 1968.
44. DDL to DRH, 1987.
45. Fritz Cleary, "Statue Draws Thousands," *Asbury Park Sunday Press*, September 17, 1967, p. 20.

Aurora, 1945, plaster, 20 × 31 inches.

An early plaque, comparable to *Naomi It Is Time To Go* in size, this relief also uses the device of breaking the established picture plane.

DONALD HARCOURT   NAOMI CROSS
1897   1907   1982
DeLUE

SCULPTOR
WASHINGTON AT VALLEY FORGE
OMAHA BEACH, NORMANDY, FR.
GETTYSBURG, LOUISIANA AND
MISSISSIPPI STATE MEMORIALS
AT GETTYSBURG
QUEST ETERNAL, PRU. CTR. BOSTON
GREEN BERET, FT. BRAGG, N.C.
BOY SCOUT GROUP, WASH. D.C.
HARVEY FIRESTONE, AKRON, O.
THE ROCKET THROWER, N.Y.

. . . and things which are at their best are also least liable to be altered or discomposed; for example, when healthiest and strongest, the human frame is least liable to be affected by meats and drinks, and the plant which is in the fullest vigour also suffers least from winds or the heat of the sun or similar causes. Then everything which is good, whether made by art or nature, or both, is least liable to suffer change from without.

PLATO   *THE REPUBLIC II*

THE FINAL
YEARS

Study for the Tympanum of the National Cathedral, 1972, black conte drawing, 19 x 24 inches.

De Lue competed for the tympanum of the National Cathedral in Washington and drew many studies of a creator figure enveloped by swirling cosmic beings. He had been inspired in this design by the prints and paintings of William Blake. The ideas were carried out in two plaster models, but were never carved for the cathedral.

T HE *LEANDER PEREZ* MONUMENT (1976) WAS THE LAST LARGE MONUMENT that De Lue would create. It by no means marked the end of the quest for new works, new commissions, or new challenges. In the years 1971 through 1973 he was nearly awarded the commissions for the tympanum over the doorway at the National Cathedral in Washington and for the massive granite relief sculpture on the Libby Dam in Montana. Through little or no fault of his, many commissions seemed to slip through his fingers in the last dozen years of his life. The John F. Kennedy memorial in Houston and Dallas ran out of money; *Columbus* and *Isabella* had probably not been likely to meet the extensive ambitions of Mariano Lucca; *Last Heroes of the Alamo* failed through the uncompromising stubbornness of two adversarial commissioning bodies; the F.B.I. building's *Right Over Evil* came at the wrong moment in the history of the United

174
151
150
144

OPPOSITE:

Naomi, It Is Time to Go, 1982, bronze, 20½ x 29 inches.

De Lue created this relief plaque to honor and memorialize his wife after her death. It illustrates his belief in death as transition. In using this work as his own memorial, as well as his wife's, De Lue states that, for all of us, there is a moment when we should recognize "It is time to go."

States. As late as 1986, De Lue was initiating new projects. He proposed a new sculpture for the I.B.M. building in Atlanta, Georgia, and developed maquettes for it. The architects of the building, Cooper, Carry Associates of Atlanta, were enthusiastic and promoted De Lue's design, *Cosmic Being*, to the developer. The developer was looking for something entirely different. De Lue proceeded with the design, however, to finish it for his own satisfaction.

Naomi, It Is Time to Go

A chapter in De Lue's life closed with the death of his wife Naomi in September 1982. About a month later, De Lue was walking on the beach near his house and studio in Leonardo. There were crowds of people around him enjoying a local celebration. Suddenly he became aware of the presence of his wife beside him taking his arm. A lady with a dog came out of the crowd and said to him, "Mr. De Lue, are you aware that your wife is walking with you?" He assured her that he was aware. The three of them walked and talked together until a voice said, "Naomi, it is time to go."[1]

De Lue developed this powerful personal experience into a relief sculpture as a memorial to his wife. An angel gently enfolds with his wings the robed and capped figure of Naomi; the wings break out of the enclosed panel; and the message and title is lovingly inscribed below: *Naomi it is time to go*. It is, fittingly, one of the most powerful works of his entire career.

De Lue had an intuitive understanding of the power of myth and the ability to give it visual form. His recapitulation of Greek and Roman mythology and Judeo-Christian iconography reveals the power of the cultural myths that underlie Western civilization. De Lue was also a mythmaker. He believed in the "hero" and the "heroic"; he believed in the "great man" and in the "quest." De Lue believed in American ideals and amplified them not in spoken or written form, but in visual terms. He believed in man as a spiritual being who could transcend his physical limitations, and he believed in man's interrelationship with and interdependence on the forces of the cosmos. In creating the visual imagery of *The Spirit of American Youth*, *Rocket Thrower*, *Quest Eternal*, and *Right Over Evil*, De Lue gave cultural values tangible form. He believed in the "do-er" and the "hero" and he became, to a large degree, that man.

70, 110, 127 144

Through his sculpture, De Lue sought to explain the universe and man's place in it. Joseph Campbell in *The Power of Myth* suggests some of the things that make up the attributes of a hero: a calling; subordination of other interests to a great work or deed; sacrifice; and communicating a supernormal range of human experience. These truths apply not only to De Lue's mythological subjects, but also to himself. He was called to sculpture as a vocation, not as a job. He subordinated all other considerations of his life from his early teens until his death to the needs of his career in sculpture. He gave up many of the pleasures of a family and made a clear and conscious decision not to have children in order to be completely dedicated to his career. To De Lue, the act of creating in clay,

Cosmic Being, 1987, bronze, 47 inches. This figure, which was begun as an idea for the I.B.M. Building in Atlanta, Georgia, shows that De Lue's cosmic figures continued to the end of his life. This was one of his last completed works.

stone, and bronze was an act larger than himself. In Campbell's words, De Lue became a "hero who has learned or found a mode of experiencing the supernormal range of human spiritual life and come back and communicated it."[2]

De Lue strove to work and to speak through his visual images. Whatever he gave up in more transient pleasures, De Lue gained in his calling. The act of sculpting was, for him, a meditation. While sculpting late at night, every night, undisturbed, he was concentrated and centered. It was work that he chose to do, an act of bliss. His *Self Portrait* shows the intensity and concentration with which he modeled in those late-night sessions; it is clear that the sculptor has been through battles but is still resolved, determined, and unbroken in his spiritual quest to make manifest the beauty of man. He said to human beings that they were the earth, the clay, and the sculpture of cosmic forces. He put into visual terms what he perceived to be American ideals: freedom, justice, law, spiritual aspiration, democracy, brotherhood, family, honor, equality.

Evening Song, 1987, bronze, 39 inches length, 25 inches height.

The crescent moon is held outstretched by this figure that symbolizes the evening. De Lue did not call her Diana, but she may come from De Lue's understanding that the crescent moon is the symbol of the goddess and silver is her metal.

181

When he did take up his pen to write, the occasion was often to battle the dragon of modernism. De Lue simply could not see beauty, value, or meaning in the abstract works of sculpture of the 1950s and 1960s. Eventually, taste and style, everchanging as they are, began to shift in De Lue's favor.

Postmodernism

The Reintegration of Tradition

By the late 1970s modernist sculpture of the previous two decades had begun to look dated to many unbiased observers, and many of the figurative works of the same period began to look more interesting.

Since that time, collectors, critics, and museums have begun to expand their purview. But beyond the acceptance of many different forms was the sense that as a culture we had given so little credit to the accomplishments of tradition that we were on the verge of losing those accomplishments altogether. Tradition and craft, as well as myth, are a continuum that is passed from generation to generation, teacher to student, master to apprentice. But arts can be lost; crafts can disappear. As these traditions became more rare in our society, certain perceptive people, sensitive to changing social patterns, began to appreciate their value and to fear their loss. "Lost arts" could often be recovered, but at what cost? The continuity of the living art of sculpture, as passed down from the Renaissance, for a time hung by a thread. The Andrew Ritchies, John Canadays, Sanka Knoxes and Charlotte Devrees had succeeded too well. On the other hand, Modernism was always an anti-establishment art, pushing at the shocking edge of the new with force generated by pushing away from tradition. It fed its anger on the establishment. When modernists woke up one day and found that beyond their wildest dreams they had succeeded and *were* the establishment, Modernism lost the fuel of its force.

Tom Wolfe attacked the modernist establishment in *Harper's Magazine* in 1975 with criticism that became *The Painted Word*. With that, he did the spadework for the burial of modernist theory. The same year also saw favorable reviews of two exhibitions, *Academy: The Academic Tradition in American Art* at the National Museum of American Art in Washington and *A Century and a Half of American Art* at the National Academy of Design in New York. Times were changing.[3]

De Lue had fought the more extreme elements of Modernism since the early 1950s; by the middle of the 1970s, the cutting edge of architectural and monumental design had moved to "Postmodernism." To be sure, some of the early manifestations of Postmodernism represented a form of cultural sophistry, which used hollow symbols of the past that had little or no meaning divorced from their traditional context.

The difficulties that Postmodernism faced are illustrated by *Portlandia*, the 1985 emblematic female figure commissioned by the city of Portland, Oregon, to go above the portico of the new city hall designed by the architect Michael Graves. The notion of a monumental figure sweeping down from a three-story vantage to embrace the city and citizens of Portland was intriguing for the 1980s. It built a human iconography for

OPPOSITE:

Chanson d'Amour, 1986, bronze, 15½ inches.

French titles are rare in De Lue's work, although he spoke the language well. The ancient lyre in her hand suggests a classical iconography.

Libby Dam, circa 1972, plaster, 31 inches.
De Lue was one of the last two contestants
for the contract for the massive Libby Dam
granite relief. Ironically, it was won by
Albert Wein, who had been a protégé of
De Lue in the 1940s.

a city in a period with no recent precedents for doing so. Tom Wolfe, the proto-postmodernist critic, challenged critics "to think of an installation in the last fifteen years with this same emotional, sincerely felt response from the public."[4] Unfortunately, the artist, Raymond J. Kaskey, used this exercise to prove that he had little understanding of anatomy and that he lacked the craft requisite to enlarge a model competently to the size required by the building. It was his first commissioned work. The publicity surrounding the acquisition by the city of this symbol was filled with the notion of recovering crafts that were used to create the Statue of Liberty; but the least informed observer can readily discern the disparity in craft between the two works. That disparity is not merely one of "style." It proceeds from training, care, craft, artistic integrity, and, yes, money. One of the points made in the unveiling of *Portlandia* was that she was cheap for her size.

Postmodernism, at its best, can be seen as the unembarrassed reintegration of tradition and craft into the mainstream of contemporary art. The change might be put more succinctly as neo-eclecticism, but it is more than that. There has been, indeed a new tolerance for diversity, not only for the traditions that were pilloried by John Canaday, but also for the extreme modernists who filled the landscape with shocking possibilities. Contemporary art movements seem more inclusive than exclusive, even in such oddities as appropriation art. There does not seem to be a need to topple the generation of artists who have led in critical acclaim for the last three decades, and only the most political and polemical of the modernists have called for a return to strict ideological purity.

In the history of taste, generational rebellion usually takes the form of disliking what your parents bought. Now there is a younger generation that was brought up in a contemporary environment with little or no finely crafted sculpture available to be seen as part of a living tradition. This younger generation of collectors, scholars, museum curators, dealers, and artists are, in many cases, seeking out the keepers of the flame of craft and tradition in sculpture. Donald De Lue outlasted his sharpest critics and, with several of his contemporaries—among them Walker Hancock, Marshall Fredericks, Jacques Schnier and Albert Wein—survived the dark days of the 1950s and 1960s to emerge as an elder statesman and prophet of tradition.

The rule in the 1950s and 1960s was that "bigger, cheaper, and more disposable" was the constant direction for success. It is clear, with some perspective of time, that finely crafted objects have the advantage of lasting longer, and by mere survival can and do make an impact on later generations. We are witnessing a worldwide affirmation that in sculpture, as in the other arts, crafting and building well for future generations assures an object a place of integrity in our own. This is an idea that was lost, but lost ideas, as well as lost arts, can be recovered. The modernist sculpture that occupied the site on the opposite side of the Prudential building in Boston from De Lue's *Quest Eternal* is now remembered by almost no one. It removal was necessitated less than ten years after it was installed because it was structurally unsound and would cost far more to repair than its original cost. Its remains now languish in a subterranean chamber of the vast Prudential complex.

127

Contrasting Clients

In fall 1987 Donald De Lue cast, for the first time, mid-sized versions for public display of three of his better-known designs. The first of the three was dedicated on September 17 at Olympia, Washington.

155 The Grand Lodge of Washington of the Masonic Fraternity wished to make a gift to the State of Washington of appropriate patriotic significance on the occasion of the bicentennial of the Constitution. They requested the intermediate size of De Lue's design of *Washington at Prayer*, which had been designed originally for the Grand Lodge of Pennsylvania as a gift to Freedoms Foundation in Valley Forge, Pennsylvania. This was exactly the type of memorial that had occupied De Lue for most of his commissions in the previous twenty years, and precisely the type of conservative client for whom most of that work had been executed.

110, 127 On October 11 the City of Orlando, Florida, dedicated intermediate sizes of the *Rocket Thrower* and *Quest Eternal*. These latter were part of an intense program to bring to Orlando an overall design plan for civic beautification. They were to be focal points of Lockhaven Park, which a young and vigorous mayor had wrested away from developers intent on turning city land to private profit. The purpose was neither patriotic nor religious, but the beginning of a program, which continues, for the best public art available. The mayor and the Public Art Advisory Board were well aware of the availability of more modern artists and works of art, but in order to bring Orlando the best works and to begin a new tradition of public art they settled on the inspired spirituality of two of De Lue's greatest monuments. This seemingly conservative taste was actually on the cutting edge of postmodernist thinking.

A further example of this trend has become a regular issue in well-known architectural firms that have established themselves in modernist modes. Younger members of their design teams are regularly attracted by De Lue's works and present them to sometimes incredulous senior partners as solutions for the humanizing of contemporary architectural environments. As he turned ninety, De Lue became not only one of America's most venerable old masters, but one of the most active sculptors working in the vanguard of contemporary art.

The Final Small Bronzes

Paul Manship declared that 1915 to 1940 was a golden age for him for the creation and sale of small bronzes. He said, "That was a good period, that twenty-five years. I sold many, many small bronzes—pieces I made for my own pleasure and not for commissions."[5] For twenty-three of those twenty-five years, De Lue was a sculptor's assistant. In 1938, as he broke out of assistantships onto his own, he was unknown.

Whatever the taste of the public for small bronze sculptures during the war years of the 1940s, there was no bronze available for art. In the late 1940s, De Lue, having just established himself as a sculptor, was busy, as were his colleagues, preparing designs for war memorial monuments. By the early 1950s, clearly the cycle of taste had turned against realism and domestic use of sculpture. Even abstract artists did not find the kind

Donald De Lue at Tallix Foundry, 1987.

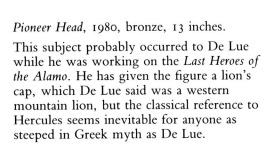

Pioneer Head, 1980, bronze, 13 inches.

This subject probably occurred to De Lue while he was working on the *Last Heroes of the Alamo*. He has given the figure a lion's cap, which De Lue said was a western mountain lion, but the classical reference to Hercules seems inevitable for anyone as steeped in Greek myth as De Lue.

reception from private collectors that sculptors like Manship had in an earlier "Golden Age."

De Lue correctly assessed that there was little purpose in attempting to promote and publish editions of his smaller works. Nevertheless, he made maquettes. The period when they were least well received by the art market was De Lue's period of greatest production. To be sure, he almost always saw the designs as potential enlargements, but he modeled them for his own pleasure and purposes. It might be argued that those works that were not done expressly for monumental commissions reveal De Lue at his most personal. De Lue derived the greatest pleasure from creative work. He modeled with intensity; periods without large commissions could be his most productive. Those periods with large commissions always had smaller works that appeared as they sprung from his mind in the breaks from the larger task.

These small sculptures, some still in plastiline, some in plaster, went almost totally uncast in bronze. A few individuals sought out De Lue and chose a work or two to have cast, and De Lue accommodated them. Occasionally, someone involved with commissioning a monument would request a bronze of the maquette. A small number of maquettes were made as "cold pour" bronze. Fewer than forty, perhaps no more than thirty small bronzes were cast by De Lue up to 1984.

By the late 1970s and early 1980s taste had again changed. The art market for small American "deco" bronzes was beginning to return. Not surprisingly, work by Paul Manship led the revival. At this time De Lue was approached by several dealers with the thought of representing him.

In 1986 he began a project that involved more than seventy of his maquettes and working models. Working with the staff at Tallix Foundry and his assistant William Kilpatrick, De Lue set about approving waxes, chasing, and patina for editions of more than a half-century of models. For the first time, De Lue knew that the time was right for his art and the collector to come together. The collecting trends of the 1980s suggested that the small figurative bronze might be entering a new "Golden Age."

This phase of De Lue's career involved new work as well as recapitulation. As he reviewed the chasing on the APEX competition models, now cast into bronze, he said, "They look pretty good after all these years and much better in bronze than I would have expected." Some work that De Lue had modeled years earlier in plastiline was completed in plaster; more recently modeled works, *Joy of Life*, *Chanson d'Amour*, *New Bedford Fisherman*, *Bearer of Good Times*, *New Day*, *Pioneer Head*, and *Evening Song*, were cast into plaster and completed as well. He was excited by the prospect of putting his first *Self Portrait*, started and finished in 1987, into bronze. He followed that with *Cosmic Being*, which was originally designed in 1987 for the I.B.M. Building in Atlanta. Ahead of him was the prospect of adding more than eight hundred separate bronze casts to his total body of work.

Leper, 1988, plastiline.
De Lue's final work of a dying figure in agony rests, nearly finished, with the artist's tools.

During this period he worked on a portrait of John P. Axelrod, which illustrates his portrait methodology. De Lue wanted to observe his subject to form his own impressions of the form and character of the sitter. He then modeled from memory a sketch study in plastiline of Axelrod. At this point he requested measured photographs of the front face, left, and right profiles so that he could create an exact size for the finished portrait. After the work was completed from the photographs, De Lue asked for as many sittings as he could get from the subject, as well as final approvals before the work was cast into plaster. *Study of John P. Axelrod* is one of the very few of De Lue's portrait sketches to survive because he almost always threw the clay back into the pile when the full-sized portrait was complete. It shows the quick impression of the sitter carried out with pills of clay rapidly applied to the head with no attempt to smooth the surface.

Friends noted the large number of works, visible in photographs, which

LEFT, ABOVE:
Sketch of John Axelrod, 1987, bronze, 10¼ inches.

This bronze was cast directly from the clay sketch that De Lue had done from memory. It preserves all of the freshness of a sketch-study and demonstrates the process of De Lue's working method in portraits.

RIGHT, ABOVE:
John Axelrod, 1987, bronze, 21½ inches.

This is the finished portrait bust of the same subject and shows the development of the sketch into the final form. It is De Lue's last portrait bust.

OPPOSITE:
Joy of Life, 1981, bronze, 30½ inches.

had been modeled in clay but apparently were never cast in plaster. When queried, De Lue admitted that he had often returned fully modeled sculpture to the pile of plastiline. Casting in plaster was expensive, he said, and the resulting plasters had to be stored. "Which ones did you like?" he asked. "I'll model them for you again." De Lue had stored the works in his mind. A lifetime of training his memory and his hands gave him the complete confidence that once modeled, once memorized, he could repeat the sculpture at will. Not only could he remake it as well as before, but with each year of growing experience his work grew better. It would be hard to number the works lost this way, but many were photographed.

His sculpture of the last dozen years of his life, drawing on a full lifetime of experience, represents the apogee of his career. The years after his last realized large commission represent a highly productive period of personal projects, interspersed with studies modeled in attempts to move forward one more grand commission. Only two years before his death, when asked if he would like to limit the size of a commission that he would entertain he replied, "No, the bigger, the better!"

With all of this progressing, De Lue began to slow down in the late spring of 1988. He sculpted less and talked more of drawing. He modeled a small and defiant *Moses Embracing the Law*, which he finished in plaster in March of his last year. He began a last work, a tortured figure caught in a block of clay, which he called *The Leper*. His spirit was still in the studio, but finally the tools were set aside. After a brief illness he died on August 26, 1988. His long-time friend, Fritz Cleary, declared, "The last of the Titans is dead!" and continued:

> De Lue's great contribution was freeing sculpture from its earth-bound position and hurling it heavenward. Donald thought of man as hero and portrayed him as such. He had little patience with the trivia that engaged the attention of so many contemporaries and made few friends with his outspoken contempt for what they turned out. Because of his fame and record, he was frequently quoted in the press. Reporters reveled in his pithy comments and wrote gleefully of his criticism of contemporary art trends and fads. His career spanned a period from the apogee of Beaux-Arts style to what he called "over-wrought iron" sculpture. While his success was determined by his unusual sculptural ability he was shrewd enough to realize that in today's world this was not enough: he appreciated that wide publicity helped.
>
> His highly muscled figures aroused the contempt, ire and spite of many New York critics with whom Donald frequently crossed swords. It was no small satisfaction to him in the last years of his life to see that most of these had become non-persons, consigned to oblivion, while his reputation (based on his remarkable bronzes) continued to grow and to appeal to each new generation.[6]

De Lue's Summary

No summary of De Lue's career could be more appropriate than his own, spoken more than a decade before his death:

Moses Embracing the Law, 1988, bronze, 8½ inches.

Moses and Isaiah are the two Old Testament figures that recur most often in De Lue's sculpture and drawing. This is the last piece of sculpture that he completed before his death.

177

In my work I try to express what I feel about life and art. I believe that art is eternal. Through art, men have striven to conquer time by immortalizing the deeper meanings of their lives. The search for these meanings, and the embodiment of them in enduring works of art, require a profound integrity of purpose and love of craftsmanship, undistracted by the transient whims and styles of the day.

The magnificent sculptures that have come down to us from the past —from Assyria, Egypt, Greece, and other ancient and Renaissance eras— have preserved, fresh and beautiful still, the spirit that animated the men of those times — their sacred beliefs, their aspirations, their ideals, the memorable events of their day.

We too have a message for the future. Men of our time have paid a heavy price in pursuance of their hopes and ideals. The nobility of their spirit, their strength, and the beauty in their lives, deserve to be told to the generations to come in great monumental works of art. That, I believe, is the challenge and the task for the sculptor of today.[7]

. . . The real artist, who knew what he was imitating, would be interested in realities and not in imitations; and would desire to leave as memorials of himself works many and fair; and instead of being the author of encomiums, would prefer to be the theme of them.

PLATO

THE REPUBLIC X

Self Portrait, 1987, bronze, 16¾ inches.

NOTES

1. DDL to DRH, 1987.

2. Joseph Campbell, interviewed by Bill Moyers, *The Power of Myth*, series on P.B.S., 1988.

3. Tom Wolfe, *The Painted Word* (New York: Bantam Press, Inc., 1976).

4. Tom Wolfe as quoted in *Art News*, December 1985, pp. 13–14, 156. *See also: Architecture*, December 1985, pp. 20–21.

5. John D. Morse, "Interview" (of Paul Manship), Archives of American Art, transcript 11, February 18, 1950.

6. Fritz Cleary, "The Last Titan," *National Sculpture Review*, Vol. 37, No. 3, August 1988, pp. 26–27.

7. Michael Lantz, *National Sculpture Review*, Vol. 23, No. 2, p. 27.

APPENDICES

New Day, 1976, bronze, 26 inches.

As with *Nymph* more than four decades earlier, De Lue has modeled an optimistic, powerful Michelangelesque female figure who reaches up to the dawn.

Be so good as to answer me a question: Do not the same magnitudes appear larger to your sight when near and smaller when at a distance? And the same holds of thickness and number; also sounds, which are in themselves equal, are greater when near, and lesser when at a distance. Now suppose happiness to consist in doing or choosing the greater, and in not doing or avoiding the less, what would be the saving principle of human life? Would not the art of measuring be the saving principle; or would the power of appearance? Is not the latter that deceiving art which makes us wander up and down and take the things at one time of which we repent at another, both in our actions and in our choice of things great and small? But the art of measurement would do away with the effect of appearances, and, showing the truth, would fain teach the soul at last to find rest in the truth, and would thus save our life. Would not mankind generally acknowledge that the art which accomplishes this result is the art of measurement?

PLATO   *PROTAGORAS*

Proportion and the Art of Donald De Lue

WHAT ARE THE IMPLIED OR REAL CONNECTIONS BETWEEN THE CLAY OF the earth and the body of mankind? What does the sculptor reveal, as he shapes forms through pressing, modeling, or carving clay, through casting and firing into durable bronze, or through chiseling in order to represent the human figure? What is the measure of mankind? These questions, linked to heaven and earth, to time and memory, are essential to understanding the work of the late Donald De Lue of Leonardo, New Jersey. As a senior sculptor and former president of the National Sculpture Society, he spoke out with vigor against the artistic currents of materialism and mediocrity so pervasive in late twentieth-century art. Unlike much of today's bland non-objective art manufactured by the yard and unlike the shockingly provocative work that thinly disguises perversion, De Lue depicted heroes and individuals worthy of society's emulation or acclaim. His subject matter was and is recognizable. However, the objective of his art was not so much the accomplished representation of a particular individual but rather the achievement of universal forms that express the "spiritual basis of sculpture namely an abiding concern for mankind's nobility." Consistently, his work evokes a large measure of poetic rapture or ecstasy akin to that found in the books of the prophets of the Old Testament.

In his ample studio, brimming over with drawings and sculpture, De Lue maintained an abiding faith that the main function of public art was to inspire the viewer with heroic and ideal visions. This attitude was in accord with age-old traditions shared by sculptors both on this continent

FORMS FROM UNCOMMON CLAY

Jonathan L. Fairbanks

Katharine Lane Weems Curator of American Decorative Arts and Sculpture at the Museum of Fine Arts, Boston

OPPOSITE:

Hand of God, 1967, bronze, 35½ inches.

Man in the hand of God was a theme that De Lue returned to many times, and which had also inspired other sculptors of the twentieth century. In this particularly fine example of De Lue's Michelangelesque style, the sculptor explores contraposto and the "figura serpentina" in a single work. Here also man is created of the clay of the earth by God at the same time the sculptor creates the "first man" with the same clay.

Figure design for a fountain in Philadelphia, *circa* 1962, black conte on paper, 24 x 19 inches.

This example of De Lue's elegant and highly atennuated figures was created for an unrealized fountain project in Philadelphia. It is one of thirteen proposed figures on one sheet and one of many sheets of drawings for the project. It is approximately a ten-head figure.

RIGHT:

Arcturus, 1980, bronze, 29½ inches.

De Lue has personified Arcturus, one of the brightest stars in the sky, as another of his light-bearing cosmic forces. The plaster model for this is in the collection of the Museum of Fine Arts, Boston.

and abroad, traditions that began with the dawn of Classicism in the Mediterranean world.

Anyone who has worked in a studio knows that the choice of a sculpture career is difficult. The profession is physically demanding and requires knowledge of many crafts. Enormous emotional and financial reserves are drained by the large studio space necessary for monumental works. Success is attained only by those who have steady hands, unwavering determination, and a philosophical frame of mind. For the figurative sculptor, a thorough understanding of anatomy is essential. Knowledge of the origins and insertions (attachments) of muscles on bones and their resultant actions is merely the beginning in the sculptor's search for form. Another artistic concern is what designers call composition—the deployment of plastic elements in space to produce visual excitement. Mastery of compositional skills must be attained. The aspiring and gifted sculptor must be so technically accomplished that no single process is so consuming that it detracts attention away from the concept expressed by the whole work. The novice sculptor makes a fetish of method or material. It is an immature viewpoint that cherishes the medium as the message in art.

While De Lue made the sculptor's task seem an easy one, the actual process is hardly simple. To demonstrate this point, we may consider one issue: that of proportions. Every sculptor must pass either consciously or subjectively through the study of proportions in order to produce coherent form. Proportional studies engaged the rapt attention of such notable masters as Leonardo Da Vinci and Albrecht Dürer. The proportional divisions of space created by Michelangelo within the Medici

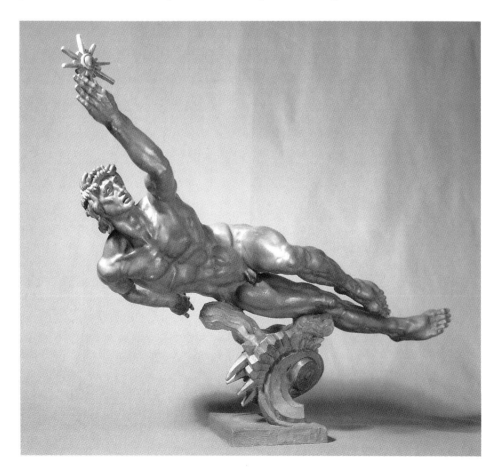

tombs made a profound impression on De Lue. The figures within that composition engaged De Lue's attention from childhood onward. It would not be inaccurate to state that as far as De Lue was concerned, Michelangelo was his master. When De Lue first saw plaster casts of the Medici tomb figures and a portion of the frieze of the *The Temple of Zeus at Pergamum* at the Museum of Fine Arts, Boston, at the age of twelve, he decided that sculpture would become his life work.

A notable feature of De Lue's figures is their small head-to-body ratio, the figures in his drawings and sculpture ranging in height from nine to eleven head lengths. Since the average adult head-to-body ratio in Western representational statuary is close to seven, it is clear that De Lue made use of attenuated proportions for expressive possibilities. In this deliberate distortion he continued a distinguished practice of ancient times.

The means by which such complex concepts were transmitted from the ancient world to the modern deserves review. A helpful reference for tracing artistic theory from classical antiquity to the Renaissance is a sixteenth-century work, *A Tract Containing the Artes of Curious Painting, Carving, Building . . .* (London, 1598). The first book printed in the English language to deal in depth with art theory, this edition is a translation of an earlier Italian treatise that dealt fully with proportional studies. The author of the original text, Giovanni Paolo Lomazzo (1538–c.1600) was a citizen of Milan and keeper of Cosimo de' Medici's picture gallery in Florence. Lomazzo's *Trattato* has become known as the "Bible of Mannerism," mannerism being a style of art that originated in mid-sixteenth-century Italy and was popularized in continental Europe and England for two centuries thereafter. The author explains that without the symmetrical measure of all parts of a body united in an orderly way, no decent thing can be made. He defines proportion as "a correspondencie and agreement of the measures of the partes betweene themselves, and with the whole, in every work. This correspondencie is by Vitruvius called Commodulation, because a model is a measure which being taken

Leda and the Swan, 1970, bronze, 8 inches.

In this beautifully integrated small sculpture, the swan nibbles at Leda's ear while Leda gently encourages Zeus by drawing him to her with her right hand.

Night, Michelangelo, *circa* 1534, on the tomb of Giuliano de Medici, Florence.

Michelangelo's influence on De Lue is evidenced by the similarity of pose, muscularity, and gesture between *Night* and *Leda and the Swan*.

The Measure of all Things, 1967, black conte on paper, 24 x 19 inches.

Few works unite De Lue as a humanist and a spiritualist better than this drawing. De Lue believed in the greatness and mastery of mankind and, at the same time, in a larger universe in which man is an honored participant.

at the first, measureth both the partes and the whole." Lomazzo cites Marcus Vitrius Pollio, the first-century B.C. Roman architect, as the ultimate authority on proportions and on the eternal principles at work. Lomazzo also adopts current art theories, as when he reports that Michelangelo once advised the painter Marcus de Siena that he should always make his figures pyramidal and serpentine in motion. From this the fashion for the "figura serpentina" presumably derived and was popularized throughout the late fifteenth century. Favored by both Vitruvius and by the late work of Michelangelo was a figural ideal of ten face or head lengths to the human body—proportions and compositional ideas closely related to those adopted by De Lue.

In America, the history of various published studies on human proportional systems is complex. A chronology of a few historic sources may help place De Lue's sculpture within the American tradition with respect to figural proportions. Books that plagiarized portions of Lomazzo's *Trattato* had appeared in Boston as early as 1670. By 1789 measured figures of antique statues in Rome (the *Venus de Medici* and the *Antinous*) were available through British engravings in the United States. The provincial but talented Salem woodcarver, Samuel McIntire (1757–1801) undoubtedly had access to such engraved measurements. By 1802 he had made his own drawings of male and female figures to record similar standards for the human body. His sketch, now in the Essex Institute, Salem, Massachusetts, includes a ruled scale between figures which makes clear that the unit of measurement is not actually dependent upon the length of either the human head or the face. The scale of the rule specifies a unit called a "part" equal to the length of the nose. This "part" is a modular unit equal in length to the space from the lower edge of the tip of the nose to the bottom of the chin, and also equal to the vertical distance from the upper edge of the eyebrow to the lower edge of the hairline of the forehead. The "part" in McIntire's drawing, multiplied thirty-one times, is equal to the entire height of either male or female figures. Each "part" is subdivided into twelve smaller units designated as "m," probably representing "module." With "parts" and "modules," McIntire and his workmen could develop through ruler and compass detailed layouts of the ideal human figure for carvings of almost any size—whether architectural, portrait, or miniature. His system was practical, direct, and capable of much refinement. But the use of rule and compass was a carpenter/carver approach.

A generation later in America, the profession of sculpture emerged with more complex notions about proportions, acquired through the experience of Americans carving marble figures in Italy and from the importation of more up-to-date illustrated books. A prime example of such a publication was produced in London in 1857 by the English sculptor John Gibson and the curator of Sir John Soane's Museum, Joseph Bonomi. Theirs was a popular book, *The Proportions of the Human Figure*, which went through several editions. Detailed charts recording precise measurements taken from antique statuary in Rome, Florence, and Paris were included to demonstrate the universality of laws on the proportions of the human body as observed by famous sculptors and painters of antiquity and the Renaissance.

Challenging the methods of Gibson and Bonomi, but not basically changing the measurable results, was the work of Boston sculptor William Wetmore Story, who published in 1866 his *Proportions of the Human Figure According to a New Canon*. This work cites the writings of Pliny the Elder and refers to a presumed lost canon of proportions defined by the famous ancient Greek sculptor Polycletus. Story concluded that the sculpture of the *Spear Bearer* or the *Doryphorous* by Polycletus embodied the proportional precepts of the classical world. Story felt that as a Christian he should improve upon pagan systems of ideal form and add to the study of proportions through the study of the Cabala, the mystical writings of ancient Jewish times. By invoking a study of Cabalistic numerology and applying it to symbolically meaningful geometric forms, Story developed a new system for human proportions meaningful to Christians at a period of time when intense religious revivalism swept the United States. His use of a geometric system, based upon the triangle, circle and square, for rationalizing the proportional divisions of the human body was simply too complex for most sculptors to grasp. His publication was a scholarly piece of work but impractical. Story's book does, however, reflect a widely shared concern and an intensity of belief in absolute rules of beauty derived from what was conceived to be an everlasting cosmic scheme.

That search for and belief in a divine plan or universal order persisted in American sculpture throughout the nineteenth and well into the twentieth centuries. While the English sculptor Albert Toft admitted in a book published in 1911 that sculpture represented "music of the spheres made visible, the Ideal manifest unchanging and unchangeable through the Ages," he did recommend that students carefully observe variability in

Adam and *Eve*, 1978, bronze, 9½ inches each.

The tension and agony developed in the crouching contraposto of the figures recalls Michelangelo. The figures hide from the anger of God in the moments before the expulsion from Eden.

actual proportions of the living model. In Cambridge, Massachusetts, at the Harvard School Gymnasium, the Boston-based sculptor Henry Hudson Kitson and the professor D. Sargent took measurements of the bodily proportions of college students in order to derive composite figural models for the ideal American female and male. In the early years of the twentieth century, at a time of rising nationalistic fervor, it was claimed that these measurements could yield an understanding of the ideal proportions that illustrated beauty's most perfect expression.

The search for relationships between observed proportions and constructs of geometry and numbers continued well into the twentieth century. This research was not restricted to sculptors, architects or artists. Harmonic unity was also the concern of Jay Hambidge in his work *Dynamic Symmetry: The Greek Vase*, 1902, where he analyzed the Golden Section. Two decades later (at a moment coincident with the rise of the art deco style), Claude Bragdon produced a poetic and inspiring work entitled *The Frozen Fountain*, which went through five editions between 1924 and 1932. While these books utilized geometric and mathematical methods to find harmonic measurements, their concerns did not focus wholly upon the design and pattern of the human body.

For much of the twentieth century, repeated measurements of living models have yielded proportions adopted by many members of the National Sculpture Society. According to this system, the torso and lower limbs are divisible into equal thirds. The head-to-body ratio is standardized at between seven and eight lengths. Although this system remains the figurative norm today, De Lue discovered greater power in sixteenth-century manneristic proportions of ten head lengths or more. That his art found spiritual and proportional kinship in the sculpture of Michelangelo Buonarotti is visually evident in the sculpture of De Lue, but the reasons go deeper than appearance would suggest. A few years before De Lue passed away he confided that years earlier, when he was visiting the Sistine Chapel, Michelangelo appeared to him as a very real person and carried on a conversation. We all have had some seemingly real/unreal experiences that have conditioned our lives and beliefs. For De Lue the vision of Michelangelo was the heartbeat of his work. This vision continued as a dialogue for De Lue, both artistically and spiritually, for the rest of his life.

Most contemporary figurative sculptors arrive at their own personal system of measuring physical man, either through study of the Euclidean ideal of commensurabiltiy of geometric proportions as applied to the human body, or by way of intuition and variables based on observation. For De Lue, human measurements were discovered intuitively. He wished to produce images of people of action—"do-ers" as he called them. He wished for his figures to have strength of body (suggested through extreme proportions) to accomplish their individual goals. His figures are robust, and in his own words, they "generally have a pretty small head." De Lue once observed that the human head, expressive of intelligence, is "almost like a world in itself." That world has its own program of harmonies to which De Lue's sculpture invites the viewer to visually "listen."

Phaeton II, 1972, bronze, 28 inches.

Phaeton II is De Lue's second essay in sculpture on this subject (see page 123). *Phaeton II* also exhibits a design that must be viewed in the round to fully understand it. The strong contraposto turns the head and the torso in opposite directions, creating two "fronts" to the work and the outline forms a figura serpentina.

OPPOSITE:

Divine Love and *Mortal Man*, 1969, bronze, 58 inches each.

De Lue united these two parts of the *Portal of Life Eternal* in 1986 to form a new composition. He created, through the extreme attenuation of the figures, an upward striving energy of great force. De Lue expressed the desire to rearrange many of the figures on the door to find new compositions and spiritual meanings in their symbols.

DONALD DE LUE
AND THE ART
OF THE MEDAL

D. Roger Howlett

Emerging from years in the shadows, the Society of Medalists seems ready to reassert itself as a major force for furthering the cause of medallic art. It has served notice with its latest issue: a stunning new medal by sculptor Donald De Lue.

NEW YORK TIMES, 1986

A Tradition of Honoring Heroes and History

ON FEBRUARY 2, 1986, ED REITER WROTE THE ABOVE QUOTATION IN THE numismatics column of the *New York Times*. *Bursting the Bounds* was the 111th medal issued by the Society of Medalists, the second design that De Lue had done for them, and De Lue's twenty-third medal. The art of the numismatist or medalist is one that fits neatly into De Lue's overall aesthetic as an artist.

It might be said that the designing and stamping of coins is the world's third oldest profession, the one that has allowed the two oldest to conduct their transactions more easily. From its beginnings in the dawn of civilization, the tradition of medallic art can trace its roots through the history of Western culture and civilization. The Greek victory at Marathon in 490 B.C. was commemorated with silver medallions. The Romans regularly congratulated their heroes with medallic honors. The traditions and technology of Imperial Roman coinage survived in the Byzantine Empire and greatly influenced Renaissance Italy.

In the seventeenth century the French established a reputation for excellence in medallic art, a reputation that continued through the eighteenth-century and into the Neo-Classicism of the Napoleonic Empire. At this time the young American republic needed its own coins and

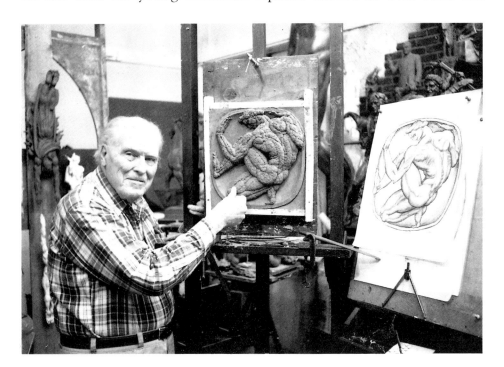

A satisfied Donald De Lue stands before his clay design and drawing for *Bursting the Bounds*.

OPPOSITE:

Bursting the Bounds, 1986, bronze, 12 × 12 inches.

Bursting the Bounds, is an appropriate title for a plaque which compositionally and thematically challenged the restraints of traditional medallic art and plaque making. Finely executed, the relatively small size of this piece does not diminish the forceful gesture of the trapped figure who strives to overcome his physical and spiritual barriers.

193

medals. From primitive designs and technology, official United States coins and medals developed to a point where, at the end of the nineteenth century, they carried among the more accomplished designs in numismatics.

Augustus Saint-Gaudens designed both the Theodore Roosevelt inaugural medal in 1905 and the Twenty Dollar Gold Piece of 1907. Saint-Gaudens's assistant, Bela Pratt, ably continued his master's numismatic tradition and, as his protegé, was asked in 1908 to redesign the five dollar and two-and-a-half-dollar gold coins. As Paula Kozol has noted: "The novel incuse, or engraved technique suggested by Egyptian intaglios, which he adopted for the coins, proved to be one of the most innovative designs in twentieth-century American medallic art."[1]

The following year, 1909, De Lue met Pratt and came under his influence. In 1912 Pratt handed fourteen-year-old De Lue one of the five-dollar gold pieces and symbolically passed on the numismatic tradition that would continue as both high craft and innovation in the medallic arts.

Fiftieth Anniversary Medal, National Sculpture Society, 1943.

Referred to by De Lue as his "learning medal," this piece is skillfully designed and very much in keeping with the artist's oeuvre of heroes and myths.

A First Medal

De Lue did not directly approach the design of medals until 1943. Although he had been a member of the august National Sculpture Society for only five years and had never designed a medal, De Lue was asked to create their fiftieth anniversary medal. Perhaps his having received the society's Lindsay Morris Prize for relief sculpture at their annual dinner in 1942 had suggested his ability to craft a medal.[2] De Lue had been taking an increasingly active part in the business of the society, attending meetings regularly as a member of the governing council. On February 15, 1943, at a meeting of the board of the National Sculpture Society, Herbert Adams (1858–1945) suggested "that at the dinner some commemorative thing, such as a coin cast in silver, made by Medallic Art Company, be placed at each plate and that this be added to the cost of the dinner. Mr. De Lue was asked to make a relief for this coin. Mr. Hering was asked to find out what the Medallic Art Company would charge."[3]

Asked later how the commission happened, De Lue said, "I don't know! Not all the members approved of the idea either, they thought I didn't have enough experience . . . and actually I was very inexperienced on the medal. There was an awful lot to learn about medals that I wasn't aware of. I know it thoroughly now and I can do it in my sleep, but in those days I couldn't."[4]

Lee Lawrie (1877–1963) had encouraged him to take up medals, because it was good money and added another area for a professional sculptor. But De Lue was reluctant to use Lawrie or other experienced members of the National Sculpture Society as teachers for his first commission for fear his work would soon take on the look of the mentor. Instead, he got support from his friend Michael Lantz, who was also struggling to learn the art of the medal, and each would visit the other's studio and criticize the work. Finally, the finished design was presented to each of the guests at the Society's fiftieth anniversary dinner at the New York Architectural League on May 27, 1943.[5] The National Sculpture Society medal was, as far as De Lue was concerned, a learning medal. He had had no experience with either of the Bakers on medals, and he had to learn new techniques.

De Lue later stressed that one of the chief things for the budding medalist to learn is to get the struck coin to pull easily from the steel die. He said, "In the plaster you can have it so it won't pull, but when you get ready for the bronze it has to pull out easily. Not fall out, but pull. I always did this after I had finished the design in clay, had it cast [into plaster] and would clean up the plaster and work out the problems. I finally became quite expert at it and can do it very easily. Or, do it quite well, anyway."[6]

A Medalist in Demand

De Lue could also easily adapt one form to another. When he received the commission for the *American Mothers Committee Medal* in 1950, he had recently completed the limestone relief on the Christian Herald House in New York on a similar subject, so it was simple to adapt the earlier design to the medal. Many of his medals related to other projects, either through inspiration or through the commissioners. His third medal, in 1950, was done in conjunction with the unveiling of the Harvey Firestone Memorial in Akron, Ohio, and the fiftieth anniversary of the Firestone Tire and Rubber Company. In the case of both the medal and the monument, De Lue did the reverse and the exedra, but not the portrait. He later remembered that Clyde Trees (1885–1960), president of Medallic Art Company, chased Harvey Firestone by telephone through Europe to get the approval for De Lue to do the reverse of that medal.[7]

Trees also commissioned De Lue to do the fifty-sixth issue of the Society of Medalists in 1957, *The Creation*. It was something of a breakthrough medal for De Lue. He was now, in his own words, "pretty experienced." He employed a subject that was perfectly adapted to his own spiritual values, and he was given great encouragement by Trees who wanted the finest medals that he could commission and to have American medals be every bit as fine as the best that were being created in Europe. According to De Lue, it was liked by almost everybody; it was especially liked by Trees. So, as people and organizations came to the Medallic Art Company over the next several years and asked who was likely to be the best sculptor to create a commemorative medal, De Lue once said, "I was pretty close to the top of the list for four or five years at least."[8]

This success resulted in a growing number of commissions. Some, like *George Washington at Prayer* and other work for the Grand Lodge of Pennsylvania, grew out of his commissions for monuments, some came from his association with the Hall of Fame of Great Americans, and some came from personal connections.

In 1959, Beverly Minster, one of England's historic churches, wanted to commemorate John of Beverly with a medal. The Baker family had long been associated with Beverly Minster as sculptors, so Bryant Baker, the last active member of the family, was asked to undertake the job. He turned to De Lue, who was now a more experienced medalist. De Lue

Drawing for the limestone relief at the Christian Herald Building, 1948, 9 × 11 inches.

In 1950, De Lue was asked to design a medal which examined the theme of motherhood and family. The end product, the *American Mothers Committee Medal*, is an almost exact duplicate of the relief that stood on the Christian Herald Building in New York.

was glad to do it but was worried about British reaction to an American doing a commission for the Minster. Baker said that they would be a little sensitive about it but it would be all right, and it was. Clyde Trees of Medallic Art was delighted. He was getting the chance to strike a medal for a British commission. Indeed the only De Lue work owned by the British Museum is the John of Beverly medal.

The *National Medal of Science* award was established by an act of Congress in 1959 in the aftermath of and as a very strong reaction to the Soviet sputnik. De Lue was selected to execute the medal and completed it in 1960. It was first awarded, however, by President Kennedy in January of 1963 for success achieved in 1962. Although the President is authorized to award up to twenty medals each year, they have generally been presented in sparing numbers. It is struck in gold and depicts a kneeling figure observing a crystal and inscribing a formula into the earth, and is the most important and prestigious American award for science.

Hall of Fame of Great Americans

By 1952 De Lue had joined the art committee for the Hall of Fame of Great Americans along with other past presidents of the National Sculpture Society Lee Lawrie, Chester Beach, James Earle Fraser, Cecil Howard, and Sidney Waugh.[9] The Hall of Fame was an institution established at the turn of the century by Henry Mitchell MacCracken, Chancellor of New York University, and Helen Gould, who generously funded the chancellor's dream. It was situated on land owned by the University at 181st Street and University Avenue in the Bronx and enshrined, in a quarter-mile long colonnade designed by Stanford White, the illustrious men and women of America.[10] The director of the hall from 1949 through De Lue's association with the project was Ralph W. Sockman. In the early 1960s De Lue became chairman of the Fine Art Committee, which also included Stanley Martineau, Michael Lantz, and Paul Jennewein.[11] The Hall had a complex system of selection of the eminent Americans who were to be enshrined. The methods tried to avoid transience in selecting the worthies and resulted in a pantheon where, in the words of Robert Moses, "Youth may find a dramatic presentation of the history of our country, the progress of democracy, the glories of free enterprise, the record of ideals in action and the promise of the future."[12]

The Fine Art Committee had the responsibility of selecting a sculptor to execute a bust of each candidate as well as a sculptor to execute a medal to commemorate the event. In 1963 the Hall of Fame had added a new dimension to its program by commissioning Medallic Art Company to issue bronze and silver medallions depicting each American enshrined in the colonnade. The Hall of Fame had received repeated requests, which they were not able to grant, for miniatures of the bronze portrait busts. To fill these requests the Fine Art Committee worked to secure sculptors for medals for each of those who had been inducted into the Hall. Where possible the sculptor of the portrait bust and the sculptor of the medal were the same.[13] The obverse of the medal showed a portrait that resembled the bust in the colonnade; on the reverse, the artist was encouraged to display his utmost creativity. For nearly fifteen years, De

National Medal of Science Medal, 1960, clay study.

OPPOSITE:

Brother Against Brother Plaque, 1971, 12 inches in diameter.

Strength, conflict and the clashing of kin are the images evoked by memories of the Civil War, a time of great disunity for America. Robert E. Lee was prominent in this period of unrest. It is fitting that *Brother Against Brother*, symbolic of this time, appears on the reverse.

Lue was pretty much in charge of the selection of the sculptors for both the busts and the medals.

The committee proved to be one of the great commissioning bodies of American medals. From 1963 through 1974 they commissioned ninety-six medals by more than forty sculptors. Most were commissioned during De Lue's tenure as chairman. De Lue felt strongly about the project and its active continuation. New York University turned the Hall and their Bronx campus over to Bronx Community College in 1973. Unfortunately, at that time the ongoing program of election and additional busts of inductees and medals was suspended, and the Fine Arts Committee was disbanded soon after.[14]

Perhaps De Lue initiated the entire medallic project when he created the Hall of Fame Medallion for the electors in 1960. His Robert E. Lee and John Adams medals followed in 1963 and 1971; and his Matthew Maury medal was issued in 1974, just before the program became inactive. The reverse of the N.Y.U. *Hall of Fame for Great Americans Medal* shows the deity and figures of fame honoring man and his art. *Brother Against Brother* on the reverse of the Lee medal is a powerful design that achieves both complexity and beauty with obvious classical references. The reverse of the Adams medal may have inspired De Lue's thinking on the *Right Over Evil* design for the F.B.I. in 1972. The motif was drawn from Adams's belief in justice as a divine attribute. De Lue depicts a war

144

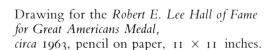

Drawing for the *Robert E. Lee Hall of Fame for Great Americans Medal,* *circa* 1963, pencil on paper, 11 × 11 inches.

in heaven between the forces of good and evil—St. Michael and Lucifer. Evil is unmasked by the sword of righteousness and is being driven from heaven by the trumpet of goodness. [15]

High Achievements in Medallic Art

In 1975 the National Academy of Design celebrated one hundred fifty years of providing academic training and standards in American art by mounting a major exhibition, *A Century and a Half of American Art*, and by arranging for a *150th Anniversary Medal*. In the words of the catalogue,

> The President and the Council of the National Academy of Design commissioned Donald De Lue, NA to design this medal to commemorate the contribution the Academy has made to the fine arts during the past 150 years since its founding: in providing training for students in painting, sculpture and the graphic arts; in exhibiting the works of professional artists; and as trustee of many and varied funds for the benefit of the public, the professional artist, and the student.
>
> The beautiful design for the medal has its basis in mythology. On the obverse side is Pegasus in flight above the clouds reaching for the stars. Prometheus is depicted on the reverse side making his gift to mankind. [16]

De Lue was perfectly at home with the classical imagery employed in the service of the Academy. *Pegasus* had been one of his first sculptures as he began his independent career, and the winged horse carrying man to the stars could hardly be more appropriate to De Lue's own imagery. *Prometheus* is, similarly, perfect in the De Lue pantheon. He recurs in De Lue's sculpture, bringing fire to mankind, but he is also one of the "cosmic beings" who come from the stars to benefit man. It is the quintessential De Lue medal.

Brookgreen Gardens in South Carolina may be the most comprehensive and distinguished collection of American twentieth-century figurative sculpture. In 1978, Brookgreen Gardens had already begun a distinguished series of medals on various themes by American sculptors. De Lue was selected and given the theme of the sculptors themselves. Joseph V. Noble, president of Brookgreen, discusses De Lue's methodology in his introduction to this book. Again, De Lue approached his subject with classical imagery. On the medal, one sculptor is creating Diana on the obverse, and another is sculpting Apollo on the reverse. Nowhere else in De Lue's work is the sculptor so obviously the creation of the gods and the creator of them, mortal clay and sculptor's clay. Noble says:

> On the obverse side of the medal, the sculptor sits before his creation modeling the clay statue of Diana. With his left hand he has rolled a pellet of clay to be applied to his work, and with his right thumb he models her arm. She is wearing a diaphanous gown, and thrown loosely over her shoulders is her cloak of night, spangled with stars. The crescent moon, her symbol, floats beside her . . . On the reverse side the sculptor, resting

23

93

Drawing for the *National Academy of Design, 150th Anniversary Medal, circa* 1975, pencil on paper, 15 × 20 inches.

De Lue working on the *Brookgreen Medal*, *circa* 1977.

on one knee, wields his mallet and chisel as he carves in stone the colossal nude figure of Apollo. The sun god is shown in the moment of his awakening at dawn as he raises the flaming sun disk to his shoulders, and the horses of the sun begin their plunging gallop across the sky. The unfinished block of stone is seen behind Apollo, while the rays of the sun fill the field of the medal. A branch of laurel rests in the area below the sculptor and is symbolic of the praise awarded great creations in sculpture. It is truly a great achievement of medallic art, and we are tremendously proud to have had Donald De Lue create this tribute to the sculptors of the world.[17]

After creating two dozen medals, De Lue reflected on both the purpose of these designs and some of his contemporaries who created them. He said, "The value of the medal is historic. It's for the purpose of recording history. For the sculptor, it is nice to be part of that in some way; you become involved and interested in the history of what the medal is about." Of the collections at the American Numismatic Society he once said, "It's fantastic, the De Lue medals are shown with the best of Greek medals and the best medals of all time. They have a marvelous collection. There is a continuation of sculpture as history and history as sculpture."[18]

De Lue had particular admiration for Saint-Gaudens. He felt that the Saint-Gaudens Victory Figure is one of the outstanding American medals. De Lue did not make many distinctions between reliefs and medals. He referred to the portrait relief that Richard Recchia did of Bela Pratt as "very much in the St. Gaudens tradition."[19] He felt that Lee Lawrie and Paul Manship were superb medalists and that Paul Jennewein and Walker Hancock were very good. He was not terribly sanguine about the immediate future of the medal: "In today's world there is almost nobody doing anything well. It's one of those things. When people are doing things well and with integrity it still has merit, I think."[20]

De Lue's work on the medal did not go unnoticed by his colleagues and by professional societies. In 1913, J. Sanford Saltus established an award for excellence in American numismatics, to be awarded by the American Numismatic Society and the National Sculpture Society once a year, but only if a worthy recipient existed. The first sculptor to be so honored was James Earle Fraser in 1919. Since then it has been sparingly awarded for distinction in medals to a select group of sculptors, including Paul Manship, Adolph Weinman, Lee Lawrie, Paul Jennewein, Walker Hancock, Thomas LoMedico, Michael Lantz, and John Flanagan. De Lue was given the Saltus medal in 1967, "for distinguished achievement in the field of the art of the medal." The American Numismatic Association named him "Sculptor of the Year" in 1979 for excellence in medals.

Bursting the Bounds was his last breakthrough medal. It required a change in the bylaws of the Society of American Medalists so that a sculptor might create more than a single medal for the society so long as there was a ten-year interval between medals. De Lue had done *The Creation* for the society as his sixth medal in 1957. Joseph Veach Noble, the newly appointed director of the Society wanted to challenge the sculptor with the theme "bursting the bounds." De Lue used the theme "to symbolize mankind's eternal quest for ways to break through restraining limitation. In this medal the figure on both the obverse and reverse is the same human being bursting out of the confining boundary of the medal. I

Drawing for *Bursting the Bounds* reverse and obverse, *circa* 1985, pencil on paper, 10 × 10 inches.

wanted this single figure to personify all of us breaking out of our handicaps to freedom. The theme inspired me to try to transcend the conventional limitations of medallic sculpture, and create an image that would both literally and figuratively break the boundaries of the medium."[21]

The medal was in a sense a collaboration of De Lue and Noble. De Lue believed that the idea for a large thick medal in very high relief originated with Noble, although they were working so closely that ideas for the medal were shared. De Lue had had some experience with Medallic Art that suggested that the factory thought his designs were too strong, but Noble encouraged him to push forward. De Lue later remembered Noble saying, "I don't give a damn what they think at Medallic Art, we've got to make something that is going to have interest worldwide."[22] They both had the idea that the way to accomplish that goal was to have a strong single figure that would be the same on both sides. De Lue noted, "If I were to take the background out, it would be the same figure; it would be like a small piece of sculpture. I often wanted to do that, but Joe didn't want to try it."[23]

De Lue stretched the capacity of the Medallic Art Company, which struck the medal. The medal is a technical as well as an artistic tour-de-force. The one-inch-thick planchet of bronze was struck fourteen times with a press that developed a force of 100 tons per square inch on each strike. It had to be annealed between each strike to soften the metal to take the next blow. The result is a depth of relief never before seen in a struck medal.

De Lue's last medal looks back to its Greek and Renaissance antecedents and shows that a tradition nearly three millenia old, in the hands of an accomplished practitioner, can renew itself in breaking the boundaries of the medium.

NOTES

1. MFA Sculpture, p. 310.
2. DDL to DRH, 1987.
3. Minutes recorded from meeting at National Sculpture Society, Feb. 15, 1943.
4. *New York Times*, May 16, 1942, p. 11, col. 4.
5. *New York Times*, March 28, 1943, p. 12, col. 6.
6. DDL to DRH, March 20, 1988.

7. *New York Times*, Oct. 3, 1960, p. 31, col. 3.
8. DDL to DRH, March 28, 1988.
9. *National Sculpture Review*, Vol. 1, No. 3, June 1952, p. 12.
10. *New York Times*, May 31, 1969, p. 24, col. 4.
11. Hall of Fame for Great Americans archives, New York University.
12. *New York Times*, May 31, 1969, p. 24, col. 4.
13. Frida T. Hiddal, *National Sculpture Review*, Vol. 18, No. 2, Summer 1969, pp. 16–19.
14. *Hall of Fame for Great Americans, Bronx Community College* (guidebook), n.d.
15. *New York Times*, Feb. 13, 1972, p. 32, col. 6.
16. *A Century and a Half of American Art* (New York: National Academy of Design, 1975).
17. Joseph Veach Noble, "The Sculptor's Medal," *National Sculpture Review*, Vol. 28, No. 1, Spring 1979, pp. 18–19.
18. DDL to DRH, March 20, 1988.
19. Portrait relief by Richard Recchia now at the Museum of Fine Arts, Boston.
20. DDL to DRH, March 20, 1988.
21. Donald De Lue as quoted in the 1985/111th issue of the *Society of Medalists*, a circular accompanying the medal.
22. DDL to DRH, March 20, 1988.
23. Ibid.

A CHECKLIST OF THE MEDALS OF DONALD DE LUE

M. Darsie Alexander

1. *National Sculpture Society — 50th Anniversary Commemorative Medal*, 1943. Reissued as 90th Anniversary Medal, 1983.
   > *obverse:* Kneeling male figure with outstretched hands sits in palm of Creator.
   > *reverse:* Staff artist, Medallic Art Company, "National Sculpture Society/ Fiftieth Anniversary Medal."
   > *struck:* Medallic Art Company, Ct. (Inv. #82–221)
   > Bronze: 1½" diameter.

De Lue's earliest medal, the National Sculpture Society Medal typifies the artist's preference for strong, mythical figures. Here, the kneeling figure extends his hand in the same gesture as the palm he rests on, suggesting the possible meanings of "creator," be he God or artist. This theme is recurrent in De Lue's oeuvre.

2. *American Mothers Committee Medal*, 1950.
   > *obverse:* "American Mothers Committee Badge" (mother with two children).
   > *reverse:* (blank with pin mount).
   > *struck:* Medallic Art Company, Ct. (Inv. #50–39)
   > Bronze and silver: 1¾" diameter.

According to De Lue, this medal honored mothers of soldiers who died in World War II. The design for this medal is related to a sculpture for the Christian Herald building in New York.

3. *Firestone Tire and Rubber Company — 50th Anniversary Medal*, 1950.
   > *obverse:* by Jeno Juszko, portrait of Harvey Firestone
   > *reverse:* by De Lue, "Fifty Years of Firestone Service" (images of automobiles, tractors and rubber tires surround the proclamation of Firestone's anniversary).
   > *struck:* Medallic Art Company, Ct. (Inv. #50–16)
   > Bronze: 2¾" diameter.

The Fiftieth Anniverary Medal was used to commemorate the dedication of the Firestone Monument.

4. *American Coalition of Patriotic Service Medal*, 1954.
    obverse: Figure of female warrior soaring over waves.
    reverse: "American Coalition of Patriotic Societies, Patriotic
        Service Medal."
    struck: Medallic Art Company, Ct. (Inv. #54–22)
        Bronze, silver and gold: 2⅞″ diameter.
This medal was an award for action in the Pacific war. The female
figure is representative of a heroic naval goddess who gives soldiers courage to fight over the oceanic waves.

5. *Gold Discovery Day Medal*, 1957, for the Committee for a Free
Gold Market, Angels Camp.
    obverse: "California Gold Discovery Day Medallion/Sutter's
        Mill, Coloma/Gold found here by James Marshall started
        the growth and prosperity of America."
    reverse: "Gold is property, Freedom to buy and sell gold is
        a consitutional right, 18 carat."
    struck: Medallic Art Company, Ct. (Inv. #57–32)
        Bronze and gold: 1¼″ diameter.

6. *The Creation*, Society of Medalists, 56th issue, 1957.
    obverse: "What is man that thou art mindful of Him" (male
        figure creating heaven and earth).
    reverse: "In the image of God created He him" (reclining
        figure holding man and sun).
    struck: Medallic Art Company, Ct. (Inv. # 30–1–56)
        Bronze: 2⅞″ diameter.
            ed. of 450 ordered 8/15/57
            ed. of 25 ordered 6/2/61
        Silver and gold: 2⅞″ diameter, unknown quantity.
The Creation, winner of the Saltus Award, 1957, promoted
recognition of De Lue as a master among medallic artists.

7. *John of Beverly Medal*, 1959.
    obverse: John of Beverly.
    reverse: (blank).
    struck: Medallic Art Company, Ct. (Inv. #59–39)
        Bronze: 3″ diameter.
    signed: "De Lue, 1959"
This medal was issued as a commemoration to John of Beverly
by Beverly Minster of Great Britain. Originally, Bryant Baker
was asked to design and execute the medal, but he recommended
De Lue in his place.

8. *Hall of Fame for Great Americans Medal*, New York University, 1960.

    obverse: "Hall of Fame for Great Americans/New York University/ In noble character, in world wide good, they live forever more"(profile of a man with laurels).

    reverse: Figure of creation.

    struck: Medallic Art Company, Ct. (Inv. #60–60)

        Bronze: 3″ diameter, ed. of 1200

        Bronze: 1¾″ diameter, ed. of 2500

        Silver: 1¾″ diameter, ed. of 600

    signed: "De Lue"

This medal, catagorized as a "keystone medal," was conceived and executed as an introductory medal for the series issued by the Hall of Fame for Great Americans in New York. (D. Wayne Johnson).

9. *National Medal of Science*, first awarded by John Kennedy, 1960, for National Science Foundation, Washington, D.C.

    obverse: "National Medal of Science" (kneeling man holding crystal and scratching formula into earth).

    reverse: "Awarded by the President of the United States to . . . "

    struck: Medallic Art Company, Ct. (Inv. #60–25)

        Bronze and gold: 3¼″ and ¾″ diameters.

10. *Robert E. Lee — Hall of Fame for Great Americans Medal*, 1963.

    obverse: "Hall of Fame for Great Americans, New York University, Robert E. Lee."

    reverse: "Brother–Brother" (two mounted combatants, symbolic of brother against brother).

    struck: Medallic Art Company, Ct.

        Bronze: 3″ diameter, ed. of 1200.

        Bronze: 1 ¾″ diameter, ed. of 2500.

        Silver: 1 ¾″ diameter, ed. of 600.

    signed: "De Lue SC 1963"

11. *George Washington at Prayer — Grand Lodge of Pennsylvania Medal*, 1967.

    obverse: "George Washington at Prayer, Freedoms Foundation, Valley Forge" (Washington at prayer in low relief).

    reverse: "Grand Lodge of Pennsylvania, *Virtute Silentio Amore*" (Apollo's head surrounded by rays of light).

    struck: Medallic Art Company, Ct. (Inv. #67–98)

        Bronze and silver: 3″ diameter.

12. *Hiram P. Ball—Grand Lodge of Pennsylvania Medal*, 1969.
    obverse: standard design (see *John L McCain—Grand Lodge of Pennsylvania Medal, obverse*)
    reverse: "Grand Lodge of Pennsylvania, *Virtute Silentio Amore*" (Apollo's head surrounded by rays of light).
    struck: Medallic Art Company, Ct.(Inv. #69–153–2)
        Bronze: 3″ diameter.

13. *Societé Commemorative des Femmes Célébrés*, 1970.
    obverse: "Liberty Our Precious Heritage/Statue of Liberty Presented by the People of France to the People of the United States of America/Dedication Oct 23, 1886."
    reverse: "Let Liberty be Proclaimed" (a soaring female figure, much like figure in American Coalition Medal).
    struck: Franklin Mint, Penn.
        Silver and platinum: 2″ diameter.

De Lue was called on by the Franklin Mint to design and execute a medal of the Statue of Liberty. This medal was one in a collection of fifty medals which were issued bi-monthly from 1966 to 1974. (Smithsonian Institution and the Franklin Mint).

14. *John Adams—Hall of Fame for Great Americans Medal*, 78th issue for Hall of Fame, 1971.
    obverse: "The Hall of Fame for Great Americans at New York University/John Adams/1735–1826."
    reverse: "Right/Above/Evil/Principal" (male and female figure seem to float in space; male holds sword).
    struck: Medallic Art Company, Ct. (Inv. #63–1–77)
        Bronze: 3″ diameter, ed. of 1200.
        Bronze: 1¾″ diameter, ed. of 2500.
        Silver: 1¾″ diameter, ed. of 600.

15. *Bicentennial Medal*, Daughters of the American Revolution, 1972.
    obverse: "Home and Country, 1776" (Mother and child sending husband/father off to war).
    reverse: "American Revolution Bicentennial 1776–1976, National Society, Daughters of the American Revolution."
    struck: Medallic Art Company, Ct. (Inv. #71–174)
        Silver and bronze: 2½″ diameter.
    signed: "D. De Lue c. 1972."

This medal was the first bicentennial medal in America.

16. *Matthew Fontaine Maury — Hall of Fame for Great Americans Medal*, 1974.

    obverse: "The Hall of Fame for Great Americans at New York University/Matthew Fontaine Maury/1806–1873."

    reverse: "Science/Man/Ocean" (large figure of a whale).

    struck: Medallic Art Company, Ct. (Inv. #63–1–9)

        Bronze: 3″ diameter, ed. of 1200.

        Bronze: 1¾″ diameter, ed. of 2500.

        Silver: 1¾″ diameter, ed. of 600.

    signed: "De Lue SC"

17. *150th Anniversary Medal*, National Academy of Design, 1975.

    obverse: Pegasus with rider, climbing to heaven.

    reverse: "1825/National Academy of Design/1975, One Hundred and Fiftieth Anniversary" (image of Prometheus).

    struck: Medallic Art Company, Ct. (Inv. #74–160)

        Bronze and gold-plated: 3″ diameter.

    signed: "De Lue SC c. 73"

Commissioned by the National Academy of Design, De Lue created this medal to commemorate the long-standing contribution the Academy has made to fine arts.

18. *Bicentennial of American Independence*, 1976.

    obverse: "Bicentennial of American Independence" (soldier on horseback is being led by another figure in bicentennial garb).

    reverse: "1776/Let Freedom Ring/1976" (ascending female figure holds a torch and is surrounded by sun and stars)

    signed: "De Lue SC"

    struck: The Franklin Mint, Penn. (Inv. #143)

        Silver: 39mm, edition of 5,252

        Gold: 32mm, edition of 304

19. *John L. McCain — Grand Lodge of Pennsylvania Medal*, 1976.

    obverse: George Washington at Prayer.

    reverse: "John L. McCain/R.W. Grand Master of Masons in Pennsylvania/American Bicentennial/1976"

    struck: Medallic Art Company, Ct. (Inv. #74–214)

20. *Brookgreen Gardens — Sculptor's Medal*, 1978.
    obverse: "Brookgreen Gardens, South Carolina" (sculptor modeling Apollo and the Sun).
    reverse: Sculptor carving figure of Diana.
    struck: Medallic Art Company, Ct. (Inv. #78–65)
        Bronze: 3″ diameter.
    signed: "D. De Lue SC c78"

Brookgreen Gardens, South Carolina, honored Donald De Lue by choosing his designs for the Sculptor's Medal, a medal presented to sustaining members of the organization. The designated theme of the medal, the sculptor in the process of creating, was perfectly matched to De Lue's own iconography, which frequently touched on this subject. (Joseph Veach Noble in the *Brookgreen Bulletin*, Summer 1978).

21. *Benjamin Franklin — Grand lodge of Pennsylvania Medal*, 1978.
    obverse: "Benjamin Franklin, Printer, Philosopher, Scientist, Statesman, Diplomat, Freemason."
    reverse: "Walter Pierre Wells / R.W. Grand Master Masons of Pennsylvania."
    struck: Medallic Art Company, Ct. (Inv. #78–72)
    signed: "D. De Lue SC 78"

22. *Preservationist Foundation Commemorative Medal*, 1979.
    obverse: Whaleboatmen pushing boats out of reed, with British boat burning in background.
    reverse: "Whaleboat Warfare, Shoal Harbor, 1776–1783" (colonial woman watching as whale boat returns, British ship burns).
    struck: Sasson's, Farmingdale, N.J.
        Perry's Trophy, Longwood, N.J.
        Pewter: 2⅛″ diameter.
    signed: "De Lue."

This medal commemorates the 200th anniversary of whaleboat warfare at Raritan and Sandy Hook, marking remarkable feat of 72 continentals who defended New Jersey's shore against the attack of 800 British fighters during the Revolutionary War.

23. *Penelope Stout*, Preservationist Foundation, 1980.
    obverse: "1622 / First Lady of Monmouth" (two male figures, an Indian and a soldier, assist a woman and her baby to a boat).
    reverse: "Penelope Stout" (woman is thrown over Indian's shoulder; sun and ocean in background).
    struck: Sasson's, Farmingdale, N.J.
        Perry's Trophy, Longwood, N.J.
        Pewter.
    signed: "De Lue."

In another commemorative medal honoring American history, this piece tells the tale of Penelope Stout, a young pioneer whose will to live enabled her to survive torture by Indians in 1639 and the murder of her husband. Alive through her one hundred and tenth year, Stout fought for religious freedom and an improved relationship with native Indians.

24. *National Sculpture Society—90th Anniversary Commemorative Medal*, 1983 (see No. 1).

 obverse: Kneeling male figure with outstretched hands sits in palm of Creator.

 reverse: by Robin Warr-Hockaday, "National Sculpture Society / Ninetieth Anniversary Medal."

 struck: Medallic Art Company, Ct.

25. *Bursting the Bounds*, Society of Medalists, 111th issue, 1985.

 obverse: Male nude figure struggling against boundaries of the medal.

 reverse: Back of male nude.

 struck: Medallic Art Company, Ct.

  Bronze: 2¾" x 2¾" (square).

 signed: Both sides "De Lue, SOM 111th Issue, Aug. 1985."

In De Lue's own words, the purpose of this medal was to "transcend the conventional limitations of medallic sculpture." The dual image of man pushing against his boundaries is symbolic on both human and artistic levels. (Donald De Lue's quote taken from the *New York Times*, February 2, 1986).

26. *New Jersey Governor's Award*, 1987. Designed by Donald De Lue, sculpted by Evangelos Frudakis.

 obverse: "Pride in the Best of New Jersey" (a seated female with pen and book in hand is surrounded by images of athletes and heroes).

 reverse: "The State of New Jersey Honors with Pride . . ."

 struck: Medallic Art Company, Ct.

  Gold: unknown quantity.

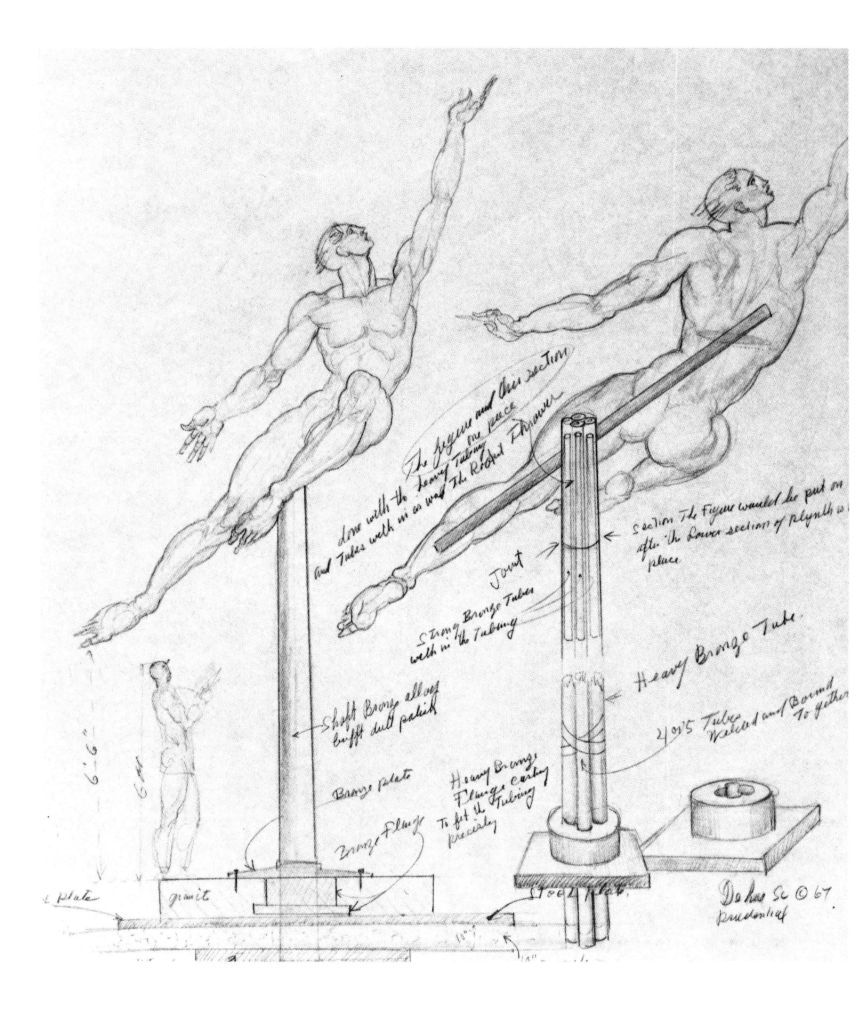

The figure and this section
done with the heavy tubing in one piece
and tubes with in as was the Rocket Thrower

section The Figure would be put on
after the lower section of plinth is in
place

Joint

Strong Bronze Tubes
with in the Tubing

Heavy Bronze Tube

Shaft Bronze alloy
buffed dull polish

2 or 5 Tubes
Welded and Boumd
To gather

Bronze plate

Heavy Bronze
Flange Casting
To fit the Tubing
precisly

Bronze Flange

6'6"

6 ft

plate

granit

Steel plate

10"

Dahm Sc © 67
providenbed

NOTES ON

BRONZE

CASTING

Bfore 1986, DONALD DE LUE EDITIONED NONE OF HIS SCULPTURE. SOME of his smaller works were cast in bronze and a few bear foundry marks. Perhaps no more than twenty bronzes were cast through 1985.

In 1986 De Lue began a major casting project at Tallix, first at their foundry in Peekskill and later at Beacon, N.Y. Each work was editioned as either twelve or fifteen. Some editions were fully cast in his lifetime and others were not. De Lue left careful instructions for continuing the casting project after his death. Editions were to remain the same and be filled out with posthumous casts if they were not yet complete. He instructed his assistant, William Kilpatrick, to continue the project with other plaster models as needed, maintaining editions as with those already cast, and following chasing, patina and base guidelines that he had established prior to his death. All posthumous casts are marked with "p" next to the foundry mark, $\overline{X}$.

The 82 Highland Avenue Corporation owns De Lue's artistic property and his copyrights. No other person or entity has the right to cast his work unless, as happened in a few well-documented cases, he ceded in writing rights to that party. The 82 Highland Avenue Corporation has announced its intention to vigorously enforce copyright to the full extent of the law.

List of works editioned by 1989:

Work:	Date	Prior to HA★	Edition size	Life casts	Potential Posthumous Casts
Pegasus	1930	0	12	6	6
Jupiter as the Bull	1931	0	15	15	0
Icarus	1934	1	12	12	0
Seated Woman	1934	0	12	12	0
Nymph	1934	0	12	6	6
Echo	1937	0	12	12	0
Faun	1937	0	12	12	0
Apex I	1937	0	12	6	6

OPPOSITE:

Studies for the engineering and installation of *Quest Eternal* at the Prudential Center, Boston, *circa* 1967, pencil on paper.

Apex II	1937	0	12	6	6
Sun God	1937	0	12	12	0
St. John the Baptist	1938	0	12	6	6
Lafayette	1938	1	12	6	6
Pegasus Plaque	1940	0	12	6	6
Cosmic Head	1943	0	12	2	10
Mighty Atom	1945	1	12	6	6
God's High Altar	1947	0	12	6	6
Airborne	1948	0	12	6	6
Jason	1948	0	12	12	0
Freedom with Wings	1948	0	12	6	6
Mother & Child	1952	0	12	6	6
Spirit of American Youth 36″	1952	1–2	12	9	3
Spirit of American Youth 11′	1952	2	12	2	8
Urn Fragment	1952	0	12	9	3
America 32½″	1955	0	12	6	6
France 32½″	1955	0	12	6	6
Three Marys	1955	0	12	6	6
Alexander Astride Bucephalus	1956–86	0	12	6	6
Phaeton I	1960	1	12	6	6
Patriotism	1962	0	12	6	6
Rocket Thrower 58″	1962	1	12	6	6
Rocket Thrower 14′	1962	1	12	0	11
Let There Be Light	1962	0	12	6	6
Brother Against Brother	1963	0	12	6	6
Orpheus	1966	1–2	12	6	6
Molly Pitcher	1966–81	0	12	6	6
Hand of God	1967	1	12	6	6
Divine Love	1969	0	12	6	6
Mortal Man	1969	0	12	6	6
Libra	1969	0	12	6	6
The Builders	1969	0	12	6	6
Moses	1970	0	12	6	6
Leda and the Swan	1970	1–2	12	12	0
Spirit Triumphant	1971	0	12	6	6
Genesis	1972	1–2	12	6	6
Phaeton II	1972	1–2	12	12	0
Right Over Evil	1972	0	12	9	3
Isaiah	1972	0	12	6	6
Poseidon	1975	1	12	6	6
Jefferson 22½″	1975	2–3	12	6	6
Jefferson 9′	1975	2	12	0	10
New Day	1976	0	12	6	6
Leander Perez	1976	4	12	2	6
Martin Luther King	1976	2	12	6	6

Prometheus	1978	1	12	6	6
Adam	1978	1	12	12	0
Eve	1978	2-3	12	12	0
Pioneer Head	1980	0	12	6	6
Arcturus	1980	1	12	9	3
Joy of Life	1981	0	12	12	0
Naomi It Is Time To Go	1982-83	1	12	6	6
Bearer of Good Times	1985	0	12	6	6
Bursting the Bounds	1985	0	12	6	6
Jobara Head	1986	0	12	6	6
Job	1986	0	12	6	6
Axelrod Head Sketch	1986	0	12	10	2
Axelrod Head	1986	0	6	2	4
Chanson d'Amour	1986	0	12	6	6
Evening Song	1987	0	12	6	6
De Lue Self Portrait	1987	0	12	4	8
Cosmic Being	1987	0	12	0	12
Moses Embracing the Law	1988	0	12	0	12

*Number of bronzes cast before the Howlett-Axelrod casting project.

Studies for *Rocket Thrower*,
1963, conte crayon on paper.

CHRONOLOGY

D. Roger Howlett

1897 · *October 5*, born to Harry T. and Ida M. (De Lue) Quigley in the Dorchester section of Boston, Massachusetts.

1909 · Drawings reviewed by Bela Pratt. De Lue begins to apprentice with Pratt and Richard Recchia.

1912 · Attends English High School in Boston, but begins to spend more time in Pratt and Recchia's studios than with conventional studies.
· *Summer*, assists Pratt on *Whaleman Memorial* in Recchia's studio at the St. Botolph Annex Studios.

1913 – 1914 · Moves to a furnished room on St. Botolph Street to be near the studios at 4 Harcourt Street.

1914 · *June 3*, De Lue's father dies in Boston.
· *October 13*, enters the modeling class of the School of the Museum of Fine Arts, Boston. Continues through the last class of the spring term, 1916.

1915 · *May*, receives Kimball Prize for modeling at the School of the Museum of Fine Arts.
· *Fall*, begins assisting Robert Baker at his studio at 26 St. Botolph St. at $6.00 per week.

1916 · Does much of the modeling on Robert Baker's *The Soul's Struggle*.
· Meets Bryant Baker and assists him at his studio at 100 Chestnut Street.

1917 · *May 18*, Bela Pratt dies.

1918 · Robert Baker's funds cut off; the studio is closed.
· Moves to New York with the sculptor Joseph Pollia.
· *November*, signs up on ship, *S.S. Minnesota*, along with sculptor, George Aarons, bound for Marseilles. Jumps ship in Marseilles and moves to Paris.

1919 – 1920 · Creates *American Soldiers* in an attempt to gain a war memorial commission.
· Works for various Paris sculptors, especially Alfredo Pina.

1920 – 1921 · Works in Lyon for Emile Vermare, a supplier of ecclesiastical sculpture.

1922 · Returns to Paris. Works for Paul Manship.
· *Summer and fall* in Chelsea, London, as assistant to Bryant Baker; stays in his 23 Fulham Road studio.
· *Mid-autumn*, returns to New York.
· *November 21*, De Lue's mother dies in Reading, Massachusetts.

1923 · Begins to assist Bryant Baker in his New York studio at 154 West 55th Street.

1926 · Helps move Baker's studio to 222 West 59th Street, the Gainsborough Studios.

1927 · Executes competition model for *The Pioneer Woman* for Bryant Baker.

1928 – 1929 · Baker wins competition for *The Pioneer Woman*. De Lue begins to enlarge and model it.

1930 · Models *Pegasus* in his studio and apartment at 4 West 40th St.

1931 · Models *Jupiter as the Bull* and *Modern Madonna*.

1933 · *October 5*, marries Martha Naomi Cross on his thirty-sixth birthday in Manhattan.
· Moves to 322 W. 72nd St., a penthouse with a small studio.

1934 · Begins a series of etchings to sell that will not compete with Bryant Baker's sculpture.
· Models *Icarus*, *Seated Woman*, and *Nymph*.

1935 · Designs Baker's competition model for the *Colonial Foot Postman* at the Post Office Building in Washington.

1937 · Models *Echo*, *Faun*, and *Sun God*.
· Executes Apex competition models for the Federal Trade Commission Building in Washington.
· Exhibits *Sun God* and *Allegorical Figure* at the Architectural League of New York.

1938 · *May 10*, is elected an associate member of the National Sculpture Society (NSS); will become a full member one year later.
· Models *Family Group* (Metropolitan Life Competition, runner-up).
· Models *St. John the Baptist* for the Church of the Epiphany in New York City and *Lafayette*.
· Exhibits *Faun* at the Architectural League of New York.

1939 · *January*, receives formal commission for Philadelphia Court House, *Law, Justice,* and *Eagle.*
· *Late summer,* moves studio to Lincoln Arcade Building, 1947 Broadway.

1940 · *April 2–May 2,* exhibits APEX model, *Trade on Sea* and *Pegasus Panel,* at the NSS special exhibition, Whitney Museum.
· Completes Philadelphia Court House reliefs, carved by Ugo and Rene Lavaggi.
· Models *Triton* for the Federal Reserve Bank and the *Alchemist* for the University of Pennsylvania, each carved by Ugo and Rene Lavaggi.

1941 · Elected to the governing council, NSS. On the membership committee and the sculpture advancement committee.
· Nominated by Adolph Weinman for Professional Sculpture Class, associate in the National Academy of Design.
· Exhibits photograph of *Law* and *Justice* from the Philadelphia Court House in the NSS traveling exhibition of enlarged photographs of sculpture, beginning May 13.
· *February 18,* submits his portrait for membership at the National Academy of Design.

1942 · *January,* prohibition of the use of bronze for sculpture instituted by the U.S. government, for war material.
· *May,* presides on the membership committee, current work committee, and library committee, NSS.
· Joins with Michael Lantz, Wheeler Williams, Eleanor Mellon, and Margaret French Cresson, the NSS committee to aid the citizens for the Army and Navy, led by Mrs. Junius Morgan and Miss Hildreth Meiere.
· Teaches at the Beaux-Arts Institute in New York. Sculptors teach in monthly rotation; De Lue teaches several of the month-long sessions over two years.
· *October,* becomes chairman of the membership committee of the NSS.
· Wins NSS Lindsay Morris Memorial Prize for *Free Man at Bay from Thermopylea to Batan.*
· Wins Architectural League of New York's Henry D. Avery Prize for *Lafayette.*
· Models for Citizens Committee: *St. Michael* and *A Knight Crusader* for the West Point and Arlington Virginia Chapels. Also, *St. Michael in Armor.*
· Models six trophies of eagles and armaments

for War Department Competition.

1943 · Designs *Cosmic Head* and NSS 50th Anniversary Medal.
· *April 28,* elected a full academician of the National Academy of Design (NAD) along with Reginald Marsh, W.L. Stevens, Everett Shinn, and J. S. Curry.
· *June,* requests extension for presentation of diploma work to NAD.
· Receives a Guggenheim Fellowship to work with Eric Gugler on "Sculpture Depicting the Heritage of America."
· Receives Avery Prize from the Architectural League of New York.

1944 · Chairs NSS Competition Program Committee, a group that establishes guidelines for potential commissioners of sculpture.

1945 · *January 9,* succeeds Paul Manship as president of the National Sculpture Society.
· *May 18,* receives a grant from the American Academy of Arts and Letters and the National Institute of Arts and Letters.
· *May 19–June 29,* exhibition of seven works at the National Institute of Arts and Letters, NYC.
· *November 27–December 23,* exhibition of De Lue sculpture at Philadelphia Art Alliance features *Woman Bearing Light, A Knight Crusader, St. Michael, North Wind, Cosmic Head,* and others.
· Models *The Mighty Atom* and twenty triptychs of *St. Michael* for the Citizens Committee.

1946 · Wins Mrs. Louis Bennett Prize for *Icarus.*
· Begins designs for the Virginia Polytechnic Institute Chapel, Blacksburg, Virginia.
· *October 7, Penelope* presented and accepted as diploma work for the NAD.

1947 · Moves studio to 225 East 67th Street.
· *March 19–April 13,* exhibits *Eve* and *Power* at the 121st Annual Exhibition of the National Academy of Design, NYC.
· Begins work on *God's High Altar.*

1948 · *January,* completes terms as president of NSS and is succeeded by Sidney Waugh.
· Models *Airborne* and *Jason.* Also works on *Family Group* for the Christian Herald House, NYC, carved by Rene Lavaggi.

1949 · Models *Benjamin Franklin* and *Joseph Willard* for Carnegie Tech in Pittsburgh, carved by Rene Lavaggi.
· *November 4–27,* exhibits preliminary work

for the Omaha Beach Memorial at the Philadelphia Art Alliance.

· *December 20–January 6, 1950*, exhibits work for the Omaha Beach Memorial at the Architectural League of New York.

· Begins work on the exedra for the Harvey Firestone Memorial.

1950 · *May 25*, exhibits plaster of *Inspiration* at the NAD-NSS exhibition at the NAD.

· Firestone Memorial dedicated.

1951 · *June 6–20*, exhibits *Icarus* in plaster in the NSS exhibition, Parke-Bernet Building, NYC.

· *June 14*, receives the gold medal of the Architectural League of New York for the exedra in the Firestone Memorial.

· *Summer*, participates in making of *Uncommon Clay*, Thomas Craven's movie on six living American sculptors.

· Models roundel of *Fleet Admiral Ernest King*.

1952 · *May 14–June 20*, exhibits *Triton* in plaster at the NSS exhibition, Parke-Bernet Building, NYC.

· Models Shelley Hayden memorial for marble, British West Indies.

· Completes commission for *Eagle* for the Federal Reserve Bank Building in Boston.

· Completes models for urns for the Omaha Beach Memorial.

· Presides over art committee for the Hall of Fame for Great Americans.

1953 · *Summer*, completes full-size plaster of the *Spirit of American Youth Rising From the Waves* for the Omaha Beach Memorial.

· Hall of Our History announced to the public and De Lue's designs shown.

· Completes commission for the doors for the Federal Reserve Bank Building in Boston.

1954 · Models *Lions of Judah*, carved in mahogany for the Germantown Jewish Center, Germantown, Penn.

· Executes *The Creation*, relief bronze for Junior High School 198, Queens, New York.

· Designs *Sun As Healer* for marble relief at Abraham Jacobi Hospital, East Bronx, New York, carved by Rene Lavaggi.

· Begins work on *Stations of the Cross* for white marble at Loyola Seminary, Shrub Oak, N.Y.

1955 · *April*, debates Lloyd Goodrich in *American Artist*; criticized by Charlotte Devree in *Art News*.

· *December 1–18*, exhibits *Cosmic Adventure*,

drawing, at "Five Arts," an exhibition at NAD.

· *America* and *France* sculpted.

1956 · *July 19*, Normandy American Cemetery and Memorial (Omaha Beach) dedicated.

· Begins and finishes modeling Edward Hull Crump Memorial, Memphis, Tenn.

· Conceives of *Alexander Astride Bucephalus*, a piece that was underway almost until the artist's death.

1957 · *April*, Crump Memorial dedicated.

· Models *Hercules* as athlete for Physical Culture Building, United States Naval Academy, Annapolis.

1958 · Serves on jury along with Paul Manship, Carl Gruppe, Wheeler Williams, and Leo Friedlander for the design of the Henry Hering Medal for the National Sculpture Society. Won by Albino Manca.

1959 · Commissioned to model *Washington as Master Mason* for New Orleans.

1960 · Wins NSS Henry Hering Prize for outstanding collaboration among architect, owner, and sculptor, for *Stations of the Cross* (Shrub Oak, New York). Also wins Henry Hering Prize for monumental sculpture in the round as a collaboration among architect, client, and sculptor, for the Omaha Beach Memorial, St. Laurent Cemetery, Normandy, France.

· *February, Washington as Master Mason* dedicated in New Orleans.

· Models four reliefs on *Life of St. Joseph* in granite for the St. Joseph Shrine at the Holy Sepulchre Cemetery in Chicago.

· *April 4–21*, exhibits *Station of the Cross #3* at the NSS exhibit, National Arts Club, NYC.

· *May 29*, Virginia Polytechnic Institute War Memorial Chapel dedicated, Blacksburg, Va.

· Models a series of reliefs for granite for the Sacred Heart Shrine, Hillside, Ill.

· Bust of Dr. Ralph Sockman sculpted for Christ Church (Methodist), NYC.

1961–1962 · Models *Rocket Thrower* for the 1964 World's Fair, Flushing Meadow, Queens, N.Y.

· Models studies except for the final enlargement for the Commemorative Tribute to the Boy Scouts of America, Washington, D.C.

· Chairs art committee for the Hall of Fame for Great Americans.

1962 · Exhibits *Birth of Jesus* at the NSS exhibition, the Glass Center, NYC.

· Wins NSS gold medal for *Urn Fragment*.

· Takes the studio building at 82 Highland Avenue, Leonardo, New Jersey, where he finishes full-sized plaster of *Rocket Thrower* by April 30.

· Begins modeling fourteen *Stations of the Cross* to be sculpted in rose marble and a *Corpus* in carved wood (Sisters of St. Joseph Chapel, Willowdale, Toronto, Canada).

1963 · Models working study for monument to the Soldiers and Sailors of the Confederacy.

1964 · New York World's Fair opens with *Rocket Thrower* as its sculptural centerpiece.

· *George Washington as Master Mason* installed in the Masonic Pavillion.

· *April 25,* John Canaday reviews *Rocket Thrower*.

· *November 7, Commemorative Tribute to the Boy Scouts of America* dedicated in Washington, D.C.

1965 · *April 25 – May 9,* exhibits *Rocket Thrower* in bronze at the NSS 32nd Exhibition, Lever House, NYC.

· Commissioned to design *Quest Eternal* for the Prudential Center in Boston.

· *June 27,* receives "Golden Plate Award" of the American Academy of Achievement for *Rocket Thrower*.

· *August 10,* receives the award of the Whistler Society of New York for *Rocket Thrower*.

· *August 25, Soldiers and Sailors of the Confederacy* dedicated on Gettysburg Battlefield, Pennsylvania.

· Models two maquettes for *Washington at Prayer*.

1966 · Wins gold medal of the NSS at 33rd Annual Exhibition for *Orpheus* (April 11 – May 1, Lever House, NYC).

· Chairs jury for NAD awards.

1967 · Wins Herbert Adams Memorial Medal of the NSS for service to sculpture.

· Wins the Samuel F.B. Morse Medal for sculpture from NAD for *Phaeton I* (February 23 — March 19).

· *March,* begins modeling *Mountaineer* for West Virginia University.

· *April 9 – 30,* exhibits *Mighty Atom* in bronze at the NSS 34th Annual, Lever House, NYC.

· *April 11,* wins the Herbert Adams Me-

morial Medal of the NSS for outstanding achievement in sculpture.

· *Quest Eternal* dedicated at the Prudential Center in Boston.

· *September 9, Washington at Prayer* dedicated at Valley Forge, Penn.

· *September,* completes half-size model of *St. Anthony* for St. Raymond Cemetery, the Bronx, N.Y. Lays up clay for *Portal of Life Eternal*, Gladwyne, Penn.

1968 · Wins Therese and Edward H. Richard Memorial Prize from the NSS for the one-third size model of *Washington at Prayer*.

· *Spring,* awarded commission for the Special Warfare Memorial Statue, Ft. Bragg, N.C.

· *September 10, Cherubim* dedicated at the Shrine to Life, Woodmont, Gladwyne, Penn.

· *October,* wins competition for *Peace and Memory,* the State of Louisiana monument at the Gettysburg Battlefield.

1969 · *June 13, St. Anthony* dedicated and blessed at St. Raymond Cemetery, the Bronx, N.Y.

· *November 19,* Special Warfare Memorial Statue dedicated, Ft. Bragg, N.C.

· Begins modeling final studies for the Mississippi Monument for Gettysburg Battlefield.

1970 · *February 26 – March 22,* chairs sculpture jury of awards at NAD.

· *April 5 – May 14,* exhibits working model in bronze for *Quest Eternal* (Prudential Building in Boston) at the 37th annual exhibition of the NSS at Lever House.

· *September 10, Portal of Life Eternal* dedicated at Woodmont, Gladwyne, Penn.

1971 · *June 11, Peace and Memory,* the State of Louisiana monument dedicated at Gettysburg Battlefield.

· *October 30, Mountaineer* dedicated at West Virginia University in Morgantown.

· Competes for sculpture on the Libby Dam in Montana.

1972 · Models *Right Over Evil* as working study for FBI building, Washington.

· *April 14,* wins competition for 150th NAD Medal.

· Competes for tympanum of the National Cathedral in Washington.

1973 · Wins the Dr. Maurice B. Hexter Prize from the NSS for *Genesis, Evening and Morning of the Second Day*.

1974 · *October*, the Mississippi Monument dedicated at Gettysburg Battlefield.
· Models *The Alamo* group for the Alamo, San Antonio, Tex.
· Wins Medal of Honor (NSS), the highest award of the society, for a lifetime of work in sculpture.

1975 · *January*, wins competition for Thomas Jefferson statue in Jefferson Parish, La.
· Designs 150th Anniversary Medal of the NAD. Exhibited at the 150th Annual Exhibition February 22 – March 16.
· *December 6*, Thomas Jefferson statue dedicated in Jefferson Parish, La.

1976 · *Leander Perez* installed at Plaquemines Parish, La.
· Models *Martin Luther King* bust for Brookdale College.
· *April 4 – 22*, exhibits *Poseidon* in bronze at the 44th Annual Exhibition of the NSS, Equitable Gallery, the Equitable Life Assurance Society, NYC.
· *May*, receives honorary degree from Monmouth College, N.J.

1978 · *March 1 – 15*, one-man show at Brookdale College, Lincroft, N.J.

1979 · Models *Columbus* and *Isabella*.

1982 · *Spring*, one-man show of 27 works at Bell Laboratories, Holmdel, N. J.
· *September*, Martha Naomi Cross De Lue dies.
· Designs *Naomi It Is Time To Go*.
· Models bust of Pope John Paul II on the occasion of his 1979 visit to the United States.

1983 · Models *John F. Kennedy* as a study for Houston, Tex., monument.

1985 · *Summer*, begins Tallix casting project

1987 · Casts *Right Over Evil* into plaster and makes final revisions.
· *February 22*, traveling exhibition of "Gods, Prophets and Heroes" opens at the Canton Art Institute. Later travels to Mabee-Gerrer Museum, McNay Art Museum, El Paso Museum of Art.
· *April 17, 1987 – July 10, 1988, Jupiter as the Bull* exhibited with traveling show of

American art deco, opening at the National Museum of American Art and closing at the Minnesota Museum.
· *September 17, Washington At Prayer* (41-inch) dedicated at State House, Olympia, Wash.
· *September 17 – November 8*, exhibits *Thomas Jefferson* and *George Washington at Prayer* (1966) at "The NSS Celebrates the Figure," Port of Our History Museum, Philadelphia.
· *October 11, Rocket Thrower* (one-third size) and *Quest Eternal* (one-half size) dedicated by City of Orlando, Fla. in Lockhaven Park.
· *October 11 – November 14*, gallery exhibition of De Lue's sculpture at Phillip's House in Orlando, Fla.
· Models *Self Portrait*.

1988 · *December 17, 1987 – February 7, 1988, Icarus* and *Sun God* exhibited at the Danforth Museum's "City Life — New York in the 1930s."
· *December 5, 1987 – February 1988*, gallery exhibition of De Lue's work at Griffith Menard Gallery, Baton Rouge, La.
· *February 2 – March 8*, sculpture exhibited at Louis Newman Gallery, Beverly Hills, Cal.
· Models *Cosmic Being* and *Moses Embracing the Law*.
· *April 14 – May 23*, selections of De Lue's sculpture exhibited at Osuna Gallery, Washington.
· Leaves *The Leper*, his last work, unfinished.
· *August 26*, dies in Leonardo, New Jersey.

1989 – 1990 · *July*, Memphis Brooks Museum, Overton Park, Memphis, Tenn. exhibits the Crump memorial.
· *September 15, 1989 – January 15, 1990, Rocket Thrower* exhibited at the Queens Museum.
· *January 22 – March 16, 1990*, Emerson Gallery, Hamilton College, exhibits work by De Lue.

1990 · *April – May*, "Gods, Prophets and Heroes" travels to the Hickory Museum.
· *October, 1990 – January, 1991*, "Gods, Prophets and Heroes" travels to the Minnesota Museum.

Standing Male Nude, circa 1938, pencil on paper, 16¾ × 13¾ inches.

BIBLIOGRAPHY

Books

Beattie, Susan. *The New Sculpture*. New Haven: Yale University Press, 1983.

Brumme, Carl Ludwig. *Contemporary American Sculpture*. New York: Crown Publishers, 1948.

Caro, Robert. *Power Broker: Robert Moses and the Fall of New York*. New York: Random House, 1975.

Clapp, Jane. *Sculpture Index*. Metuchen, New Jersey: Scarecrow Press, 1970.

Craven, Wayne. *Sculpture in America*. New York: Thomas Y. Crowell, 1968.

Duncan, Alastair. *American Art Deco*. New York: Harry N. Abrams, Inc., 1986.

Falk, Peter. *Who Was Who in American Art*. New York: Soundview Press, 1985.

Fairmont Park Art Association, *Sculpture of a City: Philadelphia's Treasures in Bronze and Stone*. New York: Walker, 1974.

Greenthal, Katherine, et. al. *American Figurative Sculpture in the Museum of Fine Arts, Boston*. Boston: Museum of Fine Arts and Northeastern University Press, 1986.

Gurney, George. *Sculpture and the Federal Triangle*. Washington, D.C.: Smithsonian Institution Press, 1985.

Havlice, Patricia. *Index to Artistic Biography*. New Jersey: Scarecrow Press, Inc., 1973.

Marion, John Francis. *Famous and Curious Cemeteries*. New York: Crown Publishing Inc., 1977.

Mayor, A. Hyatt. *A Century of American Sculpture: Treasures from Brookgreen Gardens*. New York: Abbeville Press, 1988.

Morris, Joseph F. *American Sculptors Series*. Athens, Georgia: University of Georgia Press in collaboration with the National Sculpture Society.

Opitz, Glenn B. *Dictionary of American Sculptors: 18th Century to the Present*. Poughkeepsie, N.Y.: Apollo Press, 1984.

Proske, Beatrice Gilman. *Brookgreen Gardens Sculpture*. Murels-Inlet, S.C.: Brookgreen Gardens, 1968.

Rand, Harry. *Paul Manship*. Washington, D.C.: Smithsonian Institution Press, 1989.

Schnier, Jacques. *Sculpture in Modern America*. Berkeley: University of California Press, 1948.

Short, C. W. *Public Buildings: A Survey of Architectural Projects Constructed by the Federal and Other Government Bodies Between the Years 1933–1939*. Washington, D.C.: United States Printing Office, 1939.

Taft, Lorado. *The History of American Sculpture*. New York: The Macmillan Company, 1903.

Articles

"Amateis and De Lue Do Government Reliefs." *Art Digest*, Vol. 15, No. 8 (September 1941).

Angers, Mary. "Sculptor De Lue Wins Acclaim." *Sunday Register*, Shrewsbury, New Jersey (August 12, 1979): pp. 3–4.

"Artists Living in Jersey Find that the State Nurtures the Arts." *Horizon Magazine* (October 1986): pp. 17–18.

Blair, Janet. "Sculptor's Works Symbolize Noblest of Human Efforts." *News Transcript* (August 29, 1979): sect. A, p. 3.

"Brookdale to Dedicate New Bust of Dr. King." *News Tribune*, Woodbridge, New Jersey (January 18, 1977).

"Bronze Bust of Dr. Ralph Sockman Placed in De Lue Room." *Christ Church News*, n.d.

"Bronze Door of Shrine in Woodmont Unveiled." *The Main Line Chronicle*, Ardmore, Pennsylvania (Sepetmber 5, 1968): p. 6.

Brown, Judith A. "Sculptor Meets Group for State Memorial." *Clarion Ledger*, Jackson, Mississippi (April 12, 1970): p. 2.

Canaday, John. *New York Times*, April 25, 1964.

Cleary, Fritz. "The Art Corner." *Asbury Park Press*, Asbury Park, New Jersey (November 6, 1966): p. 19.

———. "The Place for Sculpture." *Asbury Park News*, Asbury Park, New Jersey (October 29, 1967).

———. "Statue Draws Thousands." *Asbury Park Sunday Press*, Asbury Park, New Jersey (Sept. 17, 1967).

———. "De Lue Creates Third Gettysburg Statue." *Asbury Park Press*, Asbury Park, New Jersey (June 4, 1975): sect. C, p. 8.

Craven, Thomas. "The Making an Art Film." *American Artist* (November 1951): pp. 50–52.

Cresson, Margaret French. "A Minority Opinion on the Goodrich Report." *American Artist*, Vol. 18, No. 9 (November 1954): pp. 16–18, 52–58.

———. "Donald De Lue: Seventeenth President, National Sculpture Society." *National Sculpture Review*, Vol. 16, No. 2 (Summer 1967): p. 22.

Curran, Elmer. "Medals and Models are Monuments to Sculptor's Success." *Asbury Park Press*, Asbury Park, New Jersey (Feb. 3, 1980).

———. "Sculptor's Hand Guided by Forces in His Life." *Asbury Park Press* (January 27, 1980): sect. E, p. 20.

De Lue, Donald H. "Bryant Baker." *National Scultpure Review* (Fall 1964): p. 20.

———. "Edmond Amateis." *National Sculpture Review*, Vol. 15, No. 4 (Winter 1966): p. 22.

———. "In Reply to Mr. Goodrich." *American Artist* (April 1955): p. 20.

———. "Meštrović." *National Sculpture Review*, Vol. 10, No. 4 (Winter 1961): p. 5.

———. (A critique of Laurence Schmeckebier's book on Ivan Meštrović). Unpublished manuscript (October 1, 1959).

———. "Open Letter to the Metropolitan Museum." *National Sculpture Review*, Vol. 2 (March 1952): p. 5.

———. "Sculptors and Religious Art: A Symposium." *Liturgical Arts*, Vol. 13, No. 4 (August 1945): pp. 73–74.

———. "Toward a Reunion of Art and Architecture." *Journal of the American Institue of Architects*, Vol. 28, No. 3 (July 1957).

"De Lue Completing King Tribute." *The Advisor*, Middletown, New Jersey (January 19, 1977).

"De Lue Creates Third Gettysburg Sculpture." *Asbury Park Sunday Press*, Asbury Park, New Jersey (June 14, 1975): sect. C, p. 8.

"Dixie Dignitaries at Dedication." *Gettysburg Times* (June 12, 1971).

Flartey, Harold. "De Lue Captures Sculptor of the Year Laurels." *Daily Record*, Morris County, New Jersey (April 10, 1977).

"Four Sculptures Acquired to Continue the Celebration of Brookgreen Gardens Golden Anniversary." *Brookgreen Bulletin*, Vol 11, No. 3 (1981).

Friedlander, Leo. "Architecture and Sculpture." *National Sculpture Review*, Vol. 4, No. 2 (Spring 1955): p. 5.

———. "Government and Art." *National Sculpture Review*, Vol. 4, No. 4 (Fall 1954): p. 7.

———. "Modern — and All Too Modern." *National Sculpture Review*, Vol. 5, No. 2 (Summer 1956): p. 3.

"George Washington in Masonic Garb." *New York Daily News* (February 17, 1961): p. 18.

"George Washington Statue." *Times Picayune*, New Orleans, Louisiana (February 8, 1960).

"Golden Plate Event Honors 53 Leaders." *Dallas Morning News* (June 27, 1965).

Grafly, Dorothy. "Toward a Federal Art Program." *American Artist*, Vol. 18, No. 8 (October 1954): pp. 32, 68–71.

Harbison, John. "Our Memorials Abroad." *National Sculpture Review*, Vol. 4, No. 4 (1955): pp. 4–6.

"Have You a Little Orphan Model Gathering Dust in your Studio?" *Art Digest*, Vol. 13, No. 9 (January 15, 1939): p. 9.

Henderson, Maguerite. "Leonardo's De Lue Earns Sculptor of the Year Citation." *The Sunday Register*, Shrewsbury, New Jersey (July 8, 1979).

Hills, Charles M., Jr. "States Monument Being Readied for Gettysburg." *Clarion Ledger* (August 13, 1975): sect. A, p. 10.

"Icarus and Daedalus." *Brookgreen Bulletin*, Vol. 14., No. 2.

"Inspiration." *National Sculpture Review*, No. 1 (December 1951): p. 5.

Jacobson, Carol. "New Jersey Remains Unaware of Leonardo Sculptor." *Daily Register*, Shrewsbury, New Jersey (August 13, 1975): p. 10.

Lantz, Michael. "Reminiscing with Donald De Lue." *National Sculpture Review* Vol. 23, No. 2 (Summer 1974): pp. 26–27.

Le Brun, Caron. " 'Quest Eternal' For a Better Life." *Boston Sunday Herald* (April 30, 1967): p. 12.

"Leonardo Man Honored as 'Artist of the Year.' " *Hudson Dispatch*, Union City, New Jersey (November 11, 1971): p. 24.

"Leonardo Sculptor Thinks Big." *Daily Register*, Shrewsbury, New Jersey (June 26, 1975): p. 16.

Marko, Eleanor. "Fair and Square." *Red Bank Register*, Red Bank, New Jersey (March 19, 1964): p. 28.

———. "Donald De Lue: Monument to Men in His Hands." *Daily Register*, Shrewsbury, New Jersey (June 25, 1970): p. 13.

———. "Reception Set for Sculptor De Lue." *Daily Register*, Red Bank, New Jersey (September 14, 1967): p. 14.

Mazas, José Garcia. "Donald De Lue y Su Moderno Concepto del Triumfo." *Temas*, Vol. 8, No. 2 (June 1951): pp. 56–61.

McFadden, Elizabeth. "Fair Sculpture Permanent." *Newark Sunday News*, Newark, New Jersey (April 26, 1964): sect. W, p. 12.

"Medallic Memorial for Museum." *Monmouth County Panorama, General News*, Asbury Park, New Jersey (July 25, 1979): sect. W, p. 12.

"Model For Statue at Omaha Beach is Assembled in Sculptor's Studio." *New York Times* (August 6, 1953).

"Monmouth College to Confer Four Honorary Degrees." *Asbury Park Press*, Asbury Park, New Jersey (May 2, 1976): sect. D, p. 1.

"Monument Dedicated to Fallen Soldiers Unveiled at Bragg." *Fayetteville Observer* (November 27, 1969).

"Monumental Works by Sculptor De Lue." *Monmouth*, Shrewsbury, New Jersey (August 12, 1979).

"Moses Gives City Fair Site as Park." *New York Times* (June 4, 1967): p. 1, col. 2.

"Mrs. Cresson Draws Fire." *American Artist*, Vol. 19 (January 1955): pp. 12–13, 47–48, 55–56.

"New Medal for Forgotten Heroes of the Revolution." *New York Times* (August 26, 1979).

Noble, Joseph Veach. " 'Bursting the Bounds' by Donald De Lue." *11th Issue of the Society of Medalists (brochure)*, 1985.

Putnam, Brenda. "De Lue and Others Select Malvina Hoffman." *National Sculpture Review*, Vol. 3 (June 1952): p. 12.

" 'Quest Eternal,' " *Northeastern News*, Vol. 9, No. 4, Prudential Insurance Company of America.

"Recent Sculpture of Donald De Lue." *American Artist*, Vol. 21, No. 8, Issue 276: pp. 78–103.

"Sculptor De Lue to be Honored With a Degree." *Asbury Park Press*, Asbury Park, New Jersey (May 23, 1976): sect. E, p. 32.

"Sculpture Exhibit." *Daily Register*, Shrewsbury, New Jersey (April 15, 1976): p. 10.

"Sculptures at the American Academy of Arts and Letters Annual." *New York Times* (May 20, 1948).

Sheen, Fulton J. "Architecture and Courtesy." *National Sculpture Review*, Vol. 4, No. 1 (Winter 1954–55): p. 7.

Sullivan, Gary C. "I Believe in the Human Race . . . " *News Tribune*, Woodbridge, New Jersey (March 4, 1978).

Tamburo, Marianne. "Genesis in Leonardo." *Advisor*, Middletown, New Jersey (October 26, 1986): sect. A, pp. 1–2.

Thompson, Robert B. "Leonardo Sculptor, a Traditionalist, Raps Abstract Work." Associated Press, 1977.

Thompson, Robert B. "Sculptor Hews to Realism's Lines." *Asbury Park Press*, Asbury Park, New Jersey (Feb. 17, 1977): sect. C, p. 3.

Toolen, Thomas. "Noted Sculptor Raps Modernist Doodles." *Sunday News*, New York (August 28, 1966): sect. 2, p. 1.

Tortorella, Karen. "Sculptor Captures Magnificent Spirit." *New York Times* (December 10, 1982): pp. 1, 8.

Villamor, Erlinda. "Michelangelo Cast Found by Sculptor." *Asbury Park Press*, Asbury Park, New Jersey (January 7, 1979): sect. E, p. 6.

"Washington Kneeling at Prayer." *Philadelphia Inquirer* (September 10, 1967).

"Washington Statue is Unveiled." *Times Picayune*, New Orleans, Louisiana, n.d.

Watson, Ernest. "More About Standards." *American Artist*, Vol. 18, No. 3 (March 1954): p. 3.

———. "Is Representationalism Obsolete?" *American Artist*, Vol. 18, No. 1 (January 1954): p. 3.

Watson, John. "Soaring Symbol." *New York Journal American* (September 1, 1953): p. 17.

Obituaries

Boston Herald (August 28, 1988).

Cleary, Fritz. "The Last Titan." *National Sculpture Review* (November, 1988).

Driscoll, Edgar J. *Boston Globe* (August 27, 1988).

New York Times (August 27, 1988).

Exhibition Catalogues

Architectural League of New York, exhibition catalogue, 1937. (De Lue showed *Faun* and *Allegorical Figure*).

National Sculpture Society Exhibition. New York: Whitney Museum of American Art, April 3 — May 2, 1940 (De Lue exhibited *APEX* and *Pegasus Panel*).

Citizens Committee for Army and Navy, Inc., a catalogue from 1943.

American Academy of Arts and Letters and the National Institute of Arts and Letters Exhibition of Sculpture by Paul Manship, Works by Newly Elected Members of Arts and Letters Grants, May 19, 1945–June 29, 1945.

Exhibition of Ecclesiastical Sculpture. New York: National Sculpture Society, May 23 — June 9, 1950. (De Lue listed on jury of awards and on competition program committee).

An Exhibition of Sculpture. New York: National Sculpture Society, 1951 (De Lue exhibited *Icarus*).

An Exhibition of Sculpture. New York: National Sculpture Society, May 14 — June 20, 1952 (De Lue exhibited *Triton*).

National Sculpture Society and the National Arts Club Sculpture Exhibition. New York: 1961 (De Lue exhibited *Stations of the Cross*, Numbers 3 and 4).

National Sculpture Society Exhibition. New York: 1962 (De Lue served on the advisory board of past presidents, and exhibited *Urn Fragment*).

National Sculpture Society — 32nd Annual Exhibition. New York: 1965 (De Lue exhibited *Rocket Thrower*).

National Academy of Design, 143rd Annual Exhibition. New York: Feb. 22 — March 17, 1968.

Port of Our History Exhibition Catalogue. Philadelphia: 1987. (De Lue exhibited *Jefferson* and *George Washington at Prayer*).

Dedication Programs

"Mountaineer Statue Dedication." University of West Virginia, Mountainlair, West Virginia (October 30, 1971).

"National Columbus Day Committee Commissions Donald De Lue for Christopher Columbus and Queen Isabella Monuments." Christopher Columbus Award Banquet Program, Hotel Statler, Buffalo, New York (October 12, 1979).

"State of Louisiana: Gettysburg Memorial Monument." National Military Park, Gettysburg, Pennsylvania (June 11, 1971).

Archives

Archives of American Art: Watson, Ernest D. Correspondence, March 9, 1952. Microfilm No. 64.

———. Weinman Papers. Microfilm No. 100.

National Archives: Philadelphia Court House Project.

New York Public Library: 1964 World's Fair.

Film

Uncommon Clay. Produced and directed by Thomas Craven, 1951.

PHOTO CREDITS

Lisa L. Cunningham: xviii, 2, 22, 23, 30, 34, 48, 51, 52, 61, 79 (*right*), 93, 95, 112, 123, 130, 135, 146 (*left*), 153, 163, 164, 173, 178, 186 (*right*), 187 (*top*), 189, 190, 195, 212, 216, 228.

E. Ellison McKeown: vi, xix, 19, 24, 25 (*bottom*), 32 (*top*), 33 (*top*), 35, 42, 57, 63, 64, 65 (*left*), 67, 70 (*right*), 82, 87 (*middle and right*), 101, 105 (*right*), 110, 116, 119, 129, 134 (*left and middle*), 135, 144 (*right*), 147, 148, 152, 157 (*bottom*), 158 (*left*), 159, 167, 170, 171 (*top*), 174, 176, 179, 180, 181, 183, 184, 191, 192, 201, 204

De Lue Archives: xiv, 7, 9, 26, 27, 32 (*bottom*), 36 (*right*), 37, 38, 39, 40, 41, 45, 46 (*left*), 47 (*bottom*), 54, 55, 58 (*top and bottom*), 59, (*middle left*), 72, 75, 86 (*right*), 89, 94 (*right*), 104, 105 (*left*), 107, 121, 134 (*right*), 136 (*right*), 137 (*left*), 142, 146 (*right*), 150, 151, 155, 156, 158 (*right*), 181, 193, 194, 199, 230

Screened positives by Redmond and Magnell: xvii, xxii, 25 (*top*), 29, 31, 36 (*left*), 62, 65 (*right*), 66, 68 (*bottom*), 69, 70 (*left*), 81, 86 (*left*), 88, 92 (*left*), 94 (*left*), 96, 98 (*top and lower left*), 106, 111, 126, 136 (*lower left*), 137 (*right*), 144 (*left*), 157 (*top*), 169, 171 (*bottom*), 185, 186 (*left*), 188, 196, 197, 200, 202, 222

Other sources: Alinari: 187 (*lower right*); American Battle Monuments Commission: 78, 79 (*middle*); Judi Benvenuti: ii, 28, 154; Bettmann Newsphotos: 102; Bogart Studios, New York: 72; Trustees of the Boston Public Library: 11; British Library: 14; Brookgreen Gardens: 21, 56; Chet Chapman: 59 (*top right*), 168, 177; Leland Cook: 133; Thomas Craven Film Corporation: 73; Daily Register: 139; Dept. of the Army, Ft. Bragg, N.C.: 143; Father Divine's Peace Mission Movement: 160; Glass Negative, Ponca City, Ok.: 20; George Gurney: 33 (*bottom*); H2L2, Philadelphia: 75; D. Roger Howlett: 46 (*right*), 161, 162; Lenscraft Photos: 89; John Manship: 17, 124; Memphis Brooks Museum of Art: 87 (*bottom*); Museum of Fine Arts, Boston: 4 (*top*), 6; Museum of Modern Art: 114; National Academy of Design: 74; National Sculpture Society: 5, 58 (*middle*), 59 (*bottom*), 60, 71, 90, 91, 92 (*right*), 98 (*lower right*), 99, 113, 201; Joseph Veach Noble: xx; Carl Palusci: 36 (*right*); Rockport Art Association: 4 (*lower right and left*), 8; Sisters of St. Joseph: 97; University of West Virginia Libraries: 141; Virginia Polytechnic Institute: 68 (*top*)

Photos for *A Checklist for Medals* courtesy of: Lisa Cunningham, De Lue Archives, The Franklin Mint, E. Ellison McKeown, Medallic Art Company, National Sculpture Society, Smithsonian Institution, the Spy House Museum

Eve, circa 1945, plaster.

INDEX

232